BRITISH ARMY TERMINOLOGY AND ABBREVIATIONS

1939–1945

About the Author

Lt Col Dick Taylor joined the army in 1976 at the age of 16 as a junior leader Royal Armoured Corps. He spent his adult career with the Royal Tank Regiment, and was a tank commander and schools gunnery instructor, finishing his soldier career as a Warrant Officer Class 1. He was commissioned in 2000 and became a CBRN and then a survivability specialist. He completed staff college in 2009 and was promoted lieutenant colonel in 2011. After leaving the regular army he spent another eight years as a reservist and then commanded Dorset ACF for five years. During his service he deployed on 15 operational tours, including Northern Ireland, Bosnia, Kosovo, Iraq, Afghanistan, South Sudan, and Sierra Leone. He has been awarded the Queen's Commendation for Valuable Service and the US Meritorious Service Medal. He has been writing military books for over 20 years, and is the official historian of the Royal Armoured Corps. He lives in Dorset.

BRITISH ARMY TERMINOLOGY AND ABBREVIATIONS 1939–1945

Including Regiments and Corps, Battle Honours, Operational Code Words and Slang

Lt Col Dick Taylor

AMBERLEY

First published 2025

Amberley Publishing
The Hill, Stroud
Gloucestershire, GL5 4EP

www.amberley-books.com

ISBN 978 1 3981 2774 6 (paperback)
ISBN 978 1 3981 2775 3 (ebook)

British Library Cataloguing in Publication Data.
A catalogue record for this book is available from the British Library.

1 2 3 4 5 6 7 8 9 10

Typesetting by SJmagic DESIGN SERVICES, India.
Printed in the UK.

Appointed GPSR EU Representative:
Easy Access System Europe Oü, 16879218
Address: Mustamäe tee 50, 10621,
Tallinn, Estonia
Contact Details: gpsr.requests@easproject.com,
+358 40 500 3575

CONTENTS

INTRODUCTION

Wef 1200 hrs 22nd inst, LOs 1 airldg bde less BRECKNOCK will RV NNE of div CL at 0000 hrs 23/24 May 43. up & tpt will be IWT and HD, DAAG will coord. Mov at 6mi2h, 15 vtm. OsC O gp as per OO No 7 appx 2 encl A. All ack

J Smith T/Maj
BM

Although this is a fictional paragraph concocted for this volume, it is comprised entirely of official abbreviations used by the British Army during the Second World War, and as such would be decipherable and understandable to many – and equally, indecipherable and anything but understandable to many others! To the uninitiated, it appears to be close to nonsense; it could be argued that if such a document was to fall into enemy hands, unless they were privy to the standard list of abbreviations then in use the document would have a level of security that was entirely unintentional. However, the whole purpose of the abbreviations was not for security, but simply to make the passage of information quicker, particularly in the field when time is always short, and writing messages out in sentence form would simply waste it. The abbreviations therefore are just a form of military shorthand, which, in order to operate as intended, had to be standardised across the whole army. Such abbreviations and many other forms of military terminology can be immensely frustrating for the writer or researcher. When confronted with primary (and many secondary) sources, unless and until one understands the language, expressions, and terminology that were in use, he or she will struggle to comprehend what was being said. The optimistic but hopefully achievable intention behind this work therefore is to provide a single source of British Army terminology from World War 2, including abbreviations, acronyms, slang, a glossary of military terms, an overview of regiments and corps, the rank system, battle honours awarded for the conflict, and finally, a list of British Army operational code names.

A huge problem for the author in this first attempt at such an encyclopaedia was deciding where to stop! It was never the intention to reproduce all the various glossaries, terminologies, acronyms and abbreviations that were used throughout the whole of the army over the entire period of the war. Anyone who is in any way conversant with the amount of published material issued by the British Army over the period will immediately recognise that this would be an impossible task: were it possible to win a war by "out-printing" one's enemy, then the British Army surely would have been the victors by 1940. So, hopefully, sensible limits have been set here, with just enough detail to satisfy the majority of researchers. As well as general military terms, a deal of effort has gone into looking at the often deeply technical and even arcane terminology used not only by the commanders and their staff and the combat units, but also by the multitude of supporting organisations, including artillery, engineering, supply and transport, and medical.

By necessity, some of the terms herein do not strictly relate to the British Army, but refer to the other two services, civilian organisations, and Britain's allies, including the Commonwealth co-combatants. Such references have been included where, in the opinion of the author, might be encountered in archives of army documents and staff work, and do not intend in any way to represent all the complex and technical terminology belonging to the Royal Navy and the Royal Air Force; both of these services are deserving of similar treatment in their own right. German and other enemy nations' terminology has not been included, save where they were commonly used by the British, for example the Teller Mine. My guiding principle has always been to produce a reference work that is small enough to be sensible, and large enough to be useful.[1] Some of the slang terms given are today of course completely unacceptable.

A work such as this is unlikely ever to be complete; it would also be something of a miracle to be able to compile a reference work like this without occasional errors creeping in, for which I apologise in advance. This is the first edition and one which could be improved over time with additions, amendments and corrections. I therefore welcome suggestions and comments with a view to enhancing the accuracy and possibly scope of this work. It is also likely that there are other areas of reference not included herein that would benefit from a similar treatment; it is entirely possible therefore that a second and updated version of this work could be forthcoming in due course. I do hope that it is useful.

Lt Col (Retd) Dick Taylor
Blandford Forum
Dorset
Spring 2025

Part 1

A GLOSSARY OF OFFICIAL MILITARY TERMS

A major primary source in the research to begin this part of the volume was the 1939 version of the British army's "Pamphlet No 1 – Glossary of Military Terms and Organization in the Field", and its revised 1944 version. This pamphlet was intended as a handy and concise reference for the use of "Officers on active service and on manoeuvres and on instructional exercises in connection with operations". Other pamphlets in the same series covered such subjects as: orders and communication; intelligence; field engineering; billets, camps & bivouacs; movement by road, sea, air and rail; defence against gas; supply and replenishment in the field; medical services; and finally, discipline. All were regularly revised to account for changes in weaponry and technology, as well as in organisation and doctrine. Although primarily designed for use by officers, sufficient of these pamphlets were produced with the intention of being issued down to the rank of sergeant. In the glossary, direct quotations taken from Pamphlet No 1 are indicated through the use of quotation marks, with the date of the version of the pamphlet (1940 or 1944) noted in brackets. Where the definition comes from an official source other than Pamphlet No1, the details of that pamphlet are also given.

Although this is our start point, this small pamphlet was not, and is not, the answer to all the questions regarding definitions and military language. In order to keep it small enough to be a useful pocket guide, Pamphlet No 1 could only give the briefest of introductions to many topics, and it clearly relied upon other more specialist publications issued by the various corps and arms of service to go deeper into the particulars of their specific business. And there remains the issue of some military terms remaining ill-defined or, in some cases, frustratingly not defined at all. Therefore, and hopefully with the reader's forgiveness, the author has attempted to fill in those gaps by offering definitions of his own. Where this path has been taken, and this is the majority, a bracketed reference is not present.

With a greatly expanded army largely relying on territorial soldiers and then increasingly conscripted civilians, it is no surprise that mistakes were made, abbreviations were misused and definitions misunderstood, and even new terminology invented in an ad hoc manner. Lt Sydney Jary, serving in the northwest Europe campaign as a platoon commander with 4th Battalion Somerset Light Infantry, exhibited the frustration that could be caused when he wrote: 'The expression "reconnaissance in force" disturbed me. It was one of those in frequent use, the exact definition of which was suspect.'[1]

He was not alone!

The Glossary

ACCESSORY An addition to a complete article without which the article can still be used, for example a bicycle pump. Sometimes referred to as an *appurtenance*. cf *Component*

ADVANCED BASE "When a force is maintained partly from outside the actual theatre of operations, that part of the base inside the theatre will be called the advanced base". (1944) cf *Base*

ADVANCED DEPOT OF MEDICAL STORES "A corps medical unit for the supply of medical stores to medical units in corps and divisions". (1944)

ADVANCED DRESSING STATION "A divisional medical dressing station formed by one or more companies of a field ambulance or light field ambulance, where casualties are given first aid, sorted and labelled, and from which they are evacuated". (1944)

ADVANCED SURGICAL CENTRE "A corps medical unit formed by a field dressing station, to which is attached a field transfusion unit and one or more field surgical units. Casualties requiring urgent surgical treatment in the field are evacuated to this centre from the advanced dressing station". (1944)

AIRBURST Shells that are fuzed, using either time or proximity fuzes, to explode above the ground/target, in order to cause shell fragments to be driven downwards onto troops lacking overhead cover.

AIR INTELLIGENCE LIAISON SECTION "In order that the information obtained by the air may be quickly investigated and distributed, and to ensure that pilots are provided with the necessary detailed instructions to carry out their tasks, an AIL Section, consisting of two army officers with the necessary clerical staff, is attached to each army cooperation squadron, and to each bomber wing employed on strategic reconnaissance. Their duties include the annotation of air photographs". (1939)

AIR DEFENCE This refers to combined defence by aircraft and anti-aircraft units. Aircraft defence concerns defence by aircraft only, whereas anti-aircraft (AA) defence concerns defence by anti-aircraft units only; it does not imply defence by aircraft. AA defence is subdivided into *active* (measures which act directly on the attacker such as the fire of

AA guns and searchlights); and *passive* (measures taken to minimise the effect of an attack)". (1939)

AIR LIAISON OFFICER "An army officer attached to an RAF unit or formation, whose duties include the briefing and interrogation of pilots undertaking reconnaissance and assisting the commanders of squadrons carrying out any army tasks in the briefing and interrogation of air crews. He is responsible for passing on the results of the interrogation and for keeping pilots fully informed about the military situation. He also carries out a quick scrutiny of all air photographs received". (1944)

AIR OBSERVATION POST "A specially designed light aircraft from which an artillery officer directs the fire of the artillery by flying at a low altitude over our own lines". (1944)

AIR PHOTOGRAPH "A photograph of an area of ground taken from an aircraft. There are two types: Vertical photograph – presents a view of an area of country as seen from a point immediately above the centre of that area. Oblique photograph – presents a perspective view of an area of country as seen from the point of exposure". (1944)

AIR RECONNAISSANCE "Air reconnaissance is classified as strategical, tactical, and artillery reconnaissance. In addition, photographic reconnaissance may be carried out in connection with any of these categories. Night reconnaissance may be either strategical or tactical. It is impossible to define exactly where strategical reconnaissance ends and tactical reconnaissance begins. Broadly, the designation of each type of reconnaissance is indicative of the information to be obtained, strategical reconnaissance being concerned with information from rear areas on which the commander can base his general plan of operations, while tactical reconnaissance is concerned with movements and dispositions in the battle area. As a very general guide, tactical reconnaissance may extend up to about 75 miles in advance of our forward troops, and strategical reconnaissance up to the limit of the radius of action of the aircraft employed. The object of artillery reconnaissance is primarily the location of targets for the artillery and the direction of fire on them". (1939) The 1944 version added a fourth type, Contact Reconnaissance (con R), "reconnaissance to locate the position of our own forward troops".

AIR RECONNAISSANCE CODES Used as both a code and a form of shorthand, three letter codes used in signal messages were used in the early war period and were allocated to common military locations, functions and activities likely to be spotted from the air:

AAG Anti-aircraft gun(s)
ABT Airborne Troops (landed at...)
ACT Activity at...
AER Airfield
ALA All Arms (used in conjunction with COL)

ALG Air Landing Ground
AMM Ammunition
ART All Artillery (not in action)
ARV Armoured Vehicles
AMC Armoured Car(s)
ATK Anti-Tank teeth or obstacles
BAG Balloon barrage.
BDC Bridge(s) (under construction)
BDG Bridge(s)
BIV Bivouac
BLK Traffic block (in conjunction with OPN or CLO)
BUS Bus (as distinct from MET)
CAM Camouflaged
CAV Mounted men
CLM Cancel Last Message
CLO Closed
CMP Command post
CNO Cannot Observe
COL Column
DEP Defended Point
DFP Defended Post
DGR Target dangerously near own troops
DIG Digging
ELS Enemy Landing from Ships at...
ENG Engine
FAC Factory
FCG Facing
GCB Hostile batteries in action
GNF Guns Not Firing
GNS Guns in action but not firing
HAG Hangars
HAL Hostile Aircraft Landing at...
HDT Horse Drawn Transport
HOR Horses
HQS Headquarters
INF Infantry or Men
MER Merchant ship(s)
MET Mechanical Transport
MGS Machine Gun(s)
MTR Mortars
NMS No Movement Seen
OBS Observation Post
OPN Open
PAR Parachute troops landing at...
PED Civilians or refugee traffic
PET Petrol

PDG	Pontoon Bridge
PIL	Pillboxes
PLA	Planes on ground
PTG	Pontoon or improvised bridge
RAP	Ranging Point
RAR	Radar station
RED	Railhead
RES	Reserves
RFA	Reference Point A (RFB, RFC etc)
RIV	River
ROD	Road
SDG	Siding
SER	Searchlight
SIN	Single-engined aircraft
SNU	Steam Not Up (railway engine)
SSS	Splash signal (shot about to fall)
SUB	Submarine
TCH	Trench
TCK	Track
TKV	Tracked Vehicles
TMG	Target Moving
TNK	Tank
TNT	Tent
TRG	Goods trucks
TRN	Railway train (complete with engine)
TRP	Passenger coaches
TWN	Multi-engined aircraft
WAR	Warship
WTS	Wireless station

For example, the message "TRN 10 TRP W V8617" meant a passenger train of ten passenger coaches is moving west at location V8617. The same train but observed as stationary with the engine at its westerly end would be "TRN 10 TRP FCG W V8617".

AIRBORNE "The term applicable to all personnel who, normally forming part of airborne divisions, are specially organised and trained for operations involving transport by air. The term applies both to parachute troops and to air landing units, as well as to their equipment". (1944)

AIRGRAPH A system designed to reduce the huge amount of shipping space needed for mail, letters were miniaturised onto microfilm and flown to their destination where they were then enlarged. As well as saving space this also speeded up the transit time.

AIRPORTABLE "The term applicable to the equipment, modified as necessary, that accompanies air transported troops". (1944)

AIRTRANSPORTED "The term applicable only to troops who do not form part of airborne divisions but who may be transported by air for a special purpose". (1944)

ALDERSHOT OVEN A large oven of arched construction used in camps and designed to feed up to 250 troops.

ALL RANKS Used very specifically as a shorthand meaning officers *and* other ranks together. In many instances, the two were very deliberately kept separate, and many nominal rolls – and casualty lists – take care to identify officers by name whilst detailing other ranks only as numbers.

AMBULANCE As well as a vehicle designed for carrying casualties, within the Royal Army Medical Corps the term also denoted a mechanized unit used for the collection of casualties, eg 18th Light Field Ambulance RAMC.

AMMUNITION CODES To ensure that the right type of ammunition was delivered to the right type of gun or howitzer, codes were allocated to the type of shot, shell, and fuzes, as well as to the type of ordnance. These codes in combinations of two or three letters (but very rarely up to as many as five with heavy artillery) were meant to ensure that potentially dangerous mistakes could not be made. For example, in the 1939 version (the system expanded as new guns and ammunition types were added), Quick Firing (QF) fixed ammunition, including fuzes, was allocated code letters: A, B, C, E, G, H, J, L, M and BT. The associated QF guns and mortars were coded as: A, F, J, T, Y, AD, AE, AG, and AR. As an example, Code YE (the weapon code letter was always used before the ammunition/fuze code) denoted armour piercing ammunition for the 2-pounder Mk IX and X guns. In the same way, Breech Loading and QF separate loaded ammunition, again including fuzes, had the codes A, B, C, H, P, S and BE, whilst the guns and howitzers used the codes: B, C, H, K, L, M, N, P, Q, S, U, V, W, UZ and QZ. So, the direct action (DA) fuze for the 4.5" howitzer was coded HB. The system was clearly large and complicated and used mainly by the Royal Artillery and the RAOC. For the researcher needing fuller details, the appropriate Field Service Pocket Book pamphlets will need to be consulted.

AMMUNITION POINT "A forward detachment of an ammunition company to facilitate the replacement of ammunition expended. Demands by units and formations are sent to ammunition points, if found [eg established], otherwise direct to the division or corps troops ammunition company". (1939) "A point where a forward holding of ammunition on wheels is established by a second-line RASC company to facilitate rapid replacement of expended ammunition direct to units, by refilling unit ammunition vehicles, or by an artillery unit calling forward one or more vehicles to the gun or wagon lines". (1944)

AMMUNITION RAILHEAD "A terminal point on the railway line of communication at which ammunition and explosives are transferred from rail to dumps, or for onward transmission by road transport". (1944)

AMMUNITION REFILLING POINT "The place where loads are transferred from *third-line* to *second-line* transport. It is in no sense a dump". (1939)

ANT In tank fire control orders, some nicknames were used as a short and standardised form of target description. An Ant was simply an anti-tank gun. *cf Hornet, Maggie*

APPLE-PIE SHOOT An artillery shoot used by heavy regiments, in order to allow RAF aircraft to conduct missions in an area. Enemy flak positions were suppressed using airburst ammunition.

APPOINTMENT TITLES These were introduced mid-war and were used as a low-level code on the radio to refer to an appointment or role in general terms without giving away the level of the appointment. For example, SUNRAY was used for a commander; on a company net this would refer to the company commander, whereas on a brigade net it would refer to the brigade commander. The codes were as follows (with typical appointments at battalion level in brackets):

SUNRAY	Commander (CO)
SEAGULL	G staff (Adjt)
MOLAR	A/Q staff (QM)
ACORN	Intelligence staff (IO)
PRONTO	Signal staff (RSO)
SHELLDRAKE	Royal Artillery
HOLDFAST	Royal Engineers
STARLIGHT	Medical staff (RMO)
BLUEBELL	REME (EME)
RICKSHAW	Ordnance
PLAYTIME	Supply and Transport (Tech Adjt)

The deputy or 2IC could be referred to by adding MINOR after the title, so MOLAR MINOR would be the RQMS.

APPRECIATION A review of a military problem or situation based on all available information and culminating in the production of a plan; it was also used to describe the set sequence for dealing with such a tactical problem. One version of this had the following structure:

Define the objective – in other words, "ask what is to be done?"

Identify the factors affecting the attainment of the objective (eg weather, time, ground etc).

Decide what courses of action are open to both friendly and enemy troops.

Decide on the best course of action, and plan accordingly.

ARM OF THE SERVICE A method of referring to the part of the army an officer or soldier was serving in. The arm was the regiment or corps (RAC,

Welsh Guards, RASC, RAChD etc), and the service in this context meant the army as a whole.

ARMOUR SPECIFICATIONS The type and thickness of armour used in the construction of armoured fighting vehicles was labelled as follows:

IT.60	Face hardened	7 – 12mm
IT.70	Thin Homogenous Hard	3 – 30mm
IT.80	Thick Homogenous Machinable	≥ 15mm
IT.90	Cast	All thicknesses
IT.100	Thin Homogenous Machinable	3 – 14mm
IT.110[2]	Carbon Manganese Steel (Backing Plates)	All thicknesses

ARMY An operational grouping, consisting of two or more corps, and usually commanded by a General.

ARMY AIR SUPPORT "The term which, in its widest sense, includes the provision of fighter protection, air reconnaissance, attack on ground targets, and all forms of air transport. Air support may be (a) Direct – an intervention against enemy land forces actually engaged in the battle, or (b) Indirect – action having a general influence on the course of the campaign. Requests for air support are passed through air support signal units, which provide the necessary tentacles to army and RAF formations". (1944)

ARMY FORMS The army used thousands of different forms for its administration – if there was an activity, there was at least one form associated with it. All army forms begin with AF, followed by a letter denoting their usage:

A	General
B	Regiments and Corps
C	Staff & Departments
D	Reservists & Pensioners
E	Territorial Army, Supplementary Reserve, Militia and Officers' Training Corps
F	Supplies (not finance)
G	Stores (not finance)
H	Clothing & Necessities
I	Medical
K	Lands, Works, Buildings and Engineer Stores
L	Stationery, Forms and Books
M	Financial Estimates
N	Financial Accounts & Pay Lists
O	Financial Personal Vouchers
P	Financial Supply & Stores Vouchers
W	Forms issued in connection with War
X	Forms issued in connection with Demobilization

The whole system was so large and complex that a separate pamphlet of 222 pages was necessary just to list all the forms and books (AB) in use.[3] These included such invaluable documents as:

AFB 263 Dangerous Lunatic Soldier: Order for Reception (Scotland).

AFC 301 Confidential report on professional ability and qualification of Queen's Army School mistresses.

AFC 376C Application for award of a gratuity in respect of an unestablished civil servant.

AFK 1261 Roumanian Contract Form.

AFK 1264 Tender for Grazing Sheep.

AFK 3537 Stable Manure – Purchase and Removal of.

AFL 1375 Latrine paper: Annual indent.

AFO 1659A Income Tax Questionnaire: Newly appointed civilian staff (other than married women).

AFO 1780 Charges for shoeing officers' horses.

AFW 4086 Prepayment ATS hairdressing ticket.

ARMY GROUP Short for *Group of Armies*, an operational grouping of two or more armies, and usually commanded by a General or a Field Marshal.

ARMY GROUP ROYAL ARTILLERY Officially introduced towards the end of 1942 following field trials, an Army Group Royal Artillery (AGRA) was an organisation consisting of a number of field, medium and heavy regiments, which were not allocated to a division, and which were usually used to support corps-level operations. An AGRA did not 'belong' to any specific corps, but they were flexible and could be re-grouped easily and moved to where the need was greatest. Around twenty AGRAs were created, including two from the Canadian army.

ARMY TRANSPORT COMPANY RASC "Companies under the control of army HQ, primarily used to carry the requirements of corps from a L of C Terminal to within range of second-line transport". (1944)

ARMY TROOPS Those troops on the establishment of an army (eg those that do not form part of the corps, divisions or brigades under command) and which are employed to allow the army to function.

ARTILLERY FIRE According to the result desired, artillery fire was classified in three groups:

NEUTRALIZATION Applied to *covering fire* and *counter-battery fire* and is thus the usual fire employed in support of assaulting troops, when covering a withdrawal, or when dealing with hostile artillery.

DESTRUCTION Fire intended to destroy definite enemy defences and material, such as guns, dumps, railways, and bridges.

INTERFERENCE Fire directed primarily with the object of inflicting loss on enemy personnel. *Defensive fire, counter-preparation fire,* and *harassing fire* all come under this heading.

The *types* of artillery fire were also classified:

BARRAGE A barrage is a belt or curtain of fire. In attack it may be either moving or protective; a moving barrage creeps forward in front of the attacking troops thereby ensuring that all ground over which it passes is subjected to fire; a protective barrage may be employed to protect the flank of an attack, the consolidation of an objective, or as part of a defensive fire plan.

COUNTER-BATTERY FIRE This is intended to either neutralise or destroy the enemy artillery. It must therefore be considered as an integral part of the covering fire, defensive fire, and counter preparation plans.

COUNTER-PREPARATION FIRE This is fire directed on enemy forming up places and forward communications, in order to disorganize and, if possible, to break up an imminent attack. (The term was discontinued in 1941).

COVERING FIRE Fire designed to engage the enemy's attention and force him to seek cover in order that friendly units may advance or retire.

DEFENSIVE FIRE (DF) Artillery and small arms fire directed against troops actually attacking; it is usually put down in accordance with a coordinated plan in prearranged areas.

HARASSING FIRE (HF) "The object is to force on the enemy further deployment and so loss of time; to prevent or hamper the movement of reinforcements during a battle; and to reduce the morale of the enemy by interfering with the movement of troops, food and ammunition, and by disturbing the rest of reserves." (1939)

ASSAULT The final phase of an attack in which the enemy position is taken, using a combination of speed, surprise, aggression, and firepower.

ASSEMBLY AREA The ground allotted to a unit for occupation before a subsequent move. A good assembly area would be free from enemy observation and harassing fire.

ASSEMBLY POSITION "Generally. this term applies to positions where troops assemble for any particular purpose. In certain other circumstances it has a more definite significance. In night operations it is the point at which the normal march formation will be abandoned, and battle formation adopted. For a river crossing, it is a point where the assaulting troops assemble. It should be well away from the water obstacle and protected from ground and air observation". (1939)

ATTACHED To be attached to another unit meant a temporary assignment for a limited amount of time, as opposed to a posting, which was the term given to a permanent move to another unit.[4] Military documents would refer to *atts and dets*, a list of all the attachments to, and detachments from, a unit or formation. *cf Detached.*

ATTACK There are two main types of attack:

DELIBERATE The deliberate attack is mounted against strongly prepared enemy positions and aims to use the maximum weight of fire support to assist the attack. Time is allocated for a thorough reconnaissance of the likely enemy position. Also known as a *Set-Piece attack.*

QUICK The quick attack takes advantage of an unprepared enemy defence and accepts the additional risk this entails. The need for speed may reduce or remove the time available for a thorough reconnaissance. Also known as a *Hasty attack.*

AVENUE OF APPROACH A general direction that an enemy might be expected to advance along, as opposed to a specific route.

AXIS OF ADVANCE "The line given the general direction of movement astride which a formation or unit moves". (1944) The general direction of an advance towards the enemy, making best use of suitable terrain and avoiding areas that may prevent the force from manoeuvring freely.

BACKLOAD The rearward movement of damaged equipment, casualties, and material.

BACK-SQUADDING To be back-squadded meant to have to repeat a particular part of a training syllabus, usually either because the required standard could not be attained by the student, or because of medical or administrative reasons; for example, a spell in hospital or a period of unforeseen compassionate leave.

BANTAM An early name for the US vehicle that would later become universally referred to as the Jeep.

BARRAGE A generic term used for artillery fire, but more specifically used when the exact location of the enemy could not be determined.

BASE When a force is wholly maintained within the actual theatre of operations, the term *base* takes the place of the term *advanced base.*

BASE SUB-AREA "An area around a base port which contains base depots and installations required to handle the type of traffic to be imported through the port. The local administration of these depots and installations and of the port is the responsibility of the HQ base sub-area". (1944)

BASIC TRAINING See *Primary Training.*

BATTALION A battalion was a lieutenant colonel's command and comprised a number of sub-units (usually referred to as companies, squadrons, or batteries). In the infantry, a battalion would usually comprise a number of rifle companies, a fire support company, and a headquarters company. The term battalion was also used for the units that made-up the Royal Tank Regiment. Furthermore, other corps and services occasionally used the term for a similarly sized unit.

BATTERY A battery was a term solely used within the Royal Artillery for a sub-unit and that was a major's command. A battery comprised a number of troops.

BEACH BRICK/GROUP A term used in the Middle East to denote an organisation intended to administer and maintain a section of beach or landing ground, particularly during an amphibious landing. Each brick would be based upon a nominated infantry battalion, to which would be attached detachments from other corps and services as required to provide the necessary facilities. During the north-west Europe campaign these were normally referred to as *Beach Groups*.

BEACH-HEAD The initial lodgement made on the enemy bank of a river or sea, from which subsequent operations can be developed.

BEACH MAINTENANCE AREA "An area in the vicinity of the beaches comprising service units and detachments for the maintenance, in the initial stages, of troops landed in a combined operation". (1944)

BEATEN ZONE The area of ground into which all shots fired from an automatic weapon will land; it is usually oval in shape.

BEEHIVE Named for its shape, this was a shaped charge used by engineers in demolitions. A similar device using the same principle was the *Hayrick*, which was designed specifically for cutting through the steel bars in reinforced concrete. A number of different sizes of Beehive were used.

BEETLE See *Mulberry*.

BILLET "This is a form of quartering [i.e. housing] personnel, animals and transport in houses and out-houses. It is the usual form of quarters in civilized countries for forces not in close touch with the enemy. It provides concealment from air observation and gives the best form of shelter and rest. In *Close Billets* as many men as possible are billeted; the remainder are in bivouac. This system is adopted when a greater degree of readiness is required than is possible in ordinary billets. Tactical considerations will have precedence over all others". (1939) *Billets* was a common form of shorthand widely used to mean any type of accommodation.

BIVOUAC "A camp without tents or huts, where the troops make their own shelters. Its essential characteristics are concentration and readiness for action. Bivouacs enable the most favourable dispositions of troops to be made from the tactical point of view; [but] this may be injurious to the health of personnel in cold and wet weather". (1939) Troops would almost invariably shorten the name to *bivvy*.

BLANCO Originally given this trade name because it came in a white form, Blanco was a protective paste made by Pickering's and which came in a cake form; it was applied to webbing equipment with a brush. It came in a number of shades designed to be appropriate to the local terrain, although many units selected a particular shade and always used it, regardless of where they were located. (Some units did not use Blanco at all, particularly those in the western desert, and simply scrubbed the webbing to clean it).

BLIND A round of ammunition that, having been fired and landed, did not function as intended and therefore remained in a dangerous state.

BOMB LINE "A line, usually delineated by well-defined geographical feature, beyond which the air forces are free to attack any target. Targets on the friendly side of the bomb line will only be attacked by special arrangements with ground forces". (1944)

BOMBARDON See *Mulberry*.

BOUND "A tactical feature of importance used during an advance to coordinate movement. Having reached a bound, the unit or formation will continue without a pause unless otherwise ordered, or unless it is necessary to secure the feature for tactical reasons". (1944)

BOWSER A semi-official term used to donate a wheeled water or fuel tanker.

BOX BARRAGE. Three or four individual barrages used to form a box of three or four sides around an enemy position in order to isolate it and prevent movement in or out.

BOX DEFENCE A tactical layout sometimes used in the western desert, in which combined arms groups, usually infantry and artillery, formed a defensive location. Such positions wherever possible were 'anchored' to a terrain feature but in some cases were placed in open, featureless desert. They usually employed barbed wire perimeters and some digging-in. The distances between such defensive boxes usually meant that they were unable to mutually support each other and could therefore easily be defeated in detail. Because of the way they looked when represented on maps, troops sometimes referred to them as *cow pats*.

BRACKET A term used in both artillery and tank gunnery, where one shell (or number of shells) lands beyond the enemy (termed an "over"), then another shell or number of shells lands short of the enemy (a "short"), which allows the actual range to the enemy to be established.

BRASSO Originally an Australian invention, Brasso was (and still is) the trade name for the most popular brand of metal polish used by the military, to ensure that the brass elements of their equipment, such as buttons, cap badges and the fixtures on webbing equipment, would gleam on parade.

(Other similar products were Bluebell and Glitterit). When on active service all such items were meant to be left unpolished so that they would dull over time for tactical reasons. Some unfortunate units found that when they came out of the line and moved to a rear area, they were immediately expected to go back to the pre-war routine of polishing everything until it shone, which of course was unnecessary *bull* and simply meant that the process of allowing metal to tarnish would have to be repeated the next time they went into action.

BREAKING BULK In logistics, the process of splitting bulk stores into smaller component parts, often lorry loads, in order to move them forward towards the battle area. Breaking bulk normally took place at railheads.

BREASTWORK An earthwork and/or sandbags built up to breast or shoulder height to provide protection to defenders firing over it from a standing position. *cf Sangar.*

BRIDGE CLASSIFICATION A system was required to be devised to prevent military bridges from being overloaded, with potentially fatal consequences, by heavy military vehicles. Using this system a vehicle was only allowed to cross those bridges bearing a classification number that was the same as, or greater than, its own classification. For example, a vehicle of class 12 could cross any bridge marked 12 or over, but was not allowed to cross the bridge marked 5 or 9. As an additional safety measure, minimum spacings between vehicles were also used; in general terms the ideal spacing was 50 yards, and the minimum spacing was never less than 80 feet. Bridges were generally classified as 5, 9, 12, 18, 24, 30, 40, 50, 60 and 70.[5]

BRIGADE A brigadier's command, usually comprising of three combatant units, as well as a headquarters element and additional subunits as required. Brigades were intended to operate within the overall structure of a division, unless labelled as "*independent*".[6] Note: the term could also be used in other, often misleading ways, such as the infantry regiment known as the *Rifle Brigade*.[7]

BRIGADE GROUP An enhanced brigade, with additional resources to allow it to act independently of a parent division.

BRITISH WARM This was a standard pattern of double-breasted wool overcoat originally intended for general officers, but which was also worn by more junior officers in some units as an alternative to the regulation greatcoat. It was a privately purchased item and came in two colours, one a khaki which matched service dress, the other a much less practical light fawn colour chosen to match the colour of cavalry breeches.

BRYLCREEM An emulsion of mineral oil and beeswax, Brylcreem was the pre-eminent hair cream used by men at the time (although others were available, for example Anzora). Most soldiers in the army referred to the

RAF as *Brylcreem Boys*, because their more comfortable existence meant that they could still use such hair products whilst on duty.

BURBERRY A type of waterproof raincoat, which although of civilian style, was very popular among officers.

BY-PASS By-passing pockets of enemy resistance was often essential in order to maintain the speed and momentum of the main advance. Any enemy positions by-passed must be contained so that they cannot interfere with the operation, and echelon forces must be allocated to accept the surrender of, or if necessary, defeat, the by-passed enemy.

CAB RANK On-call ground attack aircraft in the air; the name comes from the supposed similarity to a rank of taxi cabs awaiting customers.

CAISSON In military engineering, a box or box-like structure used underwater or as a foundation. See *Mulberry.*

CAMOUFLET An artificial cavern or cavity created by an explosion without the surface being disturbed; if the surface is broken it is known as a *crater*.

CANNIBALISE To remove serviceable assemblies and components from a vehicle or equipment, usually one that is damaged, in order to use them elsewhere.

CAP COMFORTER A cylinder of knitted khaki wool, closed at both ends, that could be used as a scarf or, when rolled into itself, could be worn under the steel helmet for both comfort and warmth. In frontline areas, cap comforters were often worn in place of other headgear, particularly if it was cold or when going on a night patrol.

CASSINI GRID Sometimes called the military grid, the War Office grid, or the purple grid, this was a grid coordinate system used on British military mapping during the conflict, and which differs from the National Grid in use today.

CASUALTY COLLECTING POINT (Sometimes Casualty Collection Point, CCP). "A medical post formed by a section, or part of a section, of a field ambulance, to which casualties are brought from the regimental aid post, and to which ambulance cars of the field ambulance are sent to collect casualties". (1944)

CASTING The process of disposing of a vehicle or equipment that is no longer repairable.

CENSUS The census was the registration system used for all military vehicles, to allow each individual vehicle to be contracted for, built, taken on strength (TOS), maintained, transported, employed, and when necessary, struck off strength (SOS).[8] The census number acted as the vehicle registration number and consisted of two parts: a prefix letter which gave the general class of vehicle, followed by a number of digits used to identify a specific individual vehicle, eg T335335. The prefix letter was officially known as the 'vehicle classification letter':

A	Ambulance
C	Motorcycle
D	Dragon
E	Engineer
F	Armoured Car
H	Artillery Tractor (originally used pre-war for Half-Tracks, hence the H)
L	Lorry (30 Cwt and over)
M	Motor Car
P	Amphibian
R	Rotatanks & Trailers
REC	Recovery
S	Self-Propelled Gun
T	Tank
V	Van
X	Trailer
Z	Truck (up to and including 15 Cwt)

CENTRE LINE "The route along which the HQ of a formation, unit or sub-unit moves". (1944) Often referred to by using the phonetic version as the "Charlie Love".

CHARGER Originally the term given to an officer's horse, the name was adopted by the Royal Artillery towards the end of the war for a tank used as an officer's armoured runaround vehicle.

CHINAGRAPH Sometimes known as a grease pencil, a waterproof and coloured writing implement capable of writing on gloss surfaces, such as glass, metal, or celluloid. They were used to mark maps with tactical information, and employed certain standardised colours, eg red for friendly forces, and blue for enemy.

CHOKE POINT Any piece of narrow terrain or obstacle that prevents a force from using space and causes it to concentrate, often forcing vehicles or men to adopt single file.

CIRCUS A self-contained, mobile training team used to convert units and formations onto a new equipment, particularly tanks.

CLOTH MODEL See *Sand Table.*

CODE NAME "A non-secret word, standard throughout a field force, used to denote a feature, a route, or an individual at a headquarters etc". (1944)

CODE SIGN "A secret group of letters or letters and figures, which is changed at frequent intervals, and used to identify a headquarters". (1944)

These were usually a group of three letters which were changed daily at midnight.

COLUMN Used in two ways; firstly, within supply and transport organisations to denote a mobile detachment. Secondly, used for some extemporised commands, for example *Kingcol* In Iraq in 1941.

COMMAND As well as its common use as a noun (to command), a Command was an administrative formation, usually defined geographically. Both UK-based and overseas Commands were formed. At the start of the war in the UK there were six: Aldershot, Eastern, Northern, Scottish, Southern and Western Commands, joined in early 1941 by South-Eastern Command (formed by removing Kent, Surrey and Sussex from Eastern). Overseas, for example, were Ceylon Army Command and East Africa Command.[9] There was also the non-geographically defined Anti-Aircraft Command in UK, the main army part of ADGB.[10]

COMMON GRID A term used when all artillery units in a formation have a catalogue of predetermined targets against which the fire of all the guns within range can be brought to bear.

COMPANY The basic sub-unit of an infantry battalion, made up of a number of platoons and about one hundred men, if fully up to strength. A major's command, the term was also used by other arms and services, for example the Royal Army Service Corps and the Royal Engineers. With the latter, some companies could comprise more than 200 men.

COMPONENT A part of a complete article without which the article is useless, for example the track of a tank. *cf Accessory.*

COMPOSITE Made-up of more than one commodity. With units, a composite unit was a multi-function organisation; for example, a Composite Platoon RAOC could be responsible for dealing with fuel, ammunition, and general stores. Composite rations were so named because one crate would contain many different items.

CONCENTRATION AREA The area occupied by a force immediately prior to the commencement of an operation. Such areas should be occupied for as short a period as possible, only allowing enough time for the units and formations within the concentration area to "shake out" into their battle formations and be able to cross the start line at the appointed hour, otherwise the lack of dispersion brings its own risks. Concentration areas are by their very nature vulnerable to enemy fire or other interference.

CONSOLIDATE To prepare a newly won position for immediate defence against counter-attack.

CORN COB See *Mulberry.*

CORPS Coming from the French for a body (of troops), this term could be used in a number of ways. Short for Army Corps, a Corps was a tactical formation comprising two or more divisions, but usually three; it was a lieutenant general's command. The term was also applied to the various corps that made up the army, which were the supporting and administrative arms, such as the engineers, artillery, medical, signals and logistic units. Note: the term could also be used in other ways, such as the infantry regiment known as the King's Royal Rifle Corps, or indeed a Corps of Drums.

CORPS TROOPS Those troops on the establishment of a corps (eg those that do not form part of the divisions or brigades under command) and which are employed to allow the corps to function.

COUNTER-ATTACK The intention of a counter-attack is to destroy attacking enemy forces and/or retake ground that has been lost. A counter-attack may be either deliberate or hasty.

COUNTER-BATTERY Artillery fire designed to destroy or neutralise the enemy's own artillery. Sometimes known as *counter-bombardment*. *Counter-mortar* was also used in a more specific sense.

COVENTRY CLOCK A device used by artillery units firing from moving landing craft during the Normandy invasion, in order to ensure that they fired at the correct range.

CRATER See *Camouflet.*

CREEPING (or ROLLING or MOVING) BARRAGE An artillery barrage designed to move in small increments (usually of 50 to 100 yards) and timed to move forward (or otherwise controlled) in order to continue to provide protection to advancing infantry.

CURTAIN SHOOT An anti-aircraft technique, used by light anti-aircraft guns in which all fired a concentration in a given direction to produce a "curtain of fire". It was impressive to see but not very effective and wasteful in ammunition. *cf Umbrella shoot*

D-DAY The day on which a specific operation was to begin. References to D-Day, whether plus or minus, were always used in increments of a day, for example, *D minus 3* meant three days before the commencement of the operation.

DANNERT WIRE A trade name, referring to a form of barbed wire made as a coil which could be "bounced open" in order to extend it over a length of ground, where it would be held in place by iron pickets.

DEAD GROUND Ground which cannot be seen from the observer's position.

DEBOUCH See *Defile.*

DEFEAT IN DETAIL See *Jock Column.*

DEFENCE Doctrine recognised two main types of defence:

DELIBERATE A deliberate defence makes use of available time to select and prepare a defensive position on the most favourable ground whilst out of contact with the enemy. In order to use the best possible terrain for the defence, some ground may be ceded to the enemy and a withdrawal ordered to conform to the new main defensive position or line.

HASTY A hasty defence is adopted when time is short, and particularly when friendly forces are under threat of an imminent attack, or under actual attack, by the enemy. Ground chosen for the defence must therefore be the best available, and other preparations for a defence (such as a coordinated obstacle plan or the creation of entrenchments of other defensive works) may have to be dispensed with.

DEFILADE A defilade position is one in which troops are on a flank (and usually) concealed from enemy observation but are able to employ *enfilade fire* against the enemy.

DEFILE A narrow pass between areas of higher ground such as mountains or hills, and which acts as a *choke point* and channels (also known as canalises) troops. On emerging into more open country after a defile, troops are able to *debouch*, meaning to disperse and adopt normal tactical formations.

DELIVERY POINT "The place where RASC transport hands over its load to unit transport". (1944) cf *Meeting Point, Supply Point*

DEMAND See *Indent.*

DEMONSTRATION To deceive the enemy using manoeuvre whilst not becoming engaged.

DEMOTION See *Relinquish.*

DENSITY "The general spacing of vehicles on a route, expressed in the number of vehicles to the mile (vtm)". (1944) See also *Minefield.*

DEPOT 1. A place of storage, usually but not always of a permanent nature. 2. The UK based headquarters of a regiment or corps, often with a training function.

DETACHED To be detached from one's usual unit, for a limited period of time. *cf Attachment*

DETACHMENT A small group of troops, formed for a particular purpose, and to which the usual nomenclature (eg section, platoon, company etc) would not apply.

DETAIL ISSUE DEPOT The DIDs were RASC-operated supply sub-units used to store and distribute (usually) non-specialist supplies, including fuel and rations.

DIRECT FIRE Fire in which the weapon crew can see the target and are therefore able to make corrections to the fire without the need of an observer.

DISTRICT An administrative formation used both in the UK and overseas, which was responsible for a geographical area, and which did not usually have an operational or combat function. Districts in the UK and overseas were usually a sub-component of Commands, for example, Northumbrian District, which was part of Northern Command, or Rawalpindi District in northern India.[11] Districts could be further divided into *sub-districts, areas, sub-areas, garrisons* etc.[12] Exceptions to this rule were made in the case of two independent districts that operated in effect as mini-commands: London and Northern Ireland.

DIVISION A major general's command, the division was the main tactical building block of the army in the field, and usually comprised three brigades, as well as headquarters, administrative, and logistic units. The division was normally the lowest tactical formation capable or fighting an independent battle, albeit for a limited amount of time. In the UK, 'county' divisions were also formed, usually for an administrative rather than a combat function, for example the Dorset Division, or the Devon and Cornwall division.

DIVISIONAL ADMINISTRATIVE AREA "An area in which the administrative units, and unit B echelon vehicles, whose functions do not require them to be elsewhere, are situated". (1944)

DIVISIONAL ADMINISTRATIVE GROUP "The administrative units, and unit B echelon vehicles, located in the administrative area". (1944)

DRAFT A number of officers and/or soldiers moving as a single group, usually for the purposes of replacing missing personnel or casualties in an active unit. Note: the US used *drafted* in a different way, meaning to be called up for national service.

DROPPING ZONE "An area onto which parachute troops land, or where stores are delivered to a formation, by dropping". (1944)

DS SOLUTION The *Directing Staff solution*. The directing staff or DS are the instructors and trainers at a military college or similar. The expression comes from their opinion of the best course of action to be taken in any theoretical military problem. Whilst under training, for a student to come up with the DS solution would be seen as a good thing by the staff; however, on operations the DS solution would often prove to be unfeasible, unworkable, or very obvious to the enemy.

DUES-OUT An unfilled demand for an item of spares or a replacement vehicle etc. The term means that the item is "*due-out from trade*" and is often accompanied by a date indicating when it is expected to become available.

DUG-OUT In tank fire control orders, a dug-out was any enemy entrenched position. *cf Slit Trench*

D3 All signal cable used began with a D (and referred to as Don). D3 was all-arms cable, D8 was mainly used by the Royal Signals.

ECHELON The term refers to a level or group of people within an organisation, so that in the military sphere the higher levels of command may also be referred to as the higher echelons of command. The term is also used to refer to the use of subsequent and reserve forces to continue the pace and momentum of an operation, eg "to echelon fresh forces through the initial assault force".The term is further used within a unit or formation to refer to the division of combat and support troops, and to describe how logistic support is organised within the unit. A common method of using echelon terminology within a combat unit (infantry or armour) would be:

F – The F echelon refers to the fighting troops.

A – The A echelon is the logistical support closest to the fighting troops and is able to provide fast replenishment of battle necessities close to the combat area. Note: Within armoured regiments the A echelon was often broken into two components: A1 echelon represented the most immediate replenishment group which was limited to ammunition and fuel only. A2 echelon included such items as food and water, mail, clothing and bedding, and repair, maintenance, and recovery facilities.

B – The B echelon was the remaining logistic support elements belonging to the unit and usually represented (in a linear battle) those elements of the unit furthest from the enemy and which included those personnel left out of battle (LOOB). Usually located in the divisional administrative area.

Alternatively, but still in a combat setting, the different elements in an attack could also be referred to as echelons – the assault echelon, the fire support echelon, and the reserve echelon.

EMBARKATION The process of loading personnel, vehicles, and equipment onto ships, aircraft, railways, or road transport.

EMBODIMENT The process of a unit being mobilised and prepared for war.

ENCOUNTER BATTLE This occurs when two mobile forces come together unexpectedly; a key feature of the encounter battle is the need to seize and retain the initiative.

ENFILADE Enfilade fire usually but not always comes from the flank. It occurs when the length of the *beaten zone* of fire (rifle fire, machine guns, mortar bombs or artillery shells) coincides with the longest axis of the target and is therefore able to create the maximum casualties with a minimum expenditure of ammunition.

ENVELOPMENT To pass around an enemy's defensive position.

EQUIPMENT Ordnance stores of all descriptions, including guns, machine guns, small arms, ammunition, vehicles etc, and also material for repair and preservation.

ESTABLISHMENT The official and authorised scales of manpower and equipment allocated to a specific unit. The Peace Establishment (PE) was designed to allow a unit to operate and train during peacetime, whereas the much larger and more comprehensive War Establishment WE) included a more manpower as well as specific equipment that was not often available during peacetime, usually for financial reasons. The mere fact of an establishment existing was not always a guarantee that all the manpower and equipment allocated would be forthcoming. A unit that was below its full establishment was usually referred to as being under (or below) strength.

EXIGENCIES OF THE SERVICE The phrase means that in any given situation, an emergency or other unexpected situation may have to be dealt with in such a manner that the needs of the individual are made subordinate to those of the service. It was often used as an excuse for lack of forward planning and/or poor administration.

EXPLOITATION To take advantage of a developing situation.

FANTAIL Code name sometimes used for the Landing Vehicle Tracked (LVT).

FIELD DRESSING Or First Field Dressing (FFD). Carried by every soldier (the battledress trousers had a special pocket for it on the front right thigh), two separate dressing pads with tape bandages were inside, used to apply pressure onto, and reduce contamination entering, an open wound. Often called a *shell dressing*.

FIELD SERVICE MARCHING ORDER (FSMO) All the items of personal webbing equipment, including the large pack, which would allow the user to operate in the field. (Any other items required by the user in the field, but which could not be carried in FSMO would be stowed in his canvas kit bag and held within his unit's echelon. Sometimes jokingly called *Christmas Tree Order.*

FIELDCRAFT The use of natural and artificial cover and conditions to allow tactical movement and the employment of weapons.

FIGHTING ORDER The usual amount of personal webbing equipment worn during action and designed to allow the infantryman to operate for up to 24 hours (although not in much comfort). It usually consisted of the belt, both cross-straps, both ammunition pouches, water bottle and holder, bayonet frog and bayonet, entrenching tool and holder, and small pack containing mess tins, KFS, rations, gas cape and personal cooker (or similar – it is unwise to try to be too dogmatic, as different versions of this order existed depending on the theatre, unit, soldiers' preference etc).

FIGHTING PATROL A number of men under command of a junior officer or NCO, deployed with the intention of seeking contact with the enemy, for example, to dominate an area of ground, to set an ambush, or to destroy an enemy observation post or standing patrol. It was very much

British policy to actively patrol, particularly during the hours of darkness, as a means of causing enemy casualties, lowering enemy morale, depriving the enemy of sleep, and instilling aggression into one's own troops. How the troops taking part in the activity felt about it is another matter: 'I wonder how many old soldiers still shudder at the thought of a patrol, always undertaken in apparent good spirit but in actual fact one of the most horrible of military activities'.[13]

FIRE & MOVEMENT The central tenet of manoeuvre in the face of the enemy. Wherever possible, when one element of the force was moving, another element would be static and in a position to apply firepower to known or likely enemy positions if required. This was conducted at the lowest level (within the infantry section or tank troop), all the way up to formation manoeuvre.

FIRE CONTROL The control exerted on any form of fire, with a view to making it as effective as possible (in relation to its effect upon the enemy) whilst also being as efficient as possible in terms of reducing ammunition expenditure.

FIRE PIQUET A small number of men under the command of a junior NCO, responsible for the prevention of, or fighting, fires that break out in a unit's accommodation.

FIRE PLAN Usually the responsibility of the Royal Artillery, this was the detailed planning and integration of artillery (and sometimes also mortars, naval bombardment, and air support) in order to support the tactical commander's overall plan. Depending on the circumstances and especially on the time and resources available (including ammunition supply), such plans could be very simple or exceptionally complex.

FIRST-LINE (1st LINE) Lines in this sense are the logistic arrangements for resupply and replenishment stretching from the fighting troops all the way back to the home base. First-line referred to the support available within the unit. In effect, each unit would go into battle (in theory at least) fully stocked with all the ammunition, fuel, and other supplies necessary for it to conduct its mission. Based on predicted rates of usage, the fighting troops would be resupplied and replenished as necessary from first-line stocks, which, having been used, would then be resupplied themselves from *delivery points*, manned by the second-line and so on. *cf Second-line and Third-line.*

FITNESS STATES (AFV) Usually every 24 hours, units would send a summary of the state of their armoured fighting vehicles to their higher headquarters. Different formations use different systems at various points during the war. For example, returns used by Second (British) Army during the North-West Europe campaign in 1944 employed three different categories: P, Q and R. P meant that the AFV was fit for battle; Q that it was unfit but repairable and would be fit within 24 hours; and R referred to a battle casualty or breakdown that had happened in the last 24 hours, and which would not be repairable during the next 24 hours. Similarly, and according to the Glossary of Military Terms (1944), the terminology that should be applied to *vehicle casualties* was based on X, Y and Z: "X casualty – due to a temporary stoppage only, and repairable by the crew of the vehicle without other assistance. Y casualty – requires assistance from repair personnel, and likely to be repairable by unit fitters and light aid detachments or second-line workshops. Z casualty – requires extensive repair or replacement, involving evacuation".

FLAMBO A type of engineer bridge based upon the Bailey Bridge but made of mild steel and designed and used in Italy. The name comes from "Flambeau", the code name used by the administrative echelon of HQ Allied Forces (and which was sometimes itself referred to as FLAMBO).

FLANK The side of a unit or formation. An *open flank* was one that was not covered by observation and/or fire and was therefore vulnerable to exploitation by the enemy.

FORCE Used in two ways; firstly, to denote an organization of any size. Secondly, used for some extemporised commands that were neither formed units nor formations, for example *Habforce* in Syria in 1941.

FORMATION Any organisational level above that of the unit, typically applied to brigades, divisions, corps, armies, and army groups.

FORMING-UP PLACE (FUP). The FUP is the place where a unit adopts its battle formation before advancing to the objective.

FORWARD MAINTENANCE AREA "An area formed, when considered necessary, into which RASC transport under army control empties, and from which second-line transport draws, and at which small stocks are held". (1944)

GENERAL TRANSPORT COMPANY RASC "Companies provided as GHQ troops, primarily for duties on the L of C and in bases". (1944)

GOOSEBERRY See *Mulberry*.

GREEN ENVELOPE Army Form A3078, issued to troops for the transmission of letters relating to private and family matters only. The sender was required to sign a certificate to confirm the nature of its contents, but it was still liable to censorship.

GROUP "(a) A body of troops, based on the formation, unit or sub-unit specified, with the addition of other arms under command for a specified operation, eg brigade, regimental, company group. (bi) R (recce) group – Contains all the personnel a commander may require to help him during his reconnaissance and in the preparation of his plan. (bii) O (order) group – Contains the minimum personnel necessary to receive a commander's orders so as to put his plan into operation. (biii) F (fighting) group – contains the personnel, vehicles, and equipment necessary to carry out the commander's plan. (biv) T (transport) group – Contains the personnel, equipment, and A echelon transport not required in F group". (1944)

GUN In artillery usage, a gun is a long-barrelled piece of ordnance, firing a specific charge of propellant, which imparts a high velocity with a flat trajectory to the projectile.

GUN-HOWITZER In artillery usage, a piece of ordnance which combines the advantages of the gun and the howitzer.

GUNFIRE A rate of fire in which each gun crew fires (aimed shots) as fast as possible. This could be limited either by time (eg one minute) or by ammunition (eg five rounds).

GUN NUMBER A member of an RA gun crew, from the convention of numbering each member of the crew according to the task they perform, eg Number 1 (the gun commander), Number 2 (the breech operator), No 3 (the layer) etc.

GUNNER The lowest rank in the Royal Artillery equivalent to private soldier but also used to refer to an artilleryman of any rank. "The Gunners" referred to the corps as whole.

G.1098 Army Form G 1098 ("War Equipment Tables/Mobilisation Stores Tables") was a listing of all of the accountable (eg non-consumable) weapons, equipment and stores that a unit was entitled to hold, and for which support in terms of consumables, spares, maintenance and repair etc would be provided. It was invariably pronounced Gee Ten Ninety-Eight.

H-HOUR (H Hr) The time at which an operation commences, and in an attack, the time at which the first troops cross the start line. Other times are relative to H-Hour, for example preparations for an attack, including the use of artillery and air, may take place before H-hour and are thus labelled as minus relative to H-Hour, eg "H minus 2 hours" Activities after H-Hour are labelled as plus relative to H-Hour, eg "H plus 15 minutes".[14]

HANGFIRE A term used in gunnery, when an attempt to fire the gun has been made, but there is a delay in the weapon functioning and leading to a delay before the ammunition is fired. Weapon drills were designed to allow for such eventualities in order to ensure crew safety. *cf Misfire*

HARBOUR See *Leaguer.*

HAWK In tank fire control orders, a Hawk was an enemy aircraft.

HAYRICK See *Beehive.*

HEAD Used as a suffix to terms denoting the method of transportation used on the line of communication (eg railhead, roadhead, riverhead, airhead etc). It indicates a forward terminal of lines of communications. The place so named, with the exception of road head, denotes a point of transshipment from one form of transport to another". (1944)

HIPPO See *Mulberry*.

HOME Used as shorthand for the UK (and occasionally, for any other locations classified as being Home for administrative purposes). *Home Base* meant the same.

HORNET In tank fire control orders, a Hornet was an enemy tank or AFV.

HOWITZER In artillery usage, a (usually) short-barrelled, rifled piece of ordnance, firing a comparatively small charge at high elevation, producing a low velocity and a high trajectory Howitzers produced useful 'plunging' fire, which could reach positions that could not be hit by guns.

HULL DOWN A tactical position adopted by a tank or other armoured fighting vehicle, in which a crestline, ridge or similar was used to give as much physical protection as possible to the lower half of the vehicle. In order to adopt a good hull down position, the vehicle would creep forward until the gunner could just see and fire over the ridge; from the enemy perspective, all that could be seen would be the turret.

HURRICANE LAMP Sometimes called a *Storm Lamp* or *Lantern*, this was a paraffin lamp designed to withstand high winds. It was frequently used in the field to provide safe illumination; a full lamp would last about 10 hours. Commonly referred to as a *Tilley Lamp*, which was a trade name.

IMPRESSED Civilian equipment, often vehicles, taken into military service.

IMPREST A simple form of financial cash-based accounting used by paymasters in the field, generally in order to conduct local purchase of items that could not be obtained through the military system.

INDENT The method of requesting (known as *demanding)* any form of spares or materiel support that did not happen automatically. An *indent* was the form (*AB55* or similar) used to pass a demand from forward to rear, until such time as it arrived at the level responsible for satisfying the demand. Ammunition was not normally indented for, as the actual usage would be reported by units down to battery level, and the predicted rates of fire for an upcoming operation were known to the staff already.

INDIRECT FIRE Fire in which the weapon operator cannot see the target and therefore requires the assistance of an observer who can see the fall of shot and order corrections to be made.

INFILTRATE Usually conducted by small groups or even individuals, to infiltrate was to move around or through an enemy position without being detected.

INTERDICTION Measures undertaken to obstruct and/or delay movements of enemy troops, reinforcements and supplies, usually by bombing, shelling, or similar means.

INTERIOR ECONOMY A catch-all phrase applied usually when out of action, and encompassing all those necessary activities that did not form part of military training, for example, laundry, repairing and darning clothes, and preparing for inspections etc. Time allocated to IE could also be used improperly for attending the NAAFI, and, if one was very lucky, catching 'a sly forty winks' during the day.

JOCK COLUMN This term falls somewhere between officialese and slang. The term originates from the early western desert campaign, the name coming from the officer who conceived of it, Lieutenant Colonel 'Jock' Campbell. The idea behind the column was to try to compensate for a lack of numbers and resources by forming a small, mobile, and yet balanced force. This force was based around a battery of field guns, but also included anti-tank and anti-aircraft guns, a squadron of tanks, and a company of infantry. Such forces could be useful in certain circumstances but were difficult to integrate into a formation plan, particularly the artillery components, and could all too easily be isolated and destroyed piecemeal – the military term for this being *defeat in detail*. As a result of these weaknesses, they were discontinued.

LEAGUER/LAAGER This expression is probably African in origin and has at least two common spellings. It was mostly used by armoured units to denote a static formation adopted in the desert to give the best balance between the competing requirements of protection, administration, supply, maintenance, concealment, and dispersion. In a *close leaguer*, the vehicles were close to each other which facilitated easier administration, whereas in an *open leaguer*, for reasons of protection, the vehicles were spaced further apart. Units developed effective drills for forming and breaking a leaguer. The term continued in use after the desert campaign and was used to represent any administrative formation adopted, usually towards the end of the day, for overnight administrative purposes. The term *harbour* was used in a similar manner.

LINES A large barracks or camp was often broken down into a number of named *Lines*, which allowed a division of responsibilities and clarity of ownership.

LINES OF COMMUNICATION "The system of communication to a theatre of operations and [within] a theatre of operations. The latter starts at the base ports and ends at the terminal of each means of communication, ie, rail, motor transport, inland water transport". (1944)

LINES OF COMMUNICATION AREA "The area between the base ports and the rear boundaries of armies, through which the various means of transportation run. This area may be divided into two or more L of C areas, which are subdivided into L of C sub-areas". (1944)

LIFTING BARRAGE A predecessor to the creeping barrage, and useful in static trench warfare, this type of barrage was intended to drop shells onto an enemy trench until just prior to the attacking troops arriving (to a timetable), and the barrage would then lift and drop shells onto the next trench line, and so on. With its roots in the First World War, where it was used by staff planners attempting to precisely timetable attacks on enemy defences, its use was anachronistic during WW2, and better forms of fire control of artillery were rapidly developed.

LOCATING An RA term encompassing the disciplines of target acquisition, survey, and meteorology.[15]

LOGISTICS The planning and execution of the movement and maintenance of forces.

LORRY A load-carrying vehicle with a payload of one and a half tons and above (30 cwt). *cf Truck*.

MAGGIE In tank fire control orders, a Maggie was a machine gun position or nest.

MAIN BASE "When a force is partly maintained from outside the actual theatre of operations, that part of the base outside the theatre will be called the main base". (1944)

MANOUEVRE To use a combination of fire and movement in order to achieve a position of advantage.

MAPLAY A method of encoding grid (map) references. Another method was known as UNICODE.

MARCH IN/OUT The process of formally taking over accommodation from another individual or unit; the incomer would march-in whilst the former occupant would march-out.

MASK To cover a known enemy position in such a way as to prevent it interfering with your own operations. To mask such a position effectively would be to balance the competing requirements of using as small a force as possible to do so, whilst making sure that it was capable of completing the task.

MEETING POINT "A rendezvous where RASC transport is met by unit guides and guided to unit transport areas where loads are transferred (see also *Delivery Point*)". (1944)

MESS The place where one ate (and which could be separate to the place where one was accommodated). The origin of the word comes from mediaeval French *mes* meaning a portion of food. Therefore, the *messing allowance* related to payment for rations, and the officers' and sergeants' messes were the places where not only meals were taken, but were also a form of social club, exclusive to those who bore the correct rank.

MINEFIELD Five types of minefields were used:

PROTECTIVE The protective minefield was intended to provide local close protection for a unit. It would be sited and laid by the unit (as opposed to by RE).

DEFENSIVE A defensive minefield was laid to prevent enemy penetration between two units or formations; it formed part of a coordinated obstacle plan in defence.

BARRIER A barrier minefield was used to stop enemy attacks in selected areas, including flanks, or to channel enemy into a specific area.

NUISANCE The purpose of the nuisance minefield was to use a low-density minefield to impose delay and/or to cause enemy casualties in areas that could not be covered by direct fire or observed by friendly troops.

PHONY A phony/phoney or dummy minefield was used to deceive the enemy; it might contain representations of real mines, but for maximum impact had to be placed and marked as though it was a real minefield.

Such minefields could be anti-personnel, anti-tank, or a mixture of both. The *Density* was defined as the number of mines per yard of front. *Breaching* was the operation of clearing one or more lanes to allow the passage of vehicles. British policy maintained that all minefields must be laid with care, marked correctly, and accurate records (using AF W4017) taken of the position of mines.

MISFIRE Used in gunnery when an attempt has been made to fire the weapon, but it failed to fire. Weapon drills after a misfire might include attempts to use alternative methods of firing, and if these failed, safe methods of unloading the gun and removing the unfired ammunition. *cf Hangfire*

MIXED BATTERY OR REGIMENT A Royal Artillery unit or sub-unit (usually A-A) which included ATS females as well as male soldiers.

MORTAR A piece of unrifled, muzzle loading ordnance firing a bomb. It is a very low velocity weapon, has a high trajectory and a comparatively short range.

MULLBERRY These were two temporary and portable fabricated harbours used during the Normandy landings in order to provide harbour and berthing facilities until one or more channel harbours could be captured and put back into operation. *Mulberry* was used as the code name for the complete structure. *Gooseberries* were the harbour elements providing sheltered waters; *bombardons* were floating breakwaters; static breakwaters consisted of *corn cobs* (scuttled ships) and concrete *phoenix caissons*. The dock piers were floating roadways connecting the pier heads (*spuds*) to the landing beaches and were known as *whales*; these were supported on pontoons known as *beetles*. A *Hippo* was a prototype caisson to be used as a pier head that was rejected in favour of the Spud.

NAMES Certain names were always to be written in block capitals in official writing, including code names, place names and surnames, for example "*During Operation OVERLORD Lt Col TAYLOR was based in DORSET*".

NET Short for network; a radio net was made up of all the authorised *stations* under the control of a specified control station, usually the headquarters.

NIL RETURN When asked to supply information, a superior HQ could order "nil returns required" or "nil returns not required". The former was the more positive method, whereas the latter meant if a return was not received from a particular subordinate, then the assumption would be the answer was nil, no, or not applicable.

NOMENCLATURE The full and official designation given to an item of equipment, used on all items from tanks and weapons to buttons and underwear.

NOTICE (TO MOVE) "Notice is the period of time, laid down by a superior commander, that will be available for preparation after units have been named for action and before they are required to move. The length of time governs the state of readiness. Thus, 'one hour's notice' means that the unit or formation must be able to move one hour after it receives its orders to do so". (1944)

NUMBERS The army of course did not have its own system of numbers, but it was very particular about how each number should be pronounced, particularly over the radio, in order to prevent misunderstanding and to aid clarity. The approved pronunciations were:

0 = Zero (or Owe) 1 = Won 2 = Too 3 = Thuh-ree 4 = Fo-wer
5 = Fi-yiv 6 = Six 7 = Se-ven 8 = Ate 9 = Niner
10 = Wun-Zero 11 = Wun-Wun 12 = Wun-Too etc

As another aid to clarity and to prevent repetitions, the word "Figures" was to be used where required, eg "Figures zero seven hundred hours".

OBSOLESCENT No longer being manufactured, but existing stocks were to be used until exhausted.

OBSOLETE Out of date and officially withdrawn from service use.

OPEN SIGHTS "To fire over open sights" was an artillery term used to denote direct fire from a gun onto a nearby target, usually in self-defence of the battery and using direct sighting methods rather than the more complex and time-consuming use of laying instruments used for indirect fire.

ORDNANCE (1) In artillery usage, the term is applied to weapons designed for the proportion of missiles by explosive force, and includes guns, howitzers, and mortars.

ORDNANCE (2) In more general usage, the term can be applied to all stores intended to support a military force.

OUTFLANK To move around the side of an opposing unit of formation into a position of advantage.

PACK In one sense the soldiers kit bag(s), which generally consisted of a small pack (also referred to as the haversack), and a large pack. In another sense, pack is used to refer to the carrying of military stores and cargo, particularly those that can be broken down into smaller loads to make transportation easier; for example, pack mules, and pack artillery.[16]

PARK Used by RA, RE, RASC and RAOC, a somewhat outdated term used to describe a sub-unit tasked with holding reserves of commodities required to facilitate rapid resupply for a specific task.

PENETRATE To move through an enemy position. The three stages of a full penetration can be described as *break-in*, *break-through*, and then *break-out*.

PEPPERPOT (1) A technique based upon fire and movement and used by the infantry. Upon coming under effective fire, the infantry section broke down into three groups, two groups of two or three riflemen each, plus the Bren or Gun group. One group of riflemen would advance at best speed individually, usually around 20 yards at a time, before dropping into cover. As one group dropped, the other group would get up and continue the advance. The gun group moved to one or other flank in order to give covering fire.

PEPPERPOT (2) A late war artillery technique, in which a concentration of different weapons, including tank and/or anti-tank guns, and/or mortars, and/or light anti-aircraft guns, were used to fire into a given area as part of a fire plan. The idea of the pepperpot shoot was to overwhelm the enemy by weight of fire.

PETROL POINT "A point where a forward holding on wheels is established by a second-line RASC company to facilitate the replacement of petrol and lubricants to forward units". (1944)

PHASES For ease of control an operation could be divided into phases; such phases were normally sequential but there could be some concurrency (or overlap). In many instances, a subsequent phase could not begin until a previous or preliminary phase had been successfully completed.

PHONETIC ALPHABET A partial phonetic alphabet was introduced prior to the First World War but only for six letters (Ack, Beer, Emma, Esses, Toc and Vic). In 1914, Don was added. The increasing use of radio during and after the First World War made it necessary to introduce a complete phonetic alphabet and this was first done in 1927. It should be noted that the Royal Navy and the RAF both used similar but not identical systems, and these led to some confusion some might use out-dated or incorrect terminology (although in most cases it would be understood) The increasing need for cooperation between the three services, as well as with Commonwealth and allied armies (especially the USA), meant that mid-war a revised phonetic alphabet was introduced that was designed to solve this problem, the RAF adopting it before the army. (Note: The NATO phonetic alphabet still in use today was introduced in 1956).

Army 1927 to June 43	Army from June 1943	RN WW2	RAF to 1942	RAF from 1942
AC	ABLE	AC	APPLE	ABLE
BEER	BAKER	BEER	BEER	BAKER
CHARLIE	CHARLIE	CHARLIE	CHARLIE	CHARLIE
DON	DOG	DON	DON	DOG
EDWARD	EASY	EDWARD	EDWARD	EASY
FREDDIE	FOX	FOX	FREDDIE	FOX
GEORGE	GEORGE	GEORGE	GEORGE	GEORGE
HARRY	HOW	HOW	HARRY	HOW
INK	ITEM	INK	INK	ITEM
JOHNNIE	JIG	JOHNNIE	JUG	JIG
KING	KING	KING	KING	KING
LONDON	LOVE	LOVE	LONDON	LOVE
MONKEY	MIKE	MONKEY	MONKEY	MIKE
NUTS	NAN	NAN	NUTS	NAN
ORANGE	OBOE	ORANGE	ORANGE	OBOE
PIP	PETER	PIP	PIP	PETER
QUEEN	QUEEN	QUEEN	QUEEN	QUEEN
ROBERT	ROGER	ROBERT	ROBERT	ROGER
SUGAR	SUGAR	SUGAR	SUGAR	SUGAR
TOC	TARE	TOC	TOC	TARE
UNCLE	UNCLE	UNCLE	UNCLE	UNCLE
VIC	VICTOR	VIC	VIC	VICTOR
WILLIAM	WILLIAM	WILLIAM	WILLIAM	WILLIAM
X-RAY	X-RAY	XRAY	XRAY	XRAY
YORKER	YOKE	YOKE	YORKER	YOKE
ZEBRA	ZEBRA	ZEBRA	ZEBRA	ZULU

PINPOINT TARGET A small artillery target, which required more precision than the usual area target. Because of its small size, a single gun was used.

PINTAIL A device (Simulator, Rifle Fire No 1) used to simulate weapons firing, attached to dummy parachutists (*Ruperts*) during Operation OVERLORD.

PIPE MINE Not a mine in the usual sense, the Greenlee Pipe Pusher was an RE-operated machine designed for installing piping underground without disturbing the surface.

PIVOT GUN Usually the right-hand artillery gun (when viewed from behind) and used as the reference gun (the "pivot") for other guns in the battery, in order to prevent shells landing at the target end in a linear fashion matching the battery layout.

PLATOON A basic manoeuvre element of infantry battalions, usually commanded by a Lieutenant or Second Lieutenant, and comprising about 30 men. Other arms also used the term platoon for a subaltern's command.

POINT As the highest point on hills were marked on military maps (on the continent usually) in metres, each hill could be individually identified by its height, for example Point 112.

PREMATURE With ammunition, when a round of ammunition fires but then explodes before it should, including in the barrel.

PRE-POSITION To place units, equipment, ammunition or other or supplies at or near the intended point of use.

PRIMARY TRAINING Often referred to as *basic training*, the object of primary training was to turn a civilian recruit into a soldier within a period of six weeks or so. Once primary training was completed, soldiers would move onto *specialist* or *special-to-arm* training, designed to provide them with the necessary skills for their specific role.

PRINCIPLES OF WAR A set of principles for guidance in conducting operations. These were intended to be applicable in all circumstances and in all theatres. MTP 23 of 1941 "Operations" listed them as:

Maintenance of the object (The Master Principle)
Concentration
Economy of Force
Offensive Action
Surprise
Security
Co-operation
Mobility

PULHEEMS (sometimes referred to as PULHEMS). This was the acronym for the system of medical classification of personnel. It stood for:

Physical Capacity
Upper Limbs

Locomotion
Hearing (Acuity)
Eyesight (Visual acuity) Note: one E for each eye, right then left
Mental Capacity
Stability (Emotional)

The overall result allowed personnel to be assessed as being fit for service in general terms, and could also define which regiment, corps or service they could serve in, due to the medical classification requirements of those units. Additionally, a system of code letters was used as a form of short-hand, the first letter denoting the type of theatre (Forward, Lines of Communication, or Base) and the second the climatic area (Everywhere or Temperate). A separate term Home Only was also used for those could only serve within the UK. Thus, the codes used were FE, FT, LE, LT, BE, BT or HO.

PURSUIT A pursuit operation takes place when the enemy has lost the initiative and is seeking to retreat or withdraw; speed and boldness are key to a successful pursuit, and sensible risks must be accepted.

RADIO (WIRELESS) SILENCE On a radio net, wireless/radio silence could be imposed for security reasons. Because it was well known that the enemy were able to intercept and direction-find using radio transmissions, at certain stages of operations (often in the build-up), radio silence would be ordered; although a listening watch was still maintained, stations were not allowed to transmit other than in emergency.

RAID A (usually) small-scale operation involving a rapid penetration of enemy territory, typically to gain information, to confuse the enemy, to capture equipment or prisoners, or to destroy equipment and facilities.

RATES OF FIRE (ARTILLERY) Each gun or howitzer would use a specified rate of fire under different circumstances. These were usually referred to as *intense, rapid, normal, slow,* or *very slow* and were expressed in rounds per minute.

REAR MAINTENANCE AREA "An area in which are located the temporary depots which maintain the force ashore, from the time when issues from beach maintenance areas cease, and until permanent base depots start to issue". (1944)

RECONNAISSANCE Reconnaissance is subdivided into three types or levels. "Close reconnaissance is carried out at close quarters to the enemy, to obtain detailed information of the ground and of the enemy's location, strength and movements. Medium reconnaissance is carried out to obtain general information about the enemy's movements and dispositions on which to base a plan of offensive or defensive action. Distant reconnaissance is carried out to discover the enemy's strategical movements and concentrations in a theatre of operations". (1944)

RECONNAISSANCE PATROL Reconnaissance patrols could be either mounted or on foot. They were intended to avoid combat, and to use stealth and concealment in order to gain information about the enemy.

REFILLING POINT "A place where the transfer of loads from one detachment of RASC lorries to another takes place. It will only be used when the distance between the forward maintenance area and the delivery points is beyond the range of second-line transport, or when forward formations are being maintained direct from the railhead maintenance area. It is in no sense a dump". (1944)

REFUSE A FLANK A rarely used term, indicating that a flank was solidly held, sealed off, or otherwise impassable.

REGIMENT Another organizational noun with multiple meanings. Most commonly, a regiment was the name given to an infantry unit comprising one or more battalions; for example, the Dorset Regiment were an infantry regiment which during WW2 comprised eight battalions. It was used for other units, almost invariably commanded by a Lieutenant Colonel, of a roughly equivalent size, including armour, artillery, engineers, and signals, amongst others. It was also used by training organizations. Although the full title of the Royal Artillery was The Royal Regiment of Artillery, and despite consisting of dozens of individual regiments, the Royal Regiment was not, in fact, a regiment; rather it was a huge corps.

REGULATING HQ This was an extemporised HQ temporarily formed in order to control (regulate) the movement of vehicles, particularly during complex operations.

RELIABILITY The ability of an item, not necessarily a vehicle, to perform its required functions under stated conditions for a specified period of time.

RELIEF DRIVER INCREMENT The RDI was a practical means of providing a second driver to RASC transport units without having to amend the War Establishment, which allowed only one driver per vehicle.

RELIEVE To take over responsibility of a role, a piece of terrain, or a defensive position. A relief in place meant that the (new) relieving unit would move up to the (old) unit being relieved, receive briefings on the situation, and each component of the position was handed over in turn so that the defensive posture was maintained throughout the process. At a specified time, the new unit would become formally and fully responsible for the position. The unit that had been relieved could then complete its move out, usually to the rear and rest.

RELINQUISH To relinquish rank was to request to be relieved of the responsibilities of a particular rank, often of a local or acting nature. This was different to the process of *demotion*, when rank was formally removed from a person, usually for reasons of inefficiency or because of a poor disciplinary record.

REPORT LINE "A line having no tactical significance such as a lateral road or railway, on which units report but do not halt". (1944)

REQUISITION To officially request (or take) possession of an item, with the intention of payment or replacement being made immediately or in the future.

RESERVE Forces uncommitted to a specific task in an operation, but which remain well placed and ready to be used at the time and place of the commander's choosing. A key tenet of the use of reserves which was emphasised at all levels of command training was that once the reserve is committed, another must be generated; in practice this was rarely possible.

RETIRE To move one's own forces out of contact with the enemy.

RETREAT To attempt to break clean from a successful enemy attack. As opposed to *Withdrawal,* which implies control and cohesion and often an element of pre-planning, a retreat is usually disorganised and uncontrolled.

REVETMENT Material placed against the sloping walls of a defensive position, used to break up and absorb the impact of ammunition hitting the slope, as well as to retain the shape and function of the position.

ROAD CLASSIFICATION A system of letters and numbers classifying the size and serviceability of roads/tracks and their capabilities was used as follows:

A Roads wide enough to take two lines of traffic.
B Roads wide enough to take a single line of traffic but allowing individual vehicles to pass one another.
C Roads wide enough to take a single line of traffic but on which passing is impossible other than at prepared passing places.
1 Roads capable of taking heavy motor transport for example 3-ton lorries, heavy guns etc.
2 Roads capable of taking light motor transport, for example 30 cwt lorries
3 Roads capable of taking horse transport only.
4 Roads or bridle paths capable of taking pack transport only.

Thus, a road classified as B2 would be wide enough to take a single line of light motor traffic, allowing individual vehicles to pass one another.

ROUTES Referring to the main routes of advance and supply, the UP route was the one leading towards the front line, whereas the DOWN route was the one leading towards the rear. Roads joining the main routes up were known as *laterals.*

ROVER See *Tentacle.*

RUM RATION Service rum was contained in one gallon stone jars held by the quartermaster; these were often marked SRD as they were the responsibility of Supply Reserve Depots. It was not issued automatically but only with the approval of higher authority and generally for a specific purpose, such as before a demanding operation or because of extremely cold weather.

RUPERT A fairly crude deception device consisting of a hessian sack shaped like a man and filled with sand, attached to a small parachute and used to simulate paratroop landings; officially it was the *Device Camouflage No 15* and used during Operation OVERLORD. See *Pintail*.

S-MINE From the German name, *Schrapnellmine*, this widely detested mine was nicknamed the "*Bouncing Betty*" because when it was triggered, it 'jumped' about a metre into the air before exploding at groin height. Designed to cause horrendous injuries rather than to kill, its effects can be imagined.

SALVAGE The systematic removal of serviceable or repairable weapons, components, equipment, and raw materials from the battlefield in order to reuse (recycle) them at a later date.

SALVO A barrage in which all guns involved in a fire mission fire at the same time.

SAND CHANNEL Found to be necessary during desert operations, sand channels were developed pre-war for wheeled vehicles. These comprised perforated metal planks which could be placed in front of each wheel before crossing an area of the soft sand, thereby spreading the load and in effect reducing the ground pressure of the vehicle.

SAND TABLE In its original form a sand table was exactly what the name denotes; a large shallow box was constructed and filled with sand or earth. This would then be sculpted to represent and reflect an area of terrain, with other details (roads, buildings, forests etc) added. An alternative version was the cloth model, which used hessian or similar material to replicate the terrain. Sand tables/cloth models were used in two main ways. Firstly, for general tactical training, and secondly, in preparation for a specific operation in which the ground to be crossed could be replicated in some detail and aspects of the operation demonstrated/rehearsed.

SCHU-MINE A German anti-personnel mine, it was encased in a wooden box and used only small amounts of metal so therefore was difficult to detect. The Allies trained detection dogs specifically to deal with this problem.

SCREEN Screens were forces used to give some level of protection over an area of ground in which the force would otherwise be vulnerable, for example on an *open flank*. Screening forces were usually made up from what could be spared from the main operation, and reconnaissance troops were often allocated this task. The main purpose of the screen would be to give advance warning of enemy movements, and where possible, to inflict casualties and impose some delay on the enemy force. Note: Screens in another sense were long rolls of canvas, hessian etc camouflage materials, designed to shield areas from enemy observation. A common sight in WW1, they were only used infrequently in early WW2.

SECOND-LINE (2nd LINE) The logistic second-line operated within divisions from *refilling points* forward to *delivery points*. Although the organisation may have been amended according to circumstances, in general, second-line ammunition was the responsibility of an ammunition company, one of which was established for each division, as well as one for corps troops. The same principle applied for fuel, and other items such as food, spare blankets, reserve clothing, and equipment were also catered for. *cf First-line* and *Third-line*.

SECTION Within the infantry, the lowest level manoeuvre unit, usually commanded by a corporal and consisting of around 8 men. The term was also used in many other arms and corps, to denote a small unit or detachment, and which were often much larger than an infantry section.

SECURITY CLASSIFICATIONS With effect from 1st July 1943, documents were classified in one of four ways: MOST *SECRET, SECRET, Confidential* and *Restricted* – the first two always had to be written in block capitals. On this date the two previous categories of *Security* and *Not to be Published* were abolished. In addition, some documents could also be marked *OFFICER ONLY*, as well as *TO BE KEPT UNDER LOCK AND KEY*.

SHELL SCRAPE A shallow depression made in the ground using a spade or entrenching tool, and just deep enough for a prone soldier to take cover from artillery or mortar bombardments. It was in no sense a trench or fighting position. Sometimes refer to in the vernacular as a *foxhole*.

SIGSALY Not an acronym as is often thought, but a cover name resembling an acronym; it was a high-level secure speech communication system used from 1943 between the US and the UK.

SILENT POSITION An artillery position that is ready to fire but has not yet done so.

SKELETON WEBBING The bare minimum of webbing, usually consisting of the belt, both cross-straps, both ammunition pouches, water bottle and holder, and bayonet frog and bayonet.

SLIDEX A low-level radio encoding system introduced in 1944 (and still used into the 1980s).

SLIT TRENCH A narrow trench, usually for two men. Usually of basic construction and not designed to be occupied for any length of time, the name comes from the narrowness of the trench, which reduced the amount of digging required and made it less likely to collapse from a near-miss.

The phrase *dug-out*, much used during the Great War, was still in use but much less so during WW2 and tended to refer to a better constructed and more permanent form of shelter, often with good overhead cover and which could be made, to some degree at least, more comfortable/habitable).

SMALL ARMS Weapons with a calibre below 1". Note: before WW2, the 1937 edition of Equipment Regulations defined small arms as "Rifles, bayonets, swords, lances and pistols", and classified machine guns and small cannon separately.

SORTIE Originating in siege warfare, the term originally meant a surprise attack launched by the defenders. In WW2, It meant a rapid attack or raid, usually of a set or limited duration.

SOYER STOVE A cooking boiler of 10-gallon capacity used to prepare food for up to 50 troops.

SPARE PART An *accessory* or a *component*, required to restore an article to fully operational condition.

SPECIALIST/SPECIAL-TO-ARM TRAINING See *Primary Training.*

SPOILING ATTACK An attack designed to prevent or impair an impending enemy attack.

SPUD See *Mulberry.*

SQUADRON The equivalent to a Company within the RAC and some engineer units, a squadron was a major's command.[17] It usually comprised between three and five troops plus a headquarter element. It was also used instead of *Battery* by the RA in their AOP sub-units.

STANDING PATROL A patrol pushed forward of the frontline, in order to take temporary possession of a feature or to observe a likely enemy *avenue of approach*, often during the hours of darkness. Such patrols, having arrived at their destination, were typically static, and would be unpopular because of their repetitive, predictable and therefore vulnerable nature. *Fighting patrols* were often deployed specifically to destroy an enemy standing patrol and therefore dominate ground.

STAND-TO Two types of stand-to existed. One was the routine stand-to which took place usually at dusk and dawn, as these were known to be the most common times for the enemy to attack a defensive position. The other type was in response to the urgent call of "Stand to!", to deal with an unexpected emergency. In both cases, everyone in the position would be required to immediately take up their defensive posts in expectation of the need to repel an enemy attack.

START LINE (SL) This is the line which assaulting troops cross at *H-hour*. It may be artificial (eg mine tape used) or natural (eg a road or track.)

STICK GRENADE The standard German hand grenade (or *Stielhandgranate*), due to its distinctive shape. Used in both world wars, its long handle design meant that it could be thrown further than the smaller British No 36 (or Mills) "egg" grenade. Sometimes called the *Potato-masher.*

STORM LAMP/LANTERN See *Hurricane Lamp*.

SUB-UNIT Specifically, the term was used to refer to a company, squadron or battery commanded by a major. It was sometimes also used to refer to platoons, troops, or other detachments below the *Unit* level.

SUN COMPASS An essential aid to navigation in the desert. Mounting standard magnetic compasses on vehicles would not work as the vehicles own magnetic signature would affect the accuracy of the compass. The sun compass used the same principle as the shadow cast by the gnomon of a sundial, with the shadow falling on a rotatable disc that indicated the direction of travel.

SUNSHIELD A camouflage/deception device fitted to tanks in the western desert. Designed to make them look like a lorry when observed from the air or at long range, a canvas-covered framework was erected over the tank, shaped and painted to resemble an innocuous lorry, allowing armoured formations to move up towards a battle area without unduly worrying the enemy. The device could be discarded by the crew when close to the battle area.

SUPPLY POINT The place at which supplies are transferred from RASC transport to unit transport. See *delivery point.* (1944)

SUPPRESS To degrade or prevent an enemy's ability to use its own weapons.

SURVEY Used by the RA to refer to the relative position of objects on the earth's surface, particularly guns and their targets.

SWISS ROLL This wa a floating roadway that was designed to move with the tide

TACTICS The "methods of employing military forces in battle in accordance with the *Principles of War.*" (MTP23 1941)

TAMP Used with explosives, particularly demolitions, to tamp meant to seal the explosive charge by sandbags, packed earth etc, in order to concentrate the blast against the object being demolished.

TANNOY On armoured fighting vehicles, the Tannoy (a trade name from the amalgamation of the words tantalum and alloy), was a one-way communication system used by the commander to control his driver (and sometimes referred to as ECC, or emergency crew control). More widely, the name was given to any form of loudspeaker system.

TARGETS (ARTILLERY) A *Forward Observation Officer* (FOO) would normally control all eight of the guns in the battery of the field regiment to which he belonged. However, artillery control and coordination improved greatly throughout the war. It became possible to allocate many more guns to a target of opportunity that was, in the opinion of the FOO, worthy of the effort. In order to quickly allocate the appropriate resources in firepower terms, they were given phonetic code letters as follows:

MIKE TARGET one requiring all the guns (24) in a regiment that were in range of the target.

UNCLE TARGET one requiring all the guns in the divisional artillery.

VICTOR TARGET one requiring all the guns in the corps artillery, including medium regiments.

YOKE TARGET one requiring all the guns in an AGRA.

WILLIAM TARGET one requiring all the guns in the field army, including heavy artillery. A William target was therefore of the very highest priority and was something of a rarity.

TELLER MINE A much-used German anti-tank mine; the name comes from its circular casing, as *teller* is the German word for plate.

TENTACLE A code name for a wireless detachment from the Army Air Support Control (later Air Support Signals Unit), small mobile units designed to provide rapid air support for, and liaison with, ground forces, particularly at brigade and divisional level. In Italy these were known as *ROVERs*.

THIRD-LINE (3rd LINE) The logistic third-line operated between railheads (and sometimes from ports or other storage/supply depots). These sources of supply were usually referred to as *parks* and were established and organised on a corps basis. The supplies being moved were generally the responsibility of the RAOC, assisted by the RASC in the provision of transportation. So, for example, ammunition supply would take place as follows:

Ammunition from the *home base* would arrive at an ammunition railhead (ARH).

From there, it would be delivered forward by *supply columns* to the corps *ammunition park*, which itself would be organised as a number of *sub-parks*, usually one for each division under command and one for corps troops.

Each division would move its ammunition forward to an *ammunition refilling point* (ARP), and from there forward again to a dump managed by the divisional ammunition company. The move forward from the ARP represented the switch from third to second-line.

Forward of this would be one or more *ammunition points* (AP), and even further forward, a number of *delivery points*. The delivery points where the locations that the individual units would go to in order to replenish their own first-line stocks.

The fundamental principle was the ammunition was passed systematically and automatically from rear to front, and that troops in action should "never have to turn their backs on the enemy to fetch further supplies". *cf 1st Line* and *2nd Line.*

THREE TO ONE RULE Two versions of this existed, both used in relation to making an attack on a defended position. The first rule specified that in order to successfully take a defended position, the attacking force must comprise three times the manpower of the defended location. The second rule specified that artillery and mortar etc fire support must be able to use three times the weight of fire as that employed by the defending troops.

TILLEY LAMP See *Hurricane Lamp.*

TIME As with the alphabet, the army had a particular and specific approach to dealing with time. Although this was not universally followed, in official documentation all time should have used the 24-hour clock, a group of four figures followed by "hrs". The first two figures represented the hour and the last two the minutes past the hour, eg *1445 hrs.* Midnight was officially 0000 hrs, but for some reason many units and individuals referred to it as 2359 hrs (a malpractice that continues to this day). Where operations took place overnight, to avoid any possibility of confusion, both dates were specified, for example "RV at 0000 hrs 7/8 Oct". It is worth noting that although British Summer Time (i.e. one hour ahead of Greenwich Mean Time) was due to end on 27th October 1940, the clocks were not put back in the UK. For the rest of the war the country remained on BST during the winter months and went to "British Double Summer Time" over the summer; this first happened in March 1941. This system remained in place until 1947.

TOFFEE APPLE Used in the western desert at night, a burst of tracer ammunition was fired as near vertically as possible into the sky, in order to allow vehicles to 'home in' on it and reach their destination.

TRACTOR A vehicle specifically designed for pulling a load, typically a trailer, gun, or limber.

TRIPLE A A nickname for Anti-Aircraft Artillery.

TROOP The equivalent of a platoon within a squadron or battery. Usually a lieutenant or second lieutenant's command, troops were used within the RAC, RA and also in RE squadrons, as well as Commando units (where they were a much larger organization). Note: within the RA, for historical reasons, many batteries bore honorific titles using the word, such as N Battery (The Eagle Troop). "*Troops*" was also in common usage to describe manpower within the army, as in "The troops were waiting on the dock", or "He is part of corps troops".

TROOP FIRE Firing of artillery guns but controlled so that each gun fires in turn, the intention being to have an almost constant impact of shells at the target end.

TRUCK A load-carrying vehicle with a payload of up to one ton (20 cwt). *cf Lorry.*

TURRET DOWN Applied to armoured fighting vehicles, in a turret down position the whole of the vehicle would be behind a crest or similar so that it could not be observed by the enemy, nor could it use its weapons; however, the commander would just be able to look over the obstacle and use his binoculars for observation.

UMBRELLA SHOOT A type of anti-aircraft shoot in which fire is concentrated overhead, to provide a protective 'umbrella' above an area or unit. It was wasteful of ammunition and unlikely to bring down aircraft, as its purpose was to drive off enemy aircraft. *cf Curtain shoot*

UNICODE See *MAPLAY.*

UNIT Specifically, the term was used to refer to a regiment or battalion or equivalent, commanded by a Lieutenant Colonel. More generally, the term was applied to any formed body of troops. *cf Sub-unit*

VAN A small general purpose wheeled vehicle capable of carrying a small load.

VEHICLE CASUALTIES See *Fitness States.*

VITAL GROUND Vital ground is that which, if taken by the enemy, will render the whole defensive position untenable.

WAR DIARY Army Form C2118 was used for record keeping, either as the War Diary or the Intelligence Summary. Instructions for the completion of the War Diary were contained within Field Service Regulations and its upkeep was normally the responsibility of the unit adjutant or equivalent. These records were to be completed in duplicate, classed as Secret, and completed daily from the day of mobilization (or formation of the unit). Depending upon the inclination and time available to this person, War Diaries can be extensively detailed or frustratingly brief; many are typed or hand-written with care, but others are scrawled and virtually indecipherable.

WARFLAT A standard design of 'LNWR Parrot' flatbed railway wagon, designed to carry a load of up to 40 tons (later modifications produced designs capable of 45 and 50) and mainly used for the movement of tanks. Side or end ramps were required for loading and unloading; later, special ramped wagons were built.

WAR GAME Although the term could be used generally it had a very specific meaning: a two-sided tactical exercise usually conducted indoors, in which two opposing forces would attempt to better the other; the process was umpired by directing staff and followed the basic system of one side making a tactical move, which would then be countered by the other, and so on.

WEBBING The term given to the personal load carrying "web equipment" designed primarily for the infantryman but also used by other arms. It was made out of a durable cotton webbing material, with the most common pattern being the 1937 "Braithwaite" type, although at the start of the war the earlier 1908 pattern could sometimes be seen, and small amounts of an experimental 1944 pattern were in use towards the end of the war. A webbing item that was not part of the 1937 set but that was issued as personal clothing was the gaiter (or *anklet*), worn around the ankle of the boot.

WHALE See *Mulberry.*

WITHDRAWAL A withdrawal usually took place following a tactical defeat, or to avoid one. The intention would be to withdraw from unfavourable contact with the enemy, whilst retaining command, control and cohesion, and to move to a new position where reorganisation could take place. A *withdrawal in contact*, in which the rearguard of the withdrawing force remained in contact with the enemy, was generally regarded as one of the most difficult operations of war. *cf Retreat*

WORKS SERVICES This was a function of the Royal Engineers, and the term was used to denote the provision and maintenance of the army's accommodation, whether it be permanent barracks, hutted camps, or requisitioned property.

WRITE-OFF When a vehicle or piece of equipment was no longer fit for any sort of purpose, it would be "written-off", meaning that it had been officially removed from the account and therefore to all intents and purposes no longer existed. The term also had a slang usage, in that anything (or anyone) that was useless could be described as a "complete write-off".

Y-DAY Specific to Operation Overlord, this was a way of counting up to the commencement of the operation starting on 1st June 1944 (Y-Day). D-Day 6th June therefore was Y+5, thereafter all references were made to D-Day itself; 8th June 1944 was D+2 etc. In practice most documents referred to D-1 etc.

YOUNG SOLDIERS Volunteer soldiers under the age of 19, who were usually trained in special YS battalions or regiments. These youngsters were often seen as a potential source of high-quality regular servicemen for the army, and as such were a forerunner of the post-war junior soldier and junior leader units. In March 1943, the age of conscription was lowered from 20 to 18 and thus removed the need for YS units.

Y-LIST A category of troops denoting "non-effective", typically those on long-term sick leave, undergoing rehabilitation, or awaiting discharge. Similarly, the X-List was for soldiers hospitalised for a short-term (under 21 days).

Z+ Part of a method sometimes used to indicate the intended date by which progress would be made, Z related to the start of the war in September 1939, so a reference to Z+21 meant 21 months later, which equated to May 1941.

Part 2

SLANG EXPRESSIONS

"These Eytie bints are a bit manky but still better than the Gippos. Take a shufti at that bibi over there, she is a pucka bella seenyoreena."

Soldiers adore slang (and bad language), with new recruits finding it at first baffling, and then quickly adopting it into their own speech, both consciously in order to fit in but also unconsciously as it is absorbed into their vocabulary. Slang expressions can be particular to a regiment or corps or to a specific campaign, and they can of course cross nationalities. Many expressions used by the British Army in World War 2 were pre-war, from WW1, particularly from India; all expressions of Hindustani origin below are marked as (H), whilst those from Arabic are (A). Other words came in from the French (often bastardised to make pronunciation easier), from Australia and Canada, as well as from the US (both from films – "movies" – and from personal contact with GIs). Compiling a list of slang expressions is always a tricky task, particularly with regard to determining exactly when an expression was first used. The list below is hopefully, if probably not complete, at least accurate in this regard. One thing I have not attempted to do is to include common British civilian and regional expressions, eg those which would be as familiar in wider context, such as cockney rhyming slang, or the use of regional identifiers like Jock, Taffy, Mick, Paddy, Geordie etc. Another common form of slang in use was sporting terms – "to be on a sticky wicket" and similar.

ACK ACK   Anti-aircraft.

ACKERS/AKKERS (A)   Money, from the word for coins.

ACK-I   An assistant instructor.

AK DUM (H)   Hurry up, quickly.

ALL COOKING CREMATED, or ALDERSHOT CEMENT COMPANY Names for the Army Catering Corps (ACC) formed in 1941.

ALL PISS AND WIND Of no substance. Someone known to be a storyteller or a liar, in other words a *bullshitter*, would be *full of piss and wind.*

ARMY FORM BLANK Toilet paper.

ARSE ABOUT FACE Anything that was in any way different to its usual or preferred situation was *arse about face.*

ARSE CRAWLING Also known as *bum-licking, brown-nosing* and *brown-tonguing*, the act of currying favour with a superior.

BABY MAGGIE Nickname for the AA radar equipment No 3 Mk III.

BALING OUT To bale out (sometimes spelt as bail) was to evacuate a vehicle quickly, especially following a direct or close hit.

BAIT (H) Food.

BALLS-OUT To do something with maximum effort, to give 100%.

BADGIE (H) From the word *bhudgie* meaning time, used for any military trumpeter (from the practice of marking the time in the military day using bugle or trumpet calls).

BASHA (H) A native hut, used to denote any form of tent or shelter in the field. *cf Bivvy*

BATMAN An officer's servant, detailed to look after their administrative needs in order to allow the officer to concentrate on command. In the infantry, a platoon commander's batman would usually double-up as his runner, used to carry messages short distances The name is thought to come from the use of mules during the peninsula war carrying officer's baggage, with the mules being known as *bats.*

BATTLE BOWLER The steel helmet. *cf Tin Hat.*

BAZOOKA Not only the handheld American anti-tank weapon, but also applied to similar German weapons (*Panzerfaust, Panzerschreck*). One source recorded that it was also sometimes used to denote one's penis.

BED ROLL As sleeping bags were generally not issued or available during the conflict, soldiers would use their issued woollen blankets and waterproof ground sheets to make up what they called a bed roll, which became in effect their sleeping bag, and which, importantly, could be rolled up and unrolled very quickly.

BIBI (H) Woman.

BINT (A) An Arab (or any other kind of) woman, the word simply means *the daughter of.*

BIR (A) Arabic for a water well, often marked with a cairn of rocks and so in the desert frequently the only landmark for miles.

BIRD MEN Paratroops or glider troops – members of the AAC Sometimes used in documents as a very low level and obvious code for such troops.

BISCUIT A type of mattress, so-called because each of the three sections (each roughly 18″ × 2′ and somewhat thin), was said to resemble army hardtack biscuits. Straw-filled mattresses were often called *palliasses*.

BIVVY A shortened form of *bivouac*, any form of living in the field, either under canvas or by extemporised means. Small two men tents were often referred to as *bivvies*. *cf Bashas*

BLIGHTY (H) From a Hindustani word meaning a foreign country.

BLIGHTY ONE A wound serious enough to send the recipient back to the United Kingdom.

BLOOD WAGON An ambulance.

THE BLUE Used by old hands to refer to the desert, as in "we're going up the blue tomorrow". The desert of course was not blue, so this slang expression may come from the wide expanse of blue sky over an otherwise featureless landscape.

BLUE CAPS See *Red Caps*.

BLUE JOB Anyone in the RAF; also referred to as the *Brylcreem boys*, from the popular hair grease.

BLUE PENCIL Censorship, from the blue pencil required to be used by officers when censoring other rank's outgoing mail. Officers were allowed to self-certify their own mail by signing a declaration on the envelope.

BOCHE A French term from the First World War, referring to German soldiers; less frequently used in WW2. *cf Jerry, Squarehead*.

BODS Meaning bodies, but not in the sense of corpses; rather, a tank crew for example would be comprised of three, four or five bods – unless one of them happened to be an officer, in which case he would usually be a *Type*.

BOLSHIE To be bolshie was to be angry or argumentative, particularly against military authority; from Bolshevik.

BOMB-HAPPY To be nervous due to the stresses of combat – the World War One term *shell shocked* was also used in the same context.

BONDOOK (H) Spelled in any number of ways, the word originally meant musket and was used to denote any long-barrelled weapon, particularly a rifle.

BOTTLED SUNSHINE Both beer and cod liver oil, although most soldiers would probably agree that they would prefer a bottle of the former to the latter.

BOUNCE Usually used when conducting an obstacle crossing, to bounce meant to use surprise and speed to get across and onto the far bank.

BOUNCING BETTY Known by the Germans as the S-Mine (*Schrapnellmine)*, this mine was so nicknamed because when it was triggered, it 'jumped' about a metre into the air before exploding at groin height. Designed to cause horrendous injuries rather than to kill, its effects can be imagined.

BRASS HAT A general officer, the term coming from the shiny metallic leaves adorning the peak of such a personage's cap.

BRASS-UP To use automatic fire; the term comes from the amount of spent brass cases produced from such fire. Brassing-up was conducted not only against known targets, but also against places where the enemy was suspected of being located, in order to cause casualties or keep the enemy's' heads down, or to force them to withdraw or even surrender.

BREN GUN CARRIER More correctly the Universal Carrier, this was a ubiquitous small tracked armoured vehicle used in a multitude of roles by the infantry and other corps. Bren Gun Carriers were an early type of such vehicle, the name sticking when the designation and design changed.

BREW-UP (1) To make a cup of tea; famously, British soldiers of all ranks and cap badges were extremely adept in making a rapid cup of tea even under the most trying of conditions. Various techniques evolved, including the development of the so-called *Benghazi burner*, a simple improvised cooker using a sand and petrol mix in a perforated biscuit tin (or similar). Although *Tommy cookers* developed during the First World War were still used, towards the end of the war better individual *Hurlock* cookers using paraffin (kerosene) were developed. *Primus* stoves, which also used paraffin, and *Cookers Portable No 2*, which were much larger petrol-fuelled items, were generally used by vehicle crews rather than individuals. It is widely believed that Britain stockpiled more tea than ammunition in the United Kingdom during the mid-part of the war.

BREW-UP (2) An armoured vehicle catching fire; often with such rapidity and intensity that the crew would struggle to escape. Erroneously believed by most tank and armoured car crews to be caused by petrol, it was subsequently found that ammunition was the biggest culprit, leading to bans on the storage of ammunition in unapproved areas and the development of armoured steel lockers instead of open racks.

BROTHEL CREEPERS Rubber-soled suede or *sambhur* skin ankle boots, frequently adopted by RAC officers in the western desert campaign (hence the alternative name, still in use, *desert boots*), as a more comfortable type of footwear than heavy leather boots.

BUCKSHEE (A) From the Arabic *baksheesh*, a phrase picked up from beggars asking for some money. It came to be employed as a word for anything free or extra, particularly an additional item of army equipment that was not accounted for, as in: "I got hold of a buckshee pair of boots".

BUGGERED ABOUT To *be buggered about* meant to be messed about by any level of military authority, whilst *to bugger about* meant to be idle, to mess about, or to play the fool, the difference being the opinion of the person who had control of the activity.

BULL OR BULLSHIT Any form of military activity associated with wasting time. Originally applied to the often extreme measures necessary to make soldiers as smart as possible, it came to be used for any activity that seemed to be designed to stop soldiers from having any leisure time. "Bulling boots" meant the hours necessary to "burn down" and then highly polish their "Boots, Ammunition".[1] A *bullshitter* was either a teller of tall tales or a soldier of excessive smartness, one whose keenness reflected badly on his comrades.

BULLY BEEF Slang for Corned Beef, a regular part of a soldier's rations. The term comes either from the French *bouilli* (boiled) or more likely, from a bull's head shown on one of the most popular brand labels. The term *corned* comes from the treatment of the meat with grains of rock salt, also called "corns". There is no corn added to the ground beef, only gelatine. *Spam* on the other hand was a form of luncheon meat first produced in the US just prior to the outbreak of war, and there are at least three versions of the origin of the name: you choose. Spiced Ham, or Specially Produced American Meat, or Shoulder of Pork and Ham.

BUMF From "Bum Fodder", any army paperwork, implying that it would be better used as toilet roll. Sometimes called *bog bumph*.

BUMPER A manual method of polishing floors for an inspection; wax polish would be applied by hand on the floor and then polished using the bumper, a heavy block of metal wrapped in blanket or other material, attached to a pivoted wooden handle. The whole process was rather longwinded and messy but if done with vigour could produce an extremely glossy floor,, which the soldiers would then be afraid to walk on in case it spoiled the shine.

BUND (H) An earth or sand embankment.

BURGOO Originally from Turkish, *Burghal*, a porridge made with broken-up oatmeal (or any other type of army biscuit), mixed with water and condensed milk and, if available, sweetened with sugar.

BURQA/BERKA (A) The notorious red-light district of Cairo, the term could also be used for any other brothel in a foreign country.

BUTTERFLY BOMB An anti-personnel bomb (the *SD2*) used by the Luftwaffe. It hinged open when dropped and therefore looked like a large butterfly.

CAMEL TANK A 12½ gallon water tank made of copper and carried one each side of a baggage camel during the early western desert campaign.

CASA Italian for house and widely used during that campaign for any type of building.

CHAGGLE/CHAGAL/CHAGUL (H) A canvas water container used in hot environments, where evaporation helped to keep the contents cool – or at least, cooler than they would otherwise have been.

CHAR/CHA/CHAH (H) Tea.

CHARLIE Nickname for the CA radar equipment No 1 Mk IV

CHARPOY (H) A bed. Of Indian origin, and predating the conflict, this word for a rope bed had been in use by the British Army for many decades and is typical of the slang used by older veterans but widely adopted by younger soldiers trying to fit in.

CHIP HAT The side cap, due to its unusual shape particularly when taken off the head and turned upside down, in which form it resembled the paper bag used to contain fried potatoes. Some soldiers could also see a resemblance in it to a part of the female anatomy, giving it an equally short alternative and alliterative name that propriety prevents the author from recording here, but which ends in "cap".

CHIT OR CHITTY Any army form, most usually one giving the bearer permission to do (or not do) something.

COMPO Composite rations, introduced in 1943. They were called this because unlike earlier field rations which were often repetitive and boring, they comprised many different items to provide a more balanced and palatable ration.

CONK OUT To suddenly stop working, particularly when referring to an engine or similar apparatus.

COP A PACKET Originally meaning to be wounded, it was also used of someone who had managed to contract a venereal disease.

CROSSE & BLACKWELLS A somewhat derogatory name applied to members of the General Service Corps, whose cap badge, the Royal Arms, featured prominently "by appointment" on the labels of the tins and jars from that grocery company.

CUSHY Something easy, comfortable, or requiring little effort. Finding a cushy job or posting became an obsession with some soldiers, and those who managed to wangle themselves one of these were often viewed with a mixture of admiration and contempt.

DAGO A Spaniard or Spanish-speaking person.

DEIR (A) Arabic for a monastery or convent, it was frequently found on maps as one of the few recognisable features in the otherwise barren western desert.

DEKKO/DECKO/DEKHO (H) To take a look at. *cf Shufti*

THE DELTA The Nile Delta, north of Cairo and the location of much British military activity, particularly in the administrative and logistic areas.

DEMOB Demobilisation, the process of administration concerned with turning the soldier back into a civilian; talking about demob was probably one of the most frequent areas of conversation throughout the war, regardless of rank or cap badge.

DHOBI (H) Laundry.

DICKYBOW The very understandable nickname for the Divisional Counter Bombardment Officer (DCBO).

DIXIE A metal container for cooking hot food. Sometimes used to refer to the individual issue mess tins, the term was mostly used for larger containers used by crews or by cooks.

DJEBEL (A) Arabic for mountain.

DOESN'T KNOW THEIR ARSE FROM THEIR ELBOW Often used to refer to an incompetent officer or NCO, anybody who was judged to be confused or of little use.

DOOLALLY (OR DOOLALLY TAP) Mad, crazy. Originally an Indian army term referring to the town of the same name (*Deolali*) in central India near Bombay, used as a transit station, and *Tap*, the Persian/Urdu word for fever (hence also just *tapped*, or mad). One version is that soldiers sent there would go mad waiting for the transport to take them home. The other version has it that the terribly hot area had a reputation for causing sunstroke.

DROP A BOLLOCK To make a mistake, usually one that has been discovered; the severity of the offence can be modified by the use of an appropriate adjective or two, for example, "I've just dropped an enormous shagging bollock!".

DROP ONE'S GUTS To suffer from flatulence, usually of the odorous variety.

DICK SHOT OFF An officer who won the Distinguished Service Order would have the initials after his name; if he was disliked, soldiers would disagree and state that it referred to "Dick Shot Off".

EATING IRONS The issue KFS or Knife, Fork and Spoon; occasionally also *diggers*.

EFFING AND BLINDING The original meaning is a more polite representation of *Fucking and Buggering*. Used throughout the nation and not particular to the army, it was a way of referring to swearing without swearing oneself. Either word could be used on their own in the same manner, and whilst *effing about* would be used as a slightly more acceptable version of *fucking about* (to mean messing about), *blinding about* never became an expression – what would be heard was *buggering about.*

ELSIE A nickname given to Searchlight Control Radar, presumed to derive from the initials for Light Control.

ERSATZ The German for substitute or replacement, used to signify anything of low quality or not fit for purpose.

EVERY NIGHT SOMETHING AWFUL The publicly provided ENSA entertainment.

EYTIE An Italian. *cf Wop*

FAG A cigarette.

FANG FARRIER A dentist.

FIELD GLASSES A somewhat antiquated term used for binoculars.

FIZZER To be "put on a fizzer" was to be formally punished using the discipline rules laid out within Field Service Regulations (FSR).

FLAG WAGGER A signaller, both from the use of semaphore as a means of communication, and because of the trade badges warn by qualified signals personnel. Sometimes referred to as a *flag basher*.

FLASH GORDON An early form of protective helmet for parachutists, named because of its supposed similarity to the helmet worn by the science fiction character.

FLIMSY A petrol, oil or water container, with a capacity of 4 gallons and notorious for leaking, hence its name. The design was flawed in that the seams split all too easily during transportation or rough handling, and to minimise this problem two tins were meant to be transported within a lightweight wooden crate called a *shook*. Eventually, after millions of gallons of POL were lost, the design was replaced with the much more robust jerrycan (aka jerrican), copied from the Germans.[2]

FLY BOG An expression originating from the First World War meaning jam; another name for the preserve still in use in WW2 and which originated during the Boer War was *pozzy*.

FOXHOLE Informal name for a shell scrape or slit trench.

FRAT To fraternise, meaning to communicate and liaise with the local population, especially when it was forbidden to do so. Following the German capitulation in May 1945, orders were given that British soldiers were not to fraternise with the local population; the order was widely ignored and soon rescinded.[3]

FROM ARSEHOLE TO BREAKFAST TIME An undetermined period of time. Troops were often "mucked about from arsehole to breakfast time".

FULL SCREW The origin is uncertain but was very informal and referred to (in fact still does, to this day) a "full" (as opposed to lance) corporal or equivalent. Not often used by officers, who preferred the more formal use of ranks.

GABR (A) An Arabic boy's name, thought to be lucky, and often used in place names.

GEN Information, as in "What's the latest gen?"

GHARRI A horse-drawn cab or cart used in North Africa.

GIN PALACE Nickname given to any form of box body command vehicle or office caravan operated by the staff.

GIPPO OR GYPPO Egyptians. One of any number of casually racist terms frequently used by the British abroad, and not particular to the army. Although these terms are usually now considered derogatory, they were mostly applied without thinking or with any particular malice. A *Gyppy tummy* was a stomach-ache, often severe, with all the associated consequences. The term was also applied to some food, and therefore to cooks; the *Gyppo Sergeant* or *Master Gyppo* was the cook sergeant.

THE GLASSHOUSE Any military prison, believed to be named for the one at Shepton Mallet, brought back into service for the war, although the original expression may have come from the 19th century and the military prison in Aldershot.

GO ON THE PISS To engage in a bout of drinking, the piss in question usually being beer, which could be described as being *as "weak as piss"*.

GONG A medal. "Gong hunters" were dangerous and therefore despised.

GOOLIES (H) Testicles, from the Hindustani word for ball or bullet.

GOPWO A *grossly over-promoted warrant officer*; the term seems to have been used in two ways. Firstly, an officer commissioned from the ranks who was unable to "let go" of their past and who continued to behave like a sergeant major; and secondly, any commissioned officer behaving in a similar manner.

GORGONZOLA Nickname for the AA radar equipment No 4 Mk V.

GREEN To be green meant to be new, immature, or unpractised.

GREEN CAPS See *Red Caps*.

GROPPI'S HORSE Fictional unit named after the famous officers' watering hole in Talaat Harb Square, Cairo, this derisive term was used by the fighting troops in Egypt to refer to the legions of Cairo-based officers, especially those on the staff.

GROUSE To moan. Constant grousers could be a source of annoyance, although the soldier's right to grouse about any topic was tolerated to a large degree.

GUNGE OR GUNGY Also "Mank" or "Manky". Dirt in general, or to be dirty, relating to a place or a person. An unhygienic soldier could be described as either.

HARD TACK A semi-formal term, as it was often used in official documentation. Hard tack was the name given to any of the various forms of dehydrated biscuits issued to troops, and which could be eaten as they were or could become part of a more innovative and ambitious recipe. They were designed to be long lasting, and not rot or degrade easily, hence the composition. An over-reliance on the provision of hard tack and bully beef – especially in forward areas – led to a decline in the appetite and nutrition of frontline soldiers, eventually being solved by the provision of *compo rations*.

HATE Originating in World War 1, a short and intense barrage of artillery shells and/or mortar bombs.

HAY BOX An insulated container for keeping food warm whilst it was being transported to troops in remote locations away from field kitchens; early versions were extemporised from wooden crates and insulated using tightly packed hay or straw. Smaller vacuum *Thermos* containers were also used for the same purpose.

HOSE-PIPING Continuous firing of a machine gun in order to correct fire until the target is hit (often referred to as "walking fire onto the target"). Frowned upon by the weapons experts other than for anti-aircraft fire, as it wasted ammunition and caused barrels to overheat, it was nevertheless a common practice.

HUN Another WW1 word for German, but not as regularly used as *Jerry*.

HUSSIF (H) Also called a *Housewife*, a small canvas bag or pouch, containing a basic sewing kit, spare buttons and the like, and which every soldier would be required to have as part of his personal equipment.[4]

I'M ALRIGHT JACK Said to someone else and meaning that the other person had a problem, whilst implying that the speaker would do little to help and would only act in their own self-interest. The expression probably originates in the Royal Navy. Sometimes expressed as "I'm up the ladder Jack".

IN THE BAG To be captured, to be a prisoner of war. From a poacher's or gamekeeper's terminology.

IN THE SHIT To be in trouble. Particularly poor or troublesome soldiers could be described as being perpetually in the shit, with only the depth varying.

JACK A Royal Navy sailor, also sometimes a *Jack Tar* or just *Tar*.

JACKET To be awarded one's jacket meant that an officer had been accepted into the Royal Horse Artillery.

JACKSIE One's backside, as in "The sergeant major just gave me a right kick up the jacksie".

JANKERS Of unknown origin, any form of military punishment, but particularly that administered at the lower levels and often informally. To be *on jankers* meant to be undergoing some form of punishment. There is a suggestion that the word comes from *Justice Administered by NCOs*, but this seems unlikely.

JAO (H) Go! Usually repeated to imply haste, as in "Jao! Jao!"

JAP Any Japanese person or soldier; *Nip* (from Nippon) was also common.

JERRY Probably the most common form of slang applied to German soldiers, the term generally had no particular malice attached to it – to call the enemy *a Nazi* however did. *cf Boche, Hun, Kraut, Squarehead.*

JIG A JIG Sexual intercourse. Sometimes *Zig a Zig.*

JILDI (H) Originally meaning "soon", used by the army to mean to do something fast or as quickly as possible. Like *Jao*, often repeated for emphasis – "Jildi! Jildi!". The Arabic "*imshi*" was used in the same way.

JUNGLE TELEGRAPH Rumours, the informal but often very efficient passage of information within the soldiery that could sometimes be true and anticipate reality, but which very often proved to be false and ill-founded.

KAPUT From the German, used to mean broken or destroyed.

KHAD Used during the Burma campaign, a Khad is a steep slope caused by the watershed from a hill or mountain.

KHAMSEEN (A) Many Arabic words exist for specific types of winds and sandstorms in North Africa, but the *khamseen* (spellings vary) seems to have been the one almost universally adopted. Literally referring to a wind, the resultant sandstorm was universally hated and given this name.

KR "Kay Arrs", or "King's Regs". From the book of "The King's Regulations for the Army and the Army Reserve", the over-arching rules and laws for the army.

KRAUT A disparaging word for a German, probably picked up from Americans.

LARK An RA Instructor in Gunnery (IG); from the place of training, at Larkhill in Wiltshire.

LIBERATE To acquire by questionable means, covering everything from souvenir collecting on campaign to outright theft.

LIKE A PIG IN SHIT To be in a comfortable situation: "Those officers are living like pigs in shit".

LINGO Any form of language but particularly the local one, as in "Do you understand the lingo?".

LINKS Sausages.

MAIDAN (H) The parade or exercise/drill ground.

MALLAM/MALLUM (H) To understand.

MALEESH (A) Also Malesh: Arabic for (literally) "there is nothing to it", but a flexible expression used to mean "nothing", "sorry" or "never mind" or similar.

MALTA DOG A debilitating digestive illness particular to the island; different versions of similar illnesses were often named after their location; for example *Gippy tummy* and the *Bombay trots.*

MANK/MANKY See *Gungy*.

MARRA (H) A friend.

MARRY-UP To meet up with a view to coordinating future actions and operations. Usually used to indicate one unit meeting another, for example an infantry unit "marrying-up" with its supporting tanks.

MERRICAN An American-made version of the German 4-gallon POW container, used by British forces in the Middle East during 1942; around 1,000,000 were made and the name is of course a pun on Jerrican.

MOANING MINNIE The hated German Nebelwerfer multi-barrelled mortar; the alliterative name was not a fond epithet and derived from the sound made by approaching bombs. It was believed that during the Normandy campaign mortars caused more British casualties than any other type of weapon.

MOB One's unit, or whatever size, as it "Which mob do you belong to?". "The Mob" could also be used to refer to the army as a whole. *cf Shower*

MONKEY HARRY A Marmon-Herrington Armoured Car.

MONKEY TRUCK Royal Artillery slang given to a signal truck at battery level, the name coming from its code letter within the battery, M. In the days before the widespread use of radios within artillery gun positions, the monkey truck was equipped with line (cable) for communicating with the guns.

MONTY'S MOONLIGHT Shining anti-aircraft searchlights onto low cloud in order to provide a higher level of illumination during night operations.

MUCKING ABOUT Nothing to do with mucking in; the *mucking* in this case was a more polite form of a common swearword starting with F, and which, over time. came into common use in its own right.

MUCKING IN Probably coming from expressions to do with the mucking in and out of horses, mucking in was when someone got involved in completing a task that wasn't really their responsibility – it was often commented that such and such an officer was a good bloke because he mucked in with the troops.

MUFTI Civilian clothes or *civvies*. During the course of the war most soldiers had to wear uniform even when off-duty. Many private diaries refer to the strange combination of joy and unfamiliarity when putting on civilian clothes again following a long period in uniform.

MUSCLE-BOUND/MUSCLE-MAN A physical training instructor.

NAAFI BREAK The term is used to indicate a break in training of around about 30 minutes, enough time for the soldiers to go to the NAAFI canteen for a *cup of char and a wad* or similar. The term is also used in a more informal way to mean any break, particularly one where refreshments could be taken. *cf Smoke break*

NIGGER (OR SAMBO) Any black or brown person, although in practice the term could also be applied do anybody with a dusky or Mediterranean appearance. A particular paint colour was officially known as Nigger Brown, and soldiers whose surname was Brown were often nicknamed "*Nigger*", which they answered to without turning a hair.

NULLA OR NULLAH (H) The word for a riverbed, used for any form of (usually dry) river course or valley. *cf Wadi*

OFF ROAD Sometimes *off-the-road*, referring to a vehicle, that for whatever reason, was no longer roadworthy and required some form of repair or recovery before it could be used again (the full official expression was vehicle off road, VOR). It is possible that the term was originally coined to denote a vehicle that could not be legally driven on a public road, but could still be used for cross-country work etc.

OFFICERS' GROUNDSHEETS Members of the ATS.

ON THE BLINK Not working correctly and usually meaning intermittently working; radios would often be on the blink.

THE OLD MAN One's commanding officer, at almost any level.

PADRE Although officially called chaplains, most were referred to informally by all ranks as "Padre" (father).

PANEE (H) Water.

PARA BARRA The "Folding Trolley Airborne", a two-wheeled cart used by airborne forces.

PARTY A tongue-in-cheek expression sometimes used for any form of military activity, particularly if it was expected to be difficult, as in "This could be quite a tricky party".

PASSION WAGON Any vehicle used to transport off-duty soldiers to a leisure activity, not necessarily one involving the fairer sex.

PBI Poor Bloody Infantry. Used not only by the wider army but also by the infantry themselves. This enduring term remains the best possible way of summarising the truly awful experience or being an infantryman during wartime.

PIG STICKER The bayonet.

PIG'S EAR The nickname given to the Molins Fuze Setter No 11 on the 3.7-inch anti-aircraft gun.

POTATO MASHER The nickname given to the standard issue German stick grenade because of its shape; the design meant that it could be thrown much further than the British No 36 grenade. *cf Stick Grenade*

PUKKA (H) Another word derived from Hindustani or Punjabi, in this case *pakkha*, meaning literally ripe or solid. It was spelt in a number of variations and used to describe something that was real and was also used to mean *good*: "That was a pukka meal".

PULL-OFF An early term applied to military parachuting; the parachutist pulled his rip cord whilst standing on the rear of an aircraft so that as the parachute opened the slipstream pulled him off the aircraft.

POSHTEEN COAT Also known as an Afghan coat, a long sheep- or goatskin coat used mainly by officers in the Persia and Iraq campaigns.

QAIMNS The all-female army military nursing service attracted two humorous puns on their initials, which the corps history records as being "humorous and not resented". One of these was *Queer And Impossible, Mostly Not Sane*, the alternative was *Queer Assortment of Individuals, Mainly Non-Sexed.*[5]

RECCE Reconnaissance. (Note: the US version, recon, was seldom if ever used.)

RED CAPS The unloved and frequently detested members of the Corps of Military Police, so-called because of the red cloth covers worn over the crown of their service dress caps by those employed on provost (policing) duties. Members of the Field Security Police branch wore Lincoln green covers and thus were called *green caps*, whilst military policemen on vulnerable point (VP) duties wore Oxford blue covers and were known as *blue caps*.

RED TABS Any staff officer or general officer wearing the distinctive red gorget patches on his uniform collars. Generally, a term of contempt.

ROB ALL MY COMRADES A disparaging term applied to members of the Royal Army Medical Corps (RAMC), implying that front-line soldiers would have their personal possessions stolen should they be unfortunate enough to be wounded. To be fair, the evidence is overwhelming that most soldiers actually engaged in fighting the enemy held the members of the corps in the highest regard. (The RAOC were sometimes similarly referred to as *Rob All Our Comrades*.)

RUN AWAY! Someone's Coming! Another term used to disparage a different corps, in this case the RASC.

SANGAR Another term coming from India, a sangar was a small, fortified position made from piling rocks up in places where it was difficult or impossible to dig down into the ground. Whilst the term could be used by old soldiers anywhere, it was mostly used in Italy.

SAPPER The lowest rank in the Corps of Royal Engineers, equivalent to a private soldier and also used to refer to a Royal Engineer of any rank. "The Sappers" referred to the corps as whole.

SCALEYBACK Any member of the Royal Signals; the expression comes from skin problems on the back of soldiers carrying heavy and uncomfortable items such as radios or line-laying cables, the trouble with the former load possibly being exacerbated by leaking battery acid.

SCHEME Generally used of a training exercise, less commonly an active operation.

SCHMEISSER Almost universally used throughout the army, the term erroneously applied to the two main German submachine guns, the MP38 and MP40.

SEAC South East Asia Command but used as slang by GIs to mean 'Saving England's Asian Colonies'.

SHAFTO'S A popular cinema located in Maadi camp in Egypt.

SHAG Sexual intercourse, also in use as a very common adjective – "Get your shagging jacksies over here!"

SHAGGED-OUT Exhausted

SHIT HOT Extremely good. Hot was an Americanism for good.

SHIT ORDER To be in a terrible mess. The army had any number of defined orders of dress, such as battle order, drill order, and fatigue order.

Therefore, to be in shit order was to be the exact opposite of being smart and soldierly.

SHOOK See *Flimsy*.

SHOWER A shortened version of *a shower of shit* and thus a derogatory term for a unit, most often not one's own, although a *browned-off* soldier might opine that "My mob is a proper shower!". *cf Mob*

SHUFTI (A) From the Arabic, to take a look or to observe. *cf Dekko*

SIDI (A) Arabic for a saint or masterful man, often used as the first word in a place name, eg Sidi Rezegh.

SMOKE BREAK A short break between periods of training, normally five minutes and therefore enough for a quick cigarette (*fag*). *cf NAAFI break*

SOFTSKIN Another one of those expressions which, although informal, was used a lot in military communications; softskins were all unarmoured vehicles.

SPANDAU Widely but erroneously used for the common German machine guns MG34 and MG42, even though neither were designed at the Spandau armaments works in Berlin. The characteristic "ripping calico" sound of the guns was very distinctive and was caused by their exceptionally high rates of fire.

SPORTAPOOL A collapsible canvas tank used for holding water in the western desert, the sides of which were supported by the pressure exerted by the contents in a manner similar to a child's paddling pool.

SQUAREHEAD A term applied to the German soldier due to the shape of his steel helmet when compared to the much rounder British version. *cf Jerry, Boche.*

SQUARE BASHING To do formal foot drill, the square in question being the unit's parade ground, even if it wasn't square. For the majority of soldiers, a hated activity.

STAG One's stag was a tour of a specified duty for a set period of time. The word comes from "Standing Guard", standing meaning regular (as in *standing patrol*), and did not necessarily imply an upright posture.

STICKY A term of abuse, applied to individuals or units, implying cowardice or at the very least, a slowness or lack of willingness to push forward.

STONK Originally meaning a "standard concentration", the term came to be used for any form of artillery attack. Early in the war the German word *blitz* was sometimes used in a similar fashion but soon fell out of favour.

STOP A full stop (or period), used on a written message or telegraph.

SWANNING An expression from the desert campaign, *swanning around* meant to move around the battlefield in a fairly aimless way. It was used again in north-west Europe during August and September 1944 to describe the rapid advance and pursuit operations carried out after the conclusion of the Normandy campaign, which was referred to as the *Great Swan*.

TEDS From the Italian word *Tedeschi*, meaning Germans, this slang was used mainly in the Italian theatre. *cf Jerry, Bosche, Hun*

TIN HAT The most common expression for the steel helmet. *cf Battle Bowler.*

TOMMY GUN The Thompson .45" submachine gun (aka machine carbine).

TRICK CYCLIST An army psychiatrist.

TUCAN A Director of Works-produced 2-gallon welded petrol container, only used in the Middle East as a temporary solution to the *Flimsy* problem. The name is a pun on "two-gallon can".

TYPES Officers were often known as *Types*, the equivalent with other ranks were *Bods*. According to one version, all Types, regardless of rank, had been to Sandhurst, came from Tunbridge Wells, were called Biffo, and had a girlfriend called Celia.[6]

U/S Short for unserviceable, mainly used of equipment but people could also be described as being U/S.

VINO From the Italian for Wine, used for any alcoholic drink.

WAD A bun or cake; the more usual modern meaning of sandwich is post-war.

WADI (A) A riverbed. *cf Nulla*

WAGON Any form of wheeled vehicle that one could ride in or on, from a tank to an artillery limber – "*My wagon is U/S*".

WALLAH (H) A worker of any type. There were a number of common wallahs: *Char wallah* – someone who makes tea. *Chota wallah* – a person of short stature. *Desk wallah* – a clerk or staff officer, or any non-fighting soldier. *Dhobi wallah* – a laundry man. *God wallah* – the Padre or Chaplain. *Nappy wallah* – the barber.

WINDY To be windy was to be scared. Labelling a soldier as windy could cover everything from an otherwise active soldier suffering a momentary indecision, or someone reluctant to commit themselves to aggressive action, to the out-and-out coward.

WOP An Italian, the word was picked up from American GIs, the origin is believed to come from Italians arriving in the USA "*without papers*". *cf Eytie*

Part 3

ABBREVIATIONS

The Field Service Pocket Book Part 1 Pamphlet No 3 listed common army abbreviations in their official forms. As a starting point for those without immediate access to this pamphlet, the notes at the beginning of the 1944 version of the pamphlet read as follows (reproduced as accurately as possible):

General – Abbreviations, whether authorized in this pamphlet or not, will only be used if the writer is satisfied that there is no possibility of their meaning being mistaken or not understood by any one of the addressees of the document he is originating.

1. **Authorized abbreviations** – The guiding principle with abbreviations is that those in commonest use by most arms and branches of the Service should be authorized for general use, but that their number should be kept within reasonable bounds. Such authorized abbreviations are listed in this pamphlet. In the absence of some consideration that would make their use undesirable in any specific instance, these abbreviations will be used in all orders, reports, appreciations, messages, memoranda, and similar documents.

2. **Unauthorized abbreviations** – The use of unauthorized abbreviations is not encouraged. If for some reason it is considered helpful or desirable to use an unauthorized abbreviation, it must be explained or defined the first time it appears in the text, thus: EFI (Expeditionary Force Institutes), IG (Instructor in gunnery). This ruling applies particularly to specialist and technical arms and services which are in the habit of using, within their own spheres, abbreviations that, though well known by their own arm or service, are not authorized for general use.

3. **Communications with Allied formations and units** – A short list of abbreviations authorized for the combined use of British and United States Armies is given in FSPB Part II, Pamphlet

No 4A – Staff Organisation and Staff Duties in the United States Army (3 copies of which are issued to all lieutenant-colonels' commands). In communications addressed to OTHER Allied formations and units, abbreviations will NOT be used.

4. **Plurals** – Where a group of letters denotes the abbreviation for ONE word, for example adjt, the addition of letter *s* indicates the plural; but where, as with such abbreviations as AVRE, or 2IC, each letter or figure denotes a word, the plural *s* will invariably be inserted after the appropriate letter or figure, thus, AVsRE, or 2sIC. The letter *s* will NOT be added to words incapable of a plural meaning such as, for example, cav, HP, LAA; neither will it be added to abbreviations such as the following, which are either singular or plural in meaning according to the context:

aux	OR
cas	oz
cwt	PW
ft	res
fus	rfn
gdsm	sigmn
HQ	UXB
lb	X rds

5. **Punctuation** – Full stops will not be used in or after any abbreviation, but the text of any document in which abbreviations are used will be punctuated in the ordinary way, for example, *Evac, according to the cas gp, is illustrated in Appx A att.*

6. **Months and days** – The abbreviation for a calendar month or day of the week will be the first 3 letters of the name of the month or day.

7. **Points of the compass** – The four cardinal points of the compass will be written in capitals in full, for example, SOUTH; abbreviations with the letters N, S, E and W are used to denote intermediate points, for example, SSW, NE.

8. **Formations and units** – Army List abbreviations will never be used in official correspondence, instructions, memoranda, or signals. Full titles of regiments or corps, as given in the Army List, will be used only in correspondence of a very formal nature. When formations and units are described by their authorized abbreviations, ordinal numbers (written as words) are used to denote armies, for example, *First Army.* Cardinal numbers (written as figures) are used to denote particular formations or units, for example, *17 Army Gp (Seventeenth Group of Armies), 5 Corps (5th Corps), 5 Northamptons (5th Battalion, The Northamptonshire Regiment*).

9. **Abbreviated terms** – Abbreviated military terms and titles of units may be shown only by using authorized abbreviations or a combination of abbreviations; thus, *1st Field Regiment* becomes *1 Fd Regt, 105th Corps*

Field Park Company becomes *105 Corps Fd Pk Coy*, *3rd Reconnaissance Regiment* becomes *3 Recce Regt*. Compound nouns and hyphenated words can similarly be abbreviated, for example *minefield* becomes *minefd*, *re-organisation* becomes *reorg*, and *parachute troops* becomes *paratps*. The shortening of an abbreviation is forbidden, for example, *3RR* for *3 Recce Regt*.

10. **Verbs** – The ONLY present participles of verbs that may be abbreviated are: *co-ordinating, excluding, including,* and *regulating*. With these four exceptions, the abbreviation for a verb applies only to the present indicative (for example, *organize*), and to the past tense (for example, *organized*). Thus *will org* and *have org* are permissible, but *organizing* will be written in full. *Ldg*, for *landing*, and *wpfg*, for *waterproofing* are in a class by themselves, being the only present participles for which abbreviations are specifically authorized as such.

11. **Abbreviated titles** – the abbreviated titles of principal staff officers and directors of services are given in Table III. The letters A and D are used to denote their *assistant* and *deputy* subordinates, thus:-

Full title	Abbreviated title
Deputy Assistant Adjutant General	*DAAG*
Deputy Assistant Adjutant and Quartermaster General	*DAA & QMG*
Deputy Assistant Director of Supplies and Transport	*DADST*

The addition of the letter C to an arm of the service denotes *commander*, for example, *CRA, CRASC*.

Comments on the above. "Discouraging" the use of unauthorized abbreviations (as in paragraph 3) was not the same as banning them. This was clearly a compromise, an attempt to allow individuals and organisations to develop new abbreviations to meet the need, whilst trying to stop a cavalcade of new abbreviations flooding the market and confusing everyone, particularly if the same abbreviation was being used and re-used and ending up with multiple definitions – which happened. The authors of the pamphlet knew what they were talking about when they also cautioned in paragraph 3 about the tendency of certain arms to create and multiply (with a speed of which bacteria would be jealous) their own acronyms and abbreviations. The rule that the abbreviation must be explained or defined on first use remains in British doctrine to this day – if only it had been properly adhered to! Lt Bob Crisp of 3rd R Tanks in Libya in 1941 recorded that:

> There came the startling order to the remaining two squadrons to advance and engage 200 M.E.T. on the Trigh Capuzzo. I never did find out what M.E.T. stood for – mechanised enemy troops perhaps? – but we all knew what it implied. 200 M.E.T. meant a long column of German vehicles…Later we were to discover that it also meant tanks

> and anti-tank guns and the dreaded 88s. Many men were to die on each side of me in finding out exactly what M.E.T. meant.[1]

Of course, to some degree this sort of confusion was going to be unavoidable, as the army of 1944 was much larger and, in many ways, very different to that of 1939. In particular, the emergence of new forms of technology during the conflict demanded a raft of new abbreviations. And there is of course the very natural and human tendency of people joining an organisation failing to question the terminology that is being flung at them; most people prefer to remain in the background, get the gist of what the term or abbreviation means, and then begin to use it themselves, still none the wiser.[2]

Paragraph 4 makes it clear that the need for co-operation – particularly with the US military – was having an impact business. Two examples: the two countries used different phonetic alphabets, and the British began to adopt some of the American phonetic code words in place of the ones that they had been using since the First World War. Secondly, the American staff system referred to staff branches by an alpha-numerical system starting with the letter G. G1 was personnel, G2 intelligence, G3 operations, G4 logistics, and G5 civil affairs. These would be adopted by the British Army after the war and as the branch numbers and designations increased (currently standing at nine), the British Army and indeed the rest of NATO would follow suit.

Para 5 refers to the famous AVRE, which everyone now refers to as an ARMOURED Vehicle Royal Engineers – but Table II tells us a different tale; the letter A actually stood for ASSAULT.

Paragraph 6 is completely clear and was almost completely ignored. This is quite possibly because English grammar conventions of the time were insistent that words abbreviated or contracted had to use a full stop (period), so the Football Association would be written as "F.A." and etcetera as "etc.". Other examples are "i.e." or "A.E.C.". Had this diktat been obeyed, during the course of the war billions of unnecessary full stops could have been saved – but they weren't.

Paragraph 7 was generally well adhered to, so that the months of the year and the days of the week would be written as follows:

Jan	Mon
Feb	Tue
Mar	Wed
Apr	Thu
May	Fri
Jun	Sat
Jul	Sun
Aug	
Sep	
Oct	
Nov	
Dec	

Although not noted here, two other time/date conventions should be understood. Midnight was written as 0000 hrs, and operations taking place overnight were shown as the two days concerned: thus, "night 23/24 May".

Paragraph 9 refers to the Army List, this was a regularly issued publication showing the details and seniority of every officer in the army; the abbreviations used within that particular document were, for reasons of brevity, not suitable for use in operational correspondence, and a new, shorter set devised – these were always capitalised (upper case). Table I in the pamphlet gave the operational versions of the abbreviations of all the various regiments, corps and services within the army, and it was these that were to be used in most correspondence, instructions, memoranda, and signals. It should be noted that the full titles of these units were in some cases extremely long, and many included honorific titles, often, although not always, set in brackets; for example, "The North Staffordshire Regiment (The Prince of Wales's)", or "The 13th/18th Royal Hussars (Queen Mary's Own)". These were obviously much too long to be used in operational documents and so were abbreviated as N STAFFS and 13/18 H respectively. The listing of cavalry (Including yeomanry) and infantry regiments and battalions in Part 4 of this work gives the full title, the operational abbreviation, and the Army List abbreviation.[3]

The point made about the difference between ordinal and cardinal numbers was clearly made but was widely ignored, up to the present day. How many times has the reader seen "8th Army" used? All Armies should have been referred to in full, so therefore the only acceptable abbreviation – officially at least – was and is "Eighth Army".[4] A similar point can be made about abbreviating an abbreviation as mentioned in paragraph 10; it was not meant to happen, but it certainly did. So, to be clear, formations *should* be numbered as per these examples:

Full	Abbreviated
33rd Armoured Brigade	33 Armd Bde
7th Armoured Division	7 Armd Div
XXX Corps	30 Corps
Second Army	Second Army
Twenty-First Group of Armies	Twenty First Army Gp

In total, Table II of the booklet contains around 400 official abbreviations. The table below has over 3,800. Why the big difference? In part of course, it is for the reasons already discussed; that beyond the general staff requirements for official abbreviations, all the corps and arms required their own listings. (The abbreviations annotated with an * are those which are found in the pamphlet – that is not to say that the remainder are unofficial, but simply that they were not included in the official list.) Which abbreviation had the most different versions? The "winner" overall is DP, which had no fewer than nine versions, narrowly pipping MC into second place with eight, with AT and CI tied third on seven.

In selecting the additional abbreviations in this work, this author has waded through countless primary and secondary sources to flesh-out the list to make it fully – or as fully as is possible – represent what might be found within the sources (and frequently without any explanation of their meaning!). There is of course some overlap with abbreviations which most correctly belong to (or at least originate in) the other two services, the RN and the RAF – see what I did there? – and also in some cases to Commonwealth allies, mainly Canada and Australia/NZ. These have been selected on the basis that they might be encountered in army primary sources.

There is of course the worrying possibility that I may have missed some (but hopefully not too many) or indeed have included some which more properly belong to the post-1945 period, or which should have been out of use by 1939. If this is the case, I apologise but feel that is better to include something that may be anachronistic rather than omit it. only to find that it *was* in use in our period of interest. A few examples of the worst type of abbreviation are included; these are the ones that we know were used, but for which we cannot discover the exact meaning. Where there is doubt that the full title is correct, it is annotated with a question mark, and where the definition has proved impossible to decipher it has been left blank, allowing the diligent reader to insert the correct title at a later date…

Although not specifically noted, it must be realised that compound abbreviations were very common. For example, if searching for GHQ ME in the lists, it will not be found, but breaking the abbreviation down into its two elements will come up with General Headquarters and then Middle East, giving the answer. And whilst most abbreviations were innocuous to the point of banality, The FANY of course came in for some ribald comments, and who would enjoy the banter that came as a result of working for a Vehicle Detachment? And what would be the nickname of someone working as part of an Aircraft Recognition School, or indeed in the Administrative Staff School?

Finally, we come to the thorny issue of capitalization. Clearly, the army view was that an abbreviated word (rather than an acronym) should normally not be capitalised, unless it was required to be so to make it correct grammatically. So, for example, if referring to an *annexure* within the text, then the lowercase version "annx" would be used. But if the word was starting a sentence, then it would be capitalised in the normal way (eg "Annex B replaces annex A"). Acronyms, a group of letters standing for something and usually using the capital letters of each individual word, were treated differently and always capitalised, even if the individual words themselves were not capitalised when used in full. For example, the acronym for a Bath unit was BU, not Bu, and a Beach maintenance area was a BMA.[5] With regard to capitalization of ranks, generally speaking the rank would be capitalised if referring to an individual, but not capitalised if referring to the rank in more general (pun intended) terms, eg, "Sergeant Jones and Corporal Smith, plus one sergeant and three other corporals yet to be decided, are to proceed on leave".

TABLE OF ABBREVIATIONS

For reasons of space, it has not been possible to include all of the terms abbreviated within this table in the glossary. In the majority of cases, the abbreviations lacking glossary definitions are either technical in nature or refer to a particular type of unit. Where helpful, an additional remark placed in square brackets [ ] is an indication of where the abbreviation was commonly used; however, curved brackets ( ) form part of the full, unabbreviated name or title. For example: Reduced Charge [ammunition] as opposed to The Queen's Bays (2nd Dragoon Guards).

An asterix (*) in column two denotes that the acronym or abbreviation is listed in the Field Service Pocket Book of authorised abbreviations.

The alternatives noted in column three are versions of the abbreviations that, although incorrect, were frequently used in practice. These alternatives are almost certain to be incomplete but should be sufficient in most cases to allow the researcher to identify the term that is being searched for.

Abbreviation		Alternatives	Meaning
A			Angelsey [Home Guard]
A	*		Assistant
A/			Acting [rank]. EG A/Cpl = acting Corporal
AA			All After [in signal message]
AA			All Arms
AA	*	A-A	Anti-Aircraft
AA	*		Army Act
AA		Assy A	Assembly Area
AA		A/Adjt	Assistant Adjutant
AA Bde			Anti-Aircraft Brigade
AA Comd			Anti-Aircraft Command

Abbreviation		Alternatives	Meaning
AA MG			Anti-Aircraft Machine Gun
AA Tk			Anti-Aircraft Tank
AAA			Allied Airborne Army
AAA			Written message follows [in morse signalling]
AABW		AA Bde Wkshp	Anti-Aircraft Brigade Workshops [RAOC]
AAB RE			Anti-Aircraft Battalion Royal Engineers
AAC			Armoured Ammunition Carrier
AAC			Army Air Corps
AACD			Army Air Corps Depot
AA&CD		AACD	Anti-Aircraft & Coastal Defence
AAD	*		Advanced Ammunition Depot
AAD			Anti-Aircraft Defence
AADC			Anti-Aircraft Defence Commander
AADMSG			Anti-Aircraft Defence of Merchant Shipping Group
AAEE			Anti-Aircraft Experimental Establishment
AAES			Anti-Aircraft Experimental Section
AAG			Assistant Adjutant General
AAI			Allied Armies in Italy
A air SC			Army Air Support Control
AALMG			Anti-Aircraft Light Machine Gun
AAMTC			Anti-Aircraft Mobile Training Centre
AANS			Australian Army Nursing Service
AAOD			Anti-Aircraft Ordnance Depot
AAOR			Anti-Aircraft Operations Room
AAPC			African Auxiliary Pioneer Corps [June 1942 to June 1944]
AARS		AAR Sch	Anti-Aircraft Radio School
AAS			Army Air Support
AAS(I)			Anti-Aircraft School (India)
AASC			Army Air Support Control
AASC			Australian Army Service Corps
AASF			Advanced Air Striking Force [BEF]
AASL			Anti-Aircraft Searchlight
AATDC			Army Air Transport Development Centre
AATE			Anti-Aircraft Training Establishment
AATG			Anti-Aircraft Training Group

Abbreviation		Alternatives	Meaning
AATO			Army Air Transport Organization
AAW			Army Auxiliary Workshop [Ministry of Supply]
AB			Aberdeenshire [Home Guard]
AB		Adv B	Advanced Base
AB			All Before [in signal message]
AB	*		Army Book
AB115			Officer's/NCOs cover for protecting/ collecting message forms (C.2136).
AB64			A Soldier's Service and Pay Book
ABAD			Army Base Ammunition Depot
ABCA			Army Bureau of Current Affairs
ABD			Army Base Depot
ABG			Air Blast Gear
ABK			Aberdeenshire Kincardineshire Battalion [Home Guard]
ABMR		ABM	Assistant Beach Master
ABOD			Advanced Base Ordnance Depot
ABPO			Advanced Base Post Office
ABSD			Army Blood Supply Depot
ABTS			Army Blood Transfusion Service
ABTU			Army Basic Training Unit
ABW			Advanced Base Workshop
AC		A/C	Aircraft
AC			Alternating Current
AC		A/C; Armd C	Armoured Car
AC			Army Council
a/c		AC: A/C	Aircraft
AC Sqn			Army Co-operation Squadron [RAF]
ACA			Allied Control Austria
ACBC			African & Colonial Base Camp
ACBO			Assistant Counter-Battery (Bombardment) Officer
ACC			Allied Control Commission
ACC		Amb Car Coy	Ambulance Car Company [RASC]
ACC			Armoured Car Company
ACC			Army Catering Corps [from March 1941]
ACCA			Allied Control Commission Austria
ACCBD&TC			Army Catering Corps Base Depot and Training Centre [Middle East]

Abbreviation		Alternatives	Meaning
accn	*	Accn	Accommodation
Acct			Accountant
ACCTC			Army Catering Corps Training Centre
ACD			Amy Chaplain's Depertment
A Cdo			Army Commando
ACE			Army Certificate of Education
ACF			African Colonial Forces
ACF			Army Cadet Force
ACF			Army Co-operation Force
ACG		AC Gp	Airfield Construction Group [Royal Engineers]
ACG			Assistant Chaplain-General
ACI	*		Army Council Instruction
ACI			Assistant Chief Instructor
ACIGS			Assistant Chief of the Imperial General Staff
ack	*	Ack	Acknowledge/d/ment
Ack			Assistant [RA]
ACMO			Assistant Counter-Mortar Officer
ACO			Area Cash Office
ACPO			Assistant Command Post Officer
ACSRTD			Advisory Council on Scientific Research and Technical Development
ACV			Armoured Command Vehicle
AD			After Duty
AD			Air Defence
AD			Air Despatch
AD			Armoured Division
AD			Artillery Depot
AD			Assistant Director
ADAP			Assistant Director of Army Psychiatry
ADATS			Assistant Director Auxiliary Territorial Service
ADBR			Assistant Director of Biological Research
ADC			Aide-de-Camp
ADC			Air Despatch Centre
ADC			Air Dropping Container
ADC		AD Corps	Army Dental Corps
ADC Gen			Aide-de-Camp General
ADCC			Airborne Division Composite Company [RASC]

Abbreviation		Alternatives	Meaning
ADCR			Australian Divisional Cavalry Regiment
ADD			Armament Design Department
ADDS			Assistant Director Dental Services
addsd	*		Addressed
ADE		AD (E)	Armoured Division (Egypt)
ADFS			Army Department Fire Service
ADG			Air Despatch Group [RASC]
ADG			Assistant Director-General
ADGB			Air Defence of Great Britain
ADH			Assistant Director of Hygiene
adjt	*	Adjt	Adjutant
AD Lab			Army Dental Laboratory
adm	*	Adm; Ad; admin	Administration/ative
Adm O			Administrative Order
ADMS			Advanced Depot Medical Stores
ADMS		ADOMS	Assistant Director of Medical Services
ADO			Air Despatch Organisation [RASC]
ADOS			Assistant Director of Ordnance Services
ADP			Assistant Director of Pathology [RAMC]
ADPL			Assistant Director of Pioneer and Labour
ADR			Armoured Delivery Regiment
adrep			(Found in sigs message form AF C312B)
ADRU			Armoured Division Reinforcement Unit?
ADS	*		Advanced Dressing Station
ADS			Air Delivery Service
ADS		Army Del Sqn	Army Delivery Squadron
ADS			Army Dental Services
ADST			Assistant Director Supply & Transport
Adv			Advisor/Advance(d)
Adv Base			Advanced Base
Adv Dep		AD	Advanced Depot
Adv Gd			Advanced Guard
Adv Pty			Advance Party

Abbreviation		Alternatives	Meaning
Ae		AE	Aerial [or antenna]
AE			Ammunition Examiner [RAOC]
AEAF			Allied Expeditionary Air Force
AEC			Army Education Command
AEC			Army Educational Corps
AEC			Associated Equipment Company
AEF			Allied Expeditionary Force
AEME			Australian Electrical & Mechanical Engineers
A&ER		AER	Ammunition & Explosive Regulations
AES			Army Educational Section
AF		A flats	Across Flats [tools]
AF			Air Formation
AF	*		Army Form
AF			Audio Frequency
AFA			Australian Field Ambulance
AFB			Army Flying Badge
AFC			Air Force Cross
AFCC			Air Freight Control Centre
AFD			Army Forms Depot
AFDBS			Airborne Force Depot & Battle School
AFEE			Airborne Forces Experimental Establishment
AFHQ			Allied Force(s) Headquarters
afm			Aforementioned
AFPS			Army Film & Photographic Service
AFPU			Air Formation Postal Unit
AFPU			Army Film & Photographic Unit
Afr			Africa(n)
AFS			Airborne Forces Staff
AFS			Army Fire Service
AFS Coy			Army Field Survey Company
AFSD		A Fd Svy Dep	Army Field Survey Depot
AFSMD			Army Field Survey Map Depot
AFV			Armoured Fighting Vehicle
AFV (T&AC) Maint Sec			Armoured Fighting Vehicle (Tank & Armoured Car) Maintenance Section [Royal Armoured Corps]

Abbreviation		Alternatives	Meaning
AFV Insp		AFV (Ins)	Armoured Fighting Vehicle Inspectorate [REME]
AFV Serv Coy			Armoured Fighting Vehicle Servicing Company
AFV(T)			Armoured Fighting Vehicle (Technical)
AFVD		AFV dep	Armoured Fighting Vehicle Depot
AFVS			Armoured Fighting Vehicle School(s)
AFVS (D&MW)			Armoured Fighting Vehicle School Driving & Maintenance Wing
AFVS (GW)			Armoured Fighting Vehicle School Gunnery Wing
AFVS (WW)			Armoured Fighting Vehicle School Wireless Wing
AFW			Army Field Workshops
AFW			Australian Field Workshops
AG			Adjutant General
AG			Army Group
A-G		AG, A/G	Anti-Gas
AGBD			Australian General Base Depot
AGC			Automatic Gain Control [radio]
AGHQ			Aerodrome Group Headquarters
AGRA	*		Army Group Royal Artillery
AGRE	*		Army Group Royal Engineers
AGS			Army Gas School
Ah		ah; AH	Ampere-Hour
AHFS			Advanced Handling & Fieldcraft School
AHTD			Advanced Horse Transport Depot
AIA			Assistant Inspector of Armourers
AIF			Australian Imperial Force(s)
AIGU			Army Industrial Gas Unit
AILO			Air Intelligence Liaison Officer
AIR			Adviser in Radiology
Air OP			Air Observation Post
Air ph			Air Photograph
airfd			Airfield
AIR			Advisor in Radiology
Air recce			Air Reconnaissance
airtps	*		Airborne Troops

Abbreviation		Alternatives	Meaning
AIS			Assistant Instructor of Signalling
AITC&ACF			Assistant Inspector Training Corps & Army Cadet Force
AITM			Army in India Training Memorandum
AK			Army Kinema Establishment
AKE			Army Kinematography
AKS			Army Kinematograph Service [RAOC, from Aug 41]
AL		A/L	Air Landing
AL			Air Liaison
AL		A-L	Anti-Louse
AL Bde		A/L Bde	Air Landing Bde
ALFA		A/L FA	Air Landing Field Ambulance
ALFN			Allied Land Forces Norway
ALFSEA			Allied Land Forces South-East Asia
ALG	*		Advanced Landing Ground
ALO	*		Air Liaison Officer
ALS			Air Landing School
ALS			Allied Liaison Service
ALS			Apparatus Loudspeaking
ALSec	*	ALS	Air Liaison Section
ALSS(A)			Air Liaison Sub-Section (Airfield)
AM			Albert Medal
AM			Amplitude Modulation/Modulated
am		AM	Morning [ie the 12 hours before midday]
amb	*		Ambulance
AMC			Associated Motor Cycles
AMCU			Anti-Malarial Control Unit
AMD			Army Medical Directorate [sometimes Department]
AMDC			Army Mechanized Demonstration Column
Amdt			Amendment
AMF			Australian Military Forces
AMFO			Assistant Military Forwarding Officer
AMG			Allied Military Government
AMGOT			Allied Military Government of Occupied Territories

Abbreviation		Alternatives	Meaning
AMLO			Assistant Military Landing Officer
amn	*	Ammo; ammn	Ammunition
Amn Sub-Pk			Ammunition Sub-Park
Amp		amp	Ampere
Amp			Amplifier
AMPC			Auxiliary Military Pioneer Corps [to 1940]
amph			Amphibian/ious
AMS			Army Medical Services
AMS			Assistant Military Secretary
AMTD			Advanced Mechanized Transport Depot
AMTL			Amatol
AMU			Anti-Malarial Unit
AN			Assistant Nurse
ANC			American National Coarse
ANF			American National Fine
ANG			Angus [Home Guard]
ANZAC			Australian & New Zealand Army Corps
AO	*		Army Order
AOC	*		Air Officer Commanding
AOD	*		Advanced Ordnance Depot
AOER			Army Officer Emergency Reserve
AOERS			Army Officer Emergency Reserve Scheme
AofS			Angle of Sight
AOP			Air/Aerial Observation Post
AOP			Armoured Observation Post
AORE			Army Operational Research Establishment
AORG			Army Operational Research Group
AoS			Angle of Sight
AOS		AoS	Arm of Service
AOW			Army Ordnance Workshop
AP			Aiming Point [RA]
AP	*		Ammunition Point
AP	*		Armour Piercing
APC		AP Corps	African Pioneer Corps [from June 1944 to April 1946]
APC			Armour Piercing Capped

Abbreviation		Alternatives	Meaning
APC			Armoured Personnel Carrier
APC			Aspirin/Phenactin/Caffeine [drug]
APCBC			Armour Piercing Capped Ballistic Cap
APCR			Armour Piercing Composite Rigid
APD			Australian Port Detachment
APDS			Armour Piercing Discarding Sabot
APIS	*		Army Photographic Interpretation Section
APJI			Assistant Parachute Jump Instructor
APM			Assistant Provost Marshal
APO	*		Army Post Office
Approx			Approximately
Appx	*	App	Appendix
APRE			Army Personnel Research Establishment
APS			Army Postal Service [RE]
APS			Assistant Private Secretary
APT			Air Portable
APTC			Army Physical Training Corps [from 1940]
APTS			Army Physical Training Staff [to 1940]
AQ			Assistant Adjutant & Quartermaster General
AQMG(M)			Assistant Quartermaster General (Movements)
AQMS			Artificer Quartermaster Sergeant [REME]
AR			Allowance Regulations
AR			Army Reserve
AR			End of my transmission, no response required [in morse signalling]
ARA			Army Rifle Association
ARCM			Associate of the Royal College of Music
ARD			Ammunition Railhead Detachment [RAOC]
ARD			Armament Research Department
ARE			Armament Research Establishment
ARF			Ammunition Repair Factory

Abbreviation		Alternatives	Meaning
ARG			Argyllshire [Home Guard]
ARG	*		Armoured Replacement Group
ARH			Ammunition Railhead
ARK			Armoured Ramp Carrier
Arm		Armt	Armament
Armd Bde			Armoured Brigade
Armd Div		AD	Armoured Division
ARO	*		Army Routine Order
ARP	*		Air Raid Precautions
ARP	*		Ammunition Refilling Point
ARRC			Associate of the Royal Red Cross
ARS			Aircraft Recognition School
ARS			Army Remount Service
Art			Artificer
art wks coy		AWC	Artizan Workshops Company
arty	*	Arty	Artillery
Arty Coy			Artillery Company
Arty R	*	arty R	Artillery Reconnaissance
ARU			Armoured Reinforcement Unit
ARV			All-Round Vision
ARV			Armoured Recovery Vehicle
AS			Wait [in signal message]
ASA			Ammunition Small Arms
ASA			Army School of Ammunition [RAOC]
ASC			Advanced Surgical Centre
ASC			Army School of Cookery
ASC			Army Selection Centre
ASCW		A Sch of CW	Army School of Chemical Warfare
ASD			Advanced Stationery Depot
ASD			Advanced Supply Depot
ASD			Ammunition Sub-Depot
ASD			Army Spectacles Depot
ASH			Army School of Hygiene
A&SH		ASH	Argyll & Sutherland Highlanders
ASI			Air Speed Indicator
ASLS		A(S)LS	Air Survey Liaison Section [RE]
aslt	*	Asslt	Assault
aslt bde		Asslt Bde	Assault Brigade Royal Engineers
ASM			Artificer Sergeant Major [REME]

Abbreviation		Alternatives	Meaning
ASO			Assistant Section Officer
ASPT			Army School of Physical Training
ASS			Administrative Staff School
ASS		ASSigs	Air Support Signals
ASST			Air Support Signals Team
Asst			Assistant
ASSU	*		Air Support Signals Unit
Assy		assy	Assembly
ASTC			Allied Special Training Centre
ASTU			Army Selection Training Unit
ASU			Army Selection Unit
AT			Aldershot [station monogram]
AT			Ambulance Train
AT			Ammunition Technician [RAOC]
AT			Animal Transport
AT		A/T; A/Tk; Atk; A-Tk	Anti-Tank
AT		A/T, A-T	Anti-Typhus
AT			Armour Trial
ATAF			Allied Tactical Air Force
ATB			Artificer Training Battalion [RASC]
ATC			Army Transport Column [RASC]
ATC		AT Coy	Army Troops Company
ATD			Automatic Timing Device
ATDC			After Top Dead Centre
ATE			Airborne Training Establishment
ATI	*		Army Training Instruction
ATM	*		Army Training Memorandum
A tps	*	A Tps	Army Troops
ATRD			Army Troops Railhead Detachment [RAOC]
ATS			Amphibian Training School [RASC}
ATS			Army Technical School
ATS			Auxiliary Territorial Service
ATS(B)		ATS (Boys)	Army Technical School (Boys)
ATSO			Anti-Typhus Soluble Oil
ATrS			Army Transfusion Service [blood]
ATSSC			Auxiliary Territorial Service Staff College
ATSSS		ATS Sigs Sch	Auxiliary Territorial Service Signal School

Abbreviation		Alternatives	Meaning
ATSTC			Auxiliary Territorial Service Training Centre
att	*		Attach/ed/ment
ATTR			Anti-Tank Training Regiment [RA]
ATV			Auxiliary Towing Vehicle
A/U/			Acting Unpaid [rank]
Aus Div			Australian Division
Aust	*	Aus	Australia(n)
auth			Authority/ised
auto			Automatic
aux	*	Aux; auxy	Auxiliary/ies
AV			Anti-Vessicant
AVC			Automatic Volume Control [radio]
AVLB			Armoured Vehicle Launched Bridge
AVP			Advanced Vehicle Park [RAOC]
AVRE	*		Assault Vehicle Royal Engineers
AVRP			Advanced Vehicle Reception Point
AVRS			Army Veterinary & Remount Services
AVTC			Army Vocational Training Centre
A&W			Albright & Wilson
AW Grenade			Albright & Wilson Grenade
AWC			Artillery Workshop Company
AWD	*		Advanced Workshop Detachment
AWD			All Wheel Drive
AWOL		AWL	Absent Without Leave
AWOS			Army Wireless Operating Signals
AWTC			Annual Weapon Training Course
AXP			Ambulance Exchange Point
AXSS			Army X-Ray Service Store
AYR			Ayrshire [Home Guard]
Az			Azimuth
BA			British Association [screw thread]
BAD	*		Base Ammunition Depot
BANU			British Army Newspaper Unit
BAOR			British Army of the Rhine
Bap		BAP	Baptist
BAP			Battery Aiming Point [RA]
Bar			Barometer/ric
BAR			Burn After Reading

Abbreviation		Alternatives	Meaning
BARE			British Armaments Research Establishment
BARV			Beach Armoured Recovery Vehicle
BAS			British Army Staff
BB			Bailey Bridge
BB			Mustard Gas
BBE			Bailey Bridging Equipment
BBP	*		Bulk Breaking Point
BC	*		Battery Commander [RA]
BC RASC			Bridge Company Royal Army Service Corps
BCA		BC Ack	Battery Commander's Assistant [RA]
BCC			Beach Company Commander
BCF			British Concrete Fabrications
BCH			Base Clearing House
bchy			Butchery
BCOF(J)			British Commonwealth Occupation Force [in Japan]
BCP		Bty Comd Post	Battery Command Post
BCSO			
BCU			Base Censor Unit
BCWC			Birmingham Carriage & Wagon Company
BD			Barrack Department [RASC]
BD	*		Base Depot
BD			Battledress
BD	*		Bomb Disposal
BDC			Bottom Dead Centre
bde	*	Bde	Brigade
Bde Gp			Brigade Group
Bde Gp Coy			Brigade Group Company
BDF			Bedfordshire [Home Guard]
BDMS			Base Depot Medical Stores
Bdr		BDR	Bandolier [ammunition]
bdr		Bdr	Bombardier [RA]
BDS			Beach Dressing Station
BDS			Bomb Disposal Section
BDST			British Double Summer Time
BDVS			Base Depot Veterinary Stores

Abbreviation		Alternatives	Meaning
bdy	*	Bdy	Boundary
BE			Bandolier Equipment
BE			Base Ejection (Ammunition)
BE			Basic Element
BEDS		Bedfs	Bedfordshire
BEDS & HERTS		Beds & Herts	The Bedfordshire and Hertfordshire Regiment
BEF			Brazilian Expeditionary Force
BEF			British Expeditionary Force
Belg			Belgium/Belgian
BEM			British Empire Medal
BEME			Brigade Electrical & Mechanical Engineer [REME]
BEO			Battalion Education Officer
BEP			Bituminous Emulsion Paint
BER			Beyond Economic Repair
Berks			Berkshire
BETFOR			British Element Trieste Force
BFAP			British Forces Aden Protectorate
BFF			Burma Frontier Force
BFIG			British Forces in Greece
BFO			Beat Frequency Oscillator
BG		BGp	Beach Group
Bg		bg	Bearing
Bge			Barrage
BGH			British General Hospital
Bgl Maj			Bugle Major
Bglr			Bugler
BGO			Battalion Gunnery Officer
BGPC			Beach Group Commander
BGU			Beach Group Unit
BH			Base Hospital
BH			Burscough [station monogram]
BHL			Base Hospital Laundry
BHM			Birmingham [Home Guard]
BHN		bhn	Brinell Hardness Number
bhp		BHP; b/hp	Brake Horse Power
BHQ		Bn HQ	Battalion Headquarters
BHQ		Bty HQ	Battery Headquarters
BIC			Burma Intelligence Corps

Abbreviation		Alternatives	Meaning
BID			Bulk Issue Depot
BIS			Bulk Issue Store [NAAFI/EFI]
BISF			British Iron & Steel Federation
BISSB			British Inter-Services Security Board
bk		brs	Barrack(s)
BK			Battery Captain or Second-in-Command [RA]
Bk			Bulk
Bky			Bakery
BL			Base Laundry
BL			Breech Loading
BLA			British Liberation Army
BLACK WATCH		BW	Black Watch
BLFN			British Land Forces Norway
BLO			Bombardment Liaison Officer
BLP			Backloading Point
BLR			Beyond Local Repair
BLS			British Land Service
BLT			Belt [ammunition]
BM			Band Master
BM		BMR: Bmr	Beach Master
BM			Bending Moment [bridging]
BM			Bramley [station monogram]
BM			Brigade Major
BMA	*		Beach Maintenance Area
BMA			Bermuda Militia Artillery
BMFL			Base Malaria Field Laboratory
BMH			British Military Hospital
BML			Breech Mechanism Lever
BMM			British Military Mission
BMPP			British Military Printing Press
BMRA			Brigade Major Royal Artillery
BMTD (NA)			British Military Training Directorate (North Africa)
BMU			Brigade Medical Unit
BMY			Base Marshalling Yard
bn	*	Bn	Battalion
Bn HQ		BHQ	Battalion Headquarters
BNAF			British North Africa Force(s)
BNF			Banffshire [Home Guard]

Abbreviation		Alternatives	Meaning
BO			Breech Obturated
BOD	*		Base Ordnance Depot [RAOC]
BOI		BoI; BofI	Board of Inquiry
Bombardment Tp			Bombardment Troop [RA]
bomrep	*	bombrep	Bombing Report
BOR			British Other Rank(s)
BORDER		Border	Border Regiment
BOS		Bn Ord Sgt/Sjt	Battalion Orderly Sergeant
BOS		BoS; BofS	Board of Survey
BOV WING			Bovington Wing (RAC Depot)
BOW			Base Opthalmic Wing
BOW			Base Ordnance Workshop
BOWO	*		Brigade Ordnance Warrant Officer
BP			Base Plate [bridging]
BP			Bletchley Park
BP			British Pharmacopoeia [Medical]
BP			Bullet Proof
BP			Bull Point [station monogram]
BPB			Bailey Pontoon Bridge
BPC			Base Psychiatric Centre
BPC			British Pharmaceutical Codex [Medical]
BPFC			Base Petroleum Filling Centre
BPM			Balanced Pillar Mounting
BPO			Base Personnel Office
BPO			Base Post Office
BPS			Best Plough Steel
BPS			Bituminous Paint Specification
BPS			Bulk Petroleum Storage
BPSC			Bulk Petrol(eum) Storage Company
BPSP			Bullet Proof Steel Plate
BPTC		Bk Pet Tpt Coy	Bulk Petrol(eum) Transport Company
BPU			Brigade Postal Unit
BQMS	*		Battery Quartermaster Sergeant/ Serjeant
BR			Barbados Regiment
BR			Bermuda Rifles
Br			Branch
BR			Brecknockshire [Home Guard]

Abbreviation		Alternatives	Meaning
br	*	Br	Bridge(ing)
Br			British
BR			Burma Rifles [Indian Army]
Br Layer		B/L	Bridgelayer
Br Pl			Bridging Platoon
Br Tp			Bridging Troop
BRA			Brigadier Royal Artillery
BRASCO			Brigade Royal Army Service Corps Officer
BRCS			British Red Cross Society
BRD			Base Remount Depot
BREN		Bren	BRNO/Enfield
BRINDIV			British/Indian Division
Brit	*		British
BRMM			British Raw Materials Mission
BRS			Beach Recovery Section [REME]
BRS			Building Research Station
BRTCI			British Reinforcement Training Centre [India]
BRX			Berkshire [Home Guard]
BS			British Standard
BS&M			Bengal Sappers & Miners [Indian Army]
BSA			Base Sub-Area
BSA		BS-A	Beach Sub-Area
BSA			Birmingham Small Arms
BSB			Bailey Suspension Bridge
BSC			British Standard Colour
BSC			British Supply Council
BSD	*		Base Supply Depot
BSD			Boat Stores Depot [RASC]
BSF			British Standard Fine [screw thread]
BSG		Bde Sp Gp	Brigade Support Group
BSI			British Standards Institution
BSM	*		Battery Sergeant/Serjeant Major
BSM			British Supply Mission
BSO			Battalion Signals Officer
BSP			d]British Standard Pipe [screw thread]
BSS			Beach Signals Section

Abbreviation		Alternatives	Meaning
BSS			British Standard Specification
BST			British Summer Time
BSU			Base Salvage Unit
B sup airfd	*		Base Supply Airfield
BSW			British Standard Whitworth [screw thread]
Bt			Baronet
Bt			Brevet [rank]
BT			Start and end of message [in signal message]
BT			Benign Tertian [malaria]
Bt.			Baronet
BTA			Battalion Technical Adjutant
BTA			British Troops Austria
BTB			British Troops Berlin
BTC			Basic Training Centre
BTC			British Transit Centre
BTD			Base Transfusion Depot [RAMC]
BTDC			Before Top Dead Centre
BTE			British Troops Egypt
BTI			British Troops Iraq
BTLC			British Troops Low Countries
BTNI			British Troops Northern Ireland
BTO			Battalion Technical Officer
BTSO			Board of Trade Supply Organisation
BTSO			Box Terminal Signal Office
BTSRLab			Blood Transfusion and Surgical Research Laboratory
BTU			Base Transfusion Unit [RAMC]
BTU			Blood Transfusion Unit
BTU		B Th U	British Thermal Unit
bty	*	Bty	Battery
bty CP			Battery Command Post
BU	*		Bath Unit
BU			Bombardment Unit
BUCKS		Bucks	Buckinghamshire
BUCO			Build-Up Control Organization
BUFFS		Buffs	Royal East Kent Regiment
BURMARK			Burma Armoured Ramp Carrier

Abbreviation		Alternatives	Meaning
BUX			Buckinghamshire [Home Guard]
BV			Bakelite Varnish [ammunition]
BVE			Bermuda Volunteer Engineers
BVRC			Bermuda Volunteer Rifle Corps
BWIR		Br WIR; Br WI regt	British West Indies Regiment
B wkshp	*	BW; Base Wkshp	Base Workshop
Bx			Beeswax
BZ			Beaten Zone
C			Centigrade
CA			Caithness [Home Guard]
CA	*		Civil Affairs
CA	*	(CA)	Coast Artillery
CA			Current Affairs
C & A			Copper & Asbestos
CAB		CdnAB; Cdn Armd Bde	Canadian Armoured Brigade
CAD			Central Ammunition Depot [RAOC]
CADR			Canadian Armoured Delivery Regiment
CAFSO			Chief Air Force Signals Officer?
CAFV			Controller Armoured Fighting Vehicles
CAFVD			Chairman Armoured Fighting Vehicles Division
CAGRA			Commander Army Group Royal Artillery
Cal		cal	Calibrate/ion/ing
CAM			Cambridgeshire [Home Guard]
Cam			Camouflage
CAMB		Cambs; Camb R	Cambridgeshire [Regiment]
CAMERONS		Camerons	Queen's Own Cameron Highlanders
CAMS		Cams	Cameronians (Scottish Rifles)
Can		Cdn	Canada/Canadian
CANLOAN			Canadian officers loaned to the British Army
CAO			Chief Administrative Officer
CAP		Coy AP	Company Aid Post
C.A.P.			Capsule Lachrymatory

Abbreviation		Alternatives	Meaning
CAPC			Coastal Artillery Practice Camp
Capt			Captain
CAR			Canadian Armoured Regiment
Carp			Carpathian [Polish]
carr			Carrier
cart		CART	Cartridge [ammunition]
cas	*		Casualty/ies
CAS			Civil Affairs Service
CAS			Close Air Support
CAS			Coastal Artillery School
CAS(B)			Civil Affairs Service (Burma)
CASC			Civil Affairs Staff Centre
CASL			Coastal Artillery Searchlight
CASS			Civil Affairs Staff School
CASS		Corps Arty Sigs Sect	Corps Artillery Signal Section
cat		Cat	Catalogue
CATC			Coastal Artillery Training Centre
CATS			Canadian Army Trades School
C/Attk			Counter Attack
CAT WING			Catterick Wing (RAC Depot)
cav	*	Cav	Cavalry
CAV			Charles Anthony Vandervell, founder of CAV company, later part of Lucas
CAVC			Canadian Army Veterinary Corps
CB			Companion of the Most Honourable Order of the Bath
CB	*		Confined to Barracks
CB			Contact Breaker
CB	*	C/B: C/Bty	Counter-Battery
CB			Counter-Bombardment
CBE			Commander of the Most Excellent Order of the British Empire
CBI			China-Burma-India
CBLO			Chief Bombardment Liaison Officer
C/Bn			Cadet Battalion
CBO	*	C/BO; C/Bty O	Counter-Battery Officer
CBOD			Canadian Base Ordnance Depot
CBTC			Commando Basic Training Centre

Abbreviation		Alternatives	Meaning
C/bty			Counter-Battery
CBU			Commander Bombardment Units
CC			Caernarvonshire [Home Guard]
CC			Cases Charger [ammunition]
CC			Claims Commission
CC			Colonial Corps
CCAC			Combined Civil Affairs Committee
CCB			Combined Communications Board
CCB			Combined Communications Board
CCBO			Corps Counter-Bombardment Officer
CCC			Cape Coloured Corps [South Africa]
CCD			Civilian Clothing Depot [RAOC]
CCF			Combined Cadet Force
CCG			Control Commission Germany
CCGS			Chief of the Canadian General Staff
CCMA			Commander Corps Medium Artillery
CCO			Corps Camouflage Officer
CCO			Chief of Combined Operations
CCP	*		Casualty Collection/ing Point
CCR			Colchester [station monogram]
CCRA			Commander Corps Royal Artillery
CCRE			Commander Corps Royal Engineers
CCS	*		Casualty Clearing Station
CCS			Combined Chiefs of Staff
CCS			Control Commission School
CD			Circular Double [tent]
CD			Civil Defence
CD	*		Coast/Coastal Defence
CD			Convalescent Depot [RAMC]
CD			Core Diameter
CDA			Canada
CD&AA			Coatal Defence & Anti-Aircraft [artillery]
CDB		CD Bty	Coastal Defence Battery
CDC			Chemical Divisional Council
CDCE			Civil Defence Camouflage Establishment

Abbreviation		Alternatives	Meaning
CdeG			Croix de Guerre
CDES			Chemical Defence Experimental Station
CDI			Command Driver Increment
CDL			Canal Defence Light [tank]
CDLS		CDL Sch	Canal Defence Light School
CDMU			Coast Defence Maintenance Unit [REME]
Cdn			Canadian
CDN			Cardiganshire [Home Guard]
Cdn Gds			Canadian Guards
cdo	*	Cdo	Commando
CDR			Civil Defence Region
CDS			Corps Delivery Sqn [RAC]
CDS		Corps Del Sqn	Corps Dental Section
Cdt			Cadet
CD&TC			Camouflage Development & Training Centre
CE			Chief Engineer
CE		CofE	Church of England
CE			Commutator End
CE			Composition Exploding [ammunition]
CEAD			Chief Engineer & Superintendent of Armaments Design
CEAO			Chief Engineer (Administration? Accommodation? Accounting?) Officer
CEC			Corps Exhaustion Centre
CEFO			Complete Equipment Fighting Order
CEMEC			Captured Enemy Material Executive Committee
CEO			Casualty Evacuation Officer
cert			Certificate
CET			Central European Time
CETD			Chief Engineer Tank Design
CF	*		Chaplain to the Forces
CF			Combined Filling [Ammunition]
CF			Covering Fire
CFA			Cavalry Field Ambulance

Abbreviation		Alternatives	Meaning
CFF			Cavalry Frontier Force (10th Queen Victoria's Own Corps of Guides [Indian Army]
cfn	*	Cfn	Craftsman [REME]
CFPU			Canadian Film & Photographic Unit
CFS			Carrickfergus [station monogram]
CG		CofG	Centre of Gravity
CG			Chaplain General
CG R&D		CGRD	Controller General Research & Development
CGE			Controller General of Economy [War Office]
CGH			Canadian General Hospital
CGH			Combined General Hospital [British and Indian]
CGI			Corrugated Galvanised Iron
CGME			Controller General of Mechanical Equipment [from Feb 41]
CGMP			Controller General of Munitions Production
CGMT			Controller General of Machine Tools
CGT			Chevrolet Gun Tractor
CH			Cheshire [Home Guard]
CH			Companion of Honour
CHANT			Channel Tanker
chem	*		Chemical
CHESHIRE		Cheshire	Cheshire Regiment
Chev		Cvt	Chevrolet
CHO			Cameron Highlanders of Ottawa [Canada]
CHQ		Coy HQ	Company Headquarters
CHR			Civil Hospital Reserve
CI			Channel Islands
CI			Chief Inspector
CI			Chief Instructor
CI			Church of Ireland
CI			Compression-Ignition
CI			Corrugated Iron
CI			Counter-Intelligence

Abbreviation		Alternatives	Meaning
CIA			Central Inspector(ate) of Armaments
CIA			Chief Inspector of Armaments
CIABG			Czech Independent Armoured Brigade Group
CIAC		CI of AC	Chief Inspector of Army Catering
CIB		Cdn Inf Bde	Canadian Infantry Brigade
CIB			Command Interview Board
CIC			Chief Inspector of Clothing [MoS]
CIC			Combined Intelligence Committee
CID		Cdn Inf Div	Canadian Infantry Division
CID			College of Imperial Defence
CID			Committee for Imperial Defence
CIE			Companion of the Most Eminent Order of the Indian Empire
CIESS			Chief Inspector Engineer and Signals Stores
CIFV			Chief Inspector(ate) of Fighting Vehicles
CIG			Chief Instructor in Gunnery
CIGS			Chief of the Imperial General Staff
CIH			Central India Horse
CILF			Channel Islands Liberation Force
CILSA			Chief Inspector of Land Service Ammunition
CIM			Channel Islands Militia
CIM			Classroom Instructional Mounting
CIMT			Chief Inspector Mechanized Transport
CinC			Commander in Chief
CIOS		CIofS	Chief Inspector(ate) of Stores
circ			Circular
CISA			Chief Inspector of Small Arms
CIST			Chief Inspector of Supplementary Transport
CIV			Certificate Issue Voucher
civ	*		Civil/Civilian
C & J			Carpenter & Joiner
C & K			Clothing & Kit
CKD			Completely Knocked-Down
CL		C-L	Carden-Loyd

Abbreviation		Alternatives	Meaning
CL	*		Centre Line
Cl			Class
CLE			Central Landing Establishment
CLE			Container Light Equipment
Clk			Clerk
CLM			Cancel Last Message
CLN			Clackmannanshire [Home Guard]
CLO			Chief Liaison Officer
CLS			Censor Liaison Section
CLS			Central Landing School
CLU			Civilian Labour Unit
CLY			City of London Yeomanry
CLY			County of London Yeomanry
CM		Cal Meth	Calvinistic Methodist
cm			Centimeter
CM			Court Martial
CM&HC			Court Martial & Holding Centre
CMA			Controller of Military Accounts
CMA			Corps Maintenance Area
CMAB			Combined Munitions Assignment Board
CMB			Civilian Medical Board
CMC			Combined Meteorological Committee
CMD&DCU			Combined Military Dispersal & Demobilisation Camp Unit
CME			Cloth Model Exercise
CMEC			Central Medical Emergency Committee
CMF			Central Mediterranean Force(s)
CMG			Companion of the Most Distinguished Order of St Michael and St George
CMH			Cambridge Military Hospital
CMH			Connaught Military Hospital
CMHQ			Canadian Military HQ
CMO			Counter-Mortar Officer
CMP			Canadian Military Pattern
CMP			Corps of Military Police
CMP(P)			Corps of Military Police (Provost)

Abbreviation		Alternatives	Meaning
CMP(TC)			Corps of Military Police (Traffic Control)
CM&SWTC			Commando Mountain and Snow Warfare Training Centre
CMS			Carrier Maintenance Section
CMTC			Central Mediterranean Training Centre
CMTC			Combined Military Transportation Committee
CMTD			Command Mechanized Transport Depot?
CMVS			Cavalry Mobile Veterinary Section
CMWC			Central Medical War Committee
CMWTC			Commando Mountain Warfare Training Centre
CO			Combined Operations
CO	*		Commanding Officer
CO			Cornwall [Home Guard]
Coax		COAX; Co-ax	Co-axial [machine gun]
COBU			Combined Operations Bombardment Unit
COD			Chief Ordnance Officer [note: Central Ordnance Depot from 1947]
COD			Coast Observation Detachment
COE			Court of Enquiry
CofG			Centre of Gravity
CofM			Correction of the Moment [Artillery]
C of R			Commencement of Rifling
CofS			Church of Scotland
COH		CoH	Corporal of Horse
COHQ		COH	Combined Operations Headquarters
COL			City of London [Home Guard]
col	*	Col	Colonel
COLDM GDS		CG; C Gds	Coldstream Guards
coll			College
coln	*	Col; Coln	Column
Combn		combn	Combination
comd	*	Comd	Command/er/Commandant
COME			Chief Ordnance Mechanical Engineer

Abbreviation		Alternatives	Meaning
comm			Commercial
comn	*	Comm; comms	Communication
comp	*	Compo	Composite
Comp Coy		Compo Coy	Composite Company
conc	*		Concentrate/d/ion
Condr			Conductor [RAOC
Conf		confd	Confidential/Conference
Con R		con R	Contact Reconnaissance
constr	*	Constr	Construct/ed/ion
cont			Control
Conv			Convalescent
COO	*		Chief Ordnance Officer
coord	*		Coordinate/d/tion
COREP			Combined Operations Repair Organization
COS		CoS; CofS	Chief of Staff
CoS			Church of Scotland
COSSAC			Chief Of Staff to the Supreme Allied Commander
COSUP			Common Supplies Policy Committee
COV			Coventry [Home Guard]
COXE			Combined Operations Experimental Establishment
coy	*	Coy; co; cy	Company
CP			Canadian Pattern
CP			Command Post
CPB			Central Purchase Board
CPC			Combined Panel Code
CPD			Camouflage Paint Department
CPL			Camouflage Paint Levy
CPL			Central Pathology Laboratory
cpl	*	Cpl	Corporal
CPO			Command Pay Office
CPO			Command Post Officer [RA]
CPOA		CPO Ack	Command Post Officer's Assistant [RA]
CPO (FS)			Chief Provision Officer (Food Supplies)
CPPC			Corps Petrol Park Company
CPR			Cape Peninsula Rifles [South Africa]

Abbreviation		Alternatives	Meaning
CPRB			Combined Production & Resources Board
CPRSD			
CPS			Camouflage Paint Specification
cptr			Carpenter & Joiner
CPU			Cipher Producing Unit
CPU			Corps Postal Unit
CQ			Calling all stations [in signal message]
CQMS	*		Company Quartermaster Sergeant/ Serjeant
CR			Clothing Regulations
CR		CofR	Commencement of Rifling [guns]
CR			Cyprus Regiment
CR RASC			Cyprus Regiment (RASC)
CRA			Commander Royal Artillery
CRA			Consulting Radiologist to the Army
CRAC			Commander Royal Armoured Corps
CRASC			Commander Royal Army Service Corps
CRC			Combined Recruiting Centre
CRC			Corps Reinforcement Centre
CRE			Commander Royal Engineers
CREFORCE			Crete Force
CREME			Commander Royal Electrical and Mechanical Engineers
CRH			Curvature Radius Head [ammunition]
CRM			Carmathenshire [Home Guard]
CRMB			Combined Raw Materials Board
CRO			Central Recruiting Office
CRS			Camp Reception Station
CRS			Caualty Reception Station
CRU			Civil Resettlement Unit
CRU		Corps RU	Corps Reinforcement Unit
CRV			Certificate Receipt Voucher
CS			Campaign Service
CS			Central School(s)
CS			Circular Single [tent]
CS	*	C/S; CSp: Cl Sp	Close Support

Abbreviation		Alternatives	Meaning
CS			Combined Service
CSA			Chlorosulphonic Acid [ammunition]
CSCI			Christian Scientist
CSCI			Corps Supply Column
CSD			Central Salvage Depot
CSD			Cold Storage Depot
CSD			Command Supply Depot
CSDIC			Combined Service Detailed Interrogation Centre
CSEE			Clothing and Stores Experimental Establishment
CSgt		CSjt	Colour Sergeant/Serjeant
CSM	*		Company Serjeant/Sergeant Major
CSO			Chief Signals Officer
CSPC			Combined Staff Planner's Committee
C Speed			Change Speed
CT			Change To [RA gunnery]
CT			Lincolnshire [Home Guard] – means County Town
CTA			Cemented Tank Armour
CTAC		CT Ammn Coy	Corps Troops Ammunition Company [RASC]
CTC			Combined Training Centre
CTC			Commando Training Centre
CTC			Corps Training Centre
CTH			Cape Town Highlanders [South Africa]
CTN			Carton [ammunition]
C tps	*	Corps Tps	Corps Troops
CTR			Coastal Training Regiment [RA]
CTSC			Corps Troops Supply Column
CTU			Camouflage Unit
CU			Camouflage Training Unit
CU			Control Unit [radio]
cu cm			Cubic Centimetre(s)
cu ft			Cubic Foot/Feet
cu in			Cubic Inch(es)
CUM			Cumberland [Home Guard]
CV	*		Command Vehicle [noted officially as "Lorry, Command"]

Abbreviation		Alternatives	Meaning
CVC			Central Vehicle Census?
CVO			Commander of the Royal Victorian Order
CW			Central Workshop
CW	*		Chemical Warfare
CW			Chillwell [station monogram]
CW		C of W	Clerk of Works
CW			Continuous Wave
c/w			Code Word
c/w		cw;	Complete With
CWAAF			Canadian Women's Auxiliary Air Force
CWAC			Canadian Women's Army Corps
CW Coy			Chemical Warfare Company [RE]
CW Gp			Chemical Warfare Group [RE]
cwt		Cwt	Hundredweight
CWTS			Command Weapon Training School
CYPRUS R		Cyprus R	Cyprus Regiment
Cz		cz	Czechoslovak(ian)
D	*	D/	Deputy
"D"			Doubtful [RAOC use]
DA		D/A	Delayed Action [fuse]
DA			Direct Action [fuse]
DAA		div adm area	Divisional Administrative Area
DAA and QMG	*		Deputy Assistant Adjutant and Quartermaster-General
DAA&CD			Director(ate) of Anti-Aircraft & Costal Defence Artillery
DAAG	*		Deputy Assistant Adjutant General
DAC			Daimler Armoured Car
DAC			Director(ate) of Army Contracts
DAC		Div Amn Coy	Divisional Ammunition Company
DACG			Deputy Assistant Chaplain General
DAD			Deputy Assistant Director
DADAP			Deputy Assistant Director Army Psychiatry
DADBR			Deputy Assistant Director of Biological Research
DADH			Deputy Assistant Director of Hygiene
DADMS			Deputy Assistant Director of Medical Services

Abbreviation		Alternatives	Meaning
DADOS			Deputy Assistant Director of Ordnance Services
DADOS (E)			Deputy Assistant Director of Ordnance Services (Engineering)
DADST			Deputy Assistant Director of Supplies and Transport
DADVS			Deputy Assistant Director of Veterinary Services
DAE			Director(ate) of Army Education
DAER			Daily Ammunition Expenditure Rate
DAF			Desert Air Force
DAFV			Director(ate) Armoured Fighting Vehicles [from June 1940]
DAG			Deputy Adjutant General
DAG		div adm gp	Divisional Administrative Group
DAI			Direct Action Impact [fuse]
DAir			Director Air [airborne forces]
DAK			Director of Army Kinematography
DAP			Director of Army Psychiatry
DAP			Distant Aiming Point
DAP			Divisional Ammunition Park
D APS			Director(ate) of Army Postal Services
DAT			Director Army Training
DATS			Director Auxiliary Territorial Service
dB			Decibel
DB			Depot Battalion
DB			Detention Barracks
DBO			District Barracks Officer
DBO			Divisional Burials Officer
DBP			Dibutyl Phthalate
DBRE			Depot Battalion Royal Engineers
DBT			Dumbartonshire [Home Guard]
DC			Dead Centre
DC			Direct Current
DC		DofC	Director(ate) of Camouflage
D/C			Date Captured
DC(S)			Defence Committee (Supply)
DCA			Director(ate) of Civil Affairs

Abbreviation		Alternatives	Meaning
DCBO			Divisional Counter-Bombardment Officer
DCG			Deputy Chaplain General
DCI			Deputy Chief Instructor
DCIGS			Deputy Chief of the Imperial General Staff
DCLI			Duke of Cornwall's Light Infantry
DCM			Distinguished Conduct Medal
DCM			District Court Martial
DCO			Director Combined Operations
DCOS		DCoS	Deputy Chief of Staff
DCR			Divisional Cavalry Regiment
DCRE			Deputy Commander Royal Engineers
DCS			Director(ate) of Clothing & Stores
DCT			Director(ate) of Clothing & Textiles
DD			Design Department
DD		D/D	Dishonourable Discharge
DD			Double Double [Bailey Bridge]
DD			Duplex Drive
DDCS			Deputy Director of Clothing & Stores
DDE			City of Dundee [Home Guard]
DDE			Deputy Director of Equipment
DDEE			Deputy Director of Electrical Engineering
DDGTD			Deputy Director-General Tank Design
DDGTS			Deputy Director-General Tank Supply
D DIV			Deception Division
DDH			Deputy Director of Hygiene
DDL			Deputy Director of Labour
DDME			Deputy Director of Mechanical Engineering
DDMO			Deputy Director of Military Operations
DDMov		DD(Movements)	Deputy Director of Movements
DDMS			Deputy Director of Medical Services
DDMT			Deputy Director of Military Training

Abbreviation		Alternatives	Meaning
DDMT(A)			Deputy Director of Military Training (A Branch)
DDMT(B)			Deputy Director of Military Training (B Branch)
DDMT(T)			Deputy Director of Military Training (Technical)
DDofA			Deputy Director of Artillery
DDOS			Deputy Director of Ordnance Services
DDP			Deputy Director of Pathology
DDSD			Deputy Director Staff Duties
DDSP			Deputy Director Selection of Personnel
DDST			Deputy Director Supply & Transport
DE			Driving End/Driven End
DEA			Davis Escape Apparatus
DEAOS			Director(ate) of Equipment & Army Ordnance Stores
DEC			Decoppering [ammunition]
DEC			Divisional Exhaustion Centre
Def			Defence
Def & Empl Pl			Defence & Employment Platoon
Defic			Deficient
deg		°	Degree(s)
DEL			Defence Electric Light
Del			Deliver(y)
Dem			Demolition
Dem Sqn			Demolition Squadron
Demo			Demonstration
Demob			Demobilise/ation
DEMS			Defensively Equipped Merchant Shipping
DEN			Denbighshire [Home Guard]
Dent		dent	Dental
dep	*		Depot
Dep			Deputy
Dept		dept	Department
Dept of TD & E		DTDE	Department of Tank Design & Experiment
derv fuel	*	DERV	Diesel Engined Road Vehicle Fuel

Abbreviation		Alternatives	Meaning
Des			Designate(d)
DES			Director(ate) of Engineer Stores
DESE			Director of Engineer and Signal Equipment
det	*	Det	Detached, Detachment
Det			Detect/or/ed
DET		Det	Detonator [ammunition]
Dev		dev	Development
DEVON		Devons	Devonshire Regiment
DF	*	D/F	Defensive Fire
DF	*		Direction Finding
DFC			Distinguished Flying Cross
DFC			Dump Floating Crane
DFP			Disinfector Field Portable
DFS			Dumfrieshire [Home Guard]
DFV			Director(ate) Fighting Vehicles
DFV (D&L)			Director(ate) Fighting Vehicles (Design, Modifications & Manufacturing Liaison)
DG			Director General
DG			Dragoon Guards
DG of A		DGA	Director General of Artillery
DGAMS			Director General of Army Medical Services
DGAR			Director General of Army Requirements
DGAVS			Director General of Army Veterinary Services
DGC			Divisional Gas Compound
DGES			Director General of Engineer Services
DGFV (P)			Director General Fighting Vehicles (Production)
DGFV (R&D)			Director General Fighting Vehicles (Research & Development)
DGGRE			Director General Graves Registration and Enquiries
DGHG&TA			Director General Home Guard & Territorial Army
DGME			Director General Mechanical Equipment
DGME (D&D)			Director General Mechanical Equipment (Design & Development)

Abbreviation		Alternatives	Meaning
DGMP			Director General of Munitions Production
DGMS			Director General of Medical Services
DGMT			Director General of Military Training
Dgns			Dragoons
DGOF			Director General of Ordnance Factories
DGR			Director(ate) Graves Registration
DGRM			Director-General Raw Materials
DGSRD			Director-General Supply Reserve Depots?
DGTA			Director-General Territorial Army
DGTD			Director-General Transportation Services
DGTS			Director-General Tank Design
DGTT			Director-General Tank & Transport [to Feb 41]
DGWE			Director-General Welfare and Education
DGWP			Director-General Weapons Production
DH		Dir Hyg	Director(ate) of Hygiene
DHG			Director(ate) of Home Guard
DHgs			Director(ate) of Hirings
DHM			Durham [Home Guard]
DHTU			Draft Holding & Training Unit
DHU			Draft Holding Unit
DI			Dangerously Ill
dia		Diag	Diagram
diam		dia	Diameter
DID			Design & Inspection Department
DID	*		Detail Issue Depot [RASC]
Dir			Direct
DofI&S		DIS; DI&S	Directorate of Investigation & Statistics
dis P	*	Dis Pt	Dispersal Point
dist	*	Distr, DIST	District
div	*	Div; Divn	Division/al
Div Arty HQ			Divisional Artillery Headquarters
DL			Dead Load

Abbreviation		Alternatives	Meaning
DL			Deputy Lieutenant [of County]
D Lab			Director(ate) of Labour
DLI			Durban Light Infantry [South Africa]
DLI			Durham Light Infantry
DM		Dvr Mech	Driver Mechanic
D&M			Driving & Maintenance
DMA			Divisional Maintenance Area
DMC			District Movement Control
DMD			Director(ate) of Military Docks
DME			Director(ate) of Mechanical Engineering
DMGO			Deputy Master General of the Ordnance
DMI			Director(ate) of Military Intelligence
dml		Dml	Demolition
DMO			Director(ate) of Military Operations
DMO&P			Director(ate) of Military Operations & Plans
DMP			Dimethyl Phthalate
DMQ			Director(ate) of Movements & Quartering
DMR			Director(ate) of Medical Research
DMR			District Mounted Rifles [South Africa]
Dmr		Drmr	Drummer
DMS			Director(ate) of Medical Services
DMS		DMSvy	Director(ate) of Military Survey
DM(S)R			Director of Medical (Statistical) Research
DMT			Director(ate) of Military Training
DN			Diploma in Nursing
DNR			Date Not Recorded
DO			Dental Officer
DO			Design Officer
DO			District Officer [Coastal Artillery]
D-O			Demi-Official
DO(TIG)			District Officer (Technical Instructor in Gunnery)
Doc			Document(s)

Abbreviation		Alternatives	Meaning
D of A			Director(ate) of Artillery
D of H			Director of Hygiene
D of M		Dml	Director(ate) of Mechanization
D of P			Director(ate) of Plans
D of R			Director(ate) of Remounts
DOI			Died of Injuries
DOM			Director of Mechanization
DOO		DofO	Director of Organization
DOR			Dorset [Home Guard]
DORA			Defence of the Realm Act 1914
DORSET		Dorsets	Dorset Regiment
DOS			Director(ate) of Ordnance Services
DOW		DW	Died of Wounds
DOW		DofW	Director(ate) of Works
DP			Debussing Point
DP		Del Pt	Delivery Point
DP			Detraining Point
DP			Director of Pathology [RAMC]
DP		Dpers	Director(ate) of Personnel
DP			Disembarkation Point
DP			Displaced Person
DP			Disruptive Pattern
DP			Drill Purpose [Weapon]
DPB			Drill Purpose Blank Firing [Weapon]
D-P			Dual-Purpose
DP(B)		DPB	Drill Purpose (adapted for Blank firing)
DPA			Defended Port Area
DPH			Diploma in Public Health
Dpost			Director(ate) of Postal Services
DPS			Director(ate) of Personnel Services
DPSS			Director(ate) Printing & Stationery Services
DPU			Divisional Postal Unit
DPU		Div Pro Unit	Divisional Provost Unit
DPW		DPoW	Director(ate) of Prisoners of War
DQ		DofQ	Director(ate) of Quartering
DQMG			Deputy Quartermaster General
DR	*	D/R; Don R	Despatch Rider or Motor-Cyclist

Abbreviation		Alternatives	Meaning
DR			Director(ate) of Research
DR			Discrepancy Report
Dr			Doctor
Dr			Draft?
Dr		dr	Drams (weight)
DR			Dutch Reformed [South African]
DRA			Director(ate) Royal Artillery
DRAC			Director(ate) Royal Armoured Corps
DRC			Defence Requirements Committee
DREE			Director(ate) of Royal Engineer Equipment
DRemounts			Director(ate) of Remounts
DRLS	*		Despatch Rider Letter Service
DRO			Daily Routine Orders
DRO			Director(ate) of Recruiting & Organization
Drum Maj			Drum Major
DS			Directing Staff
DS			Discarding Sabot [ammunition]
DS			Dismounted Service
DS			Double Single (Bailey Bridge)
DS	*		Dressing Station
D&S			Development & Supply
DS RASC			Driving School Royal Army Service Corps
DSACEUR			Deputy Supreme Allied Commander Europe
DSACSEA			Deputy Supreme Allied Commander South East Asia
DSC			Daimler Scout Car
DSC			Distinguished Service Cross [RN]
DSD			Director(ate) of Staff Duties
DSG			Divisional Support Group
DSO			Distinguished Service Order
DSP			Director of Selection of Personnel
DSP			Divisional Sub-Park
DSR			Director(ate) of Scientific Research
DSRD			Director Supply Reserve Depots?
DST			Director(ate) of Supplies & Transport

Abbreviation		Alternatives	Meaning
DSTO			Deputy Sea Transport Officer
DSU			Divisional Salvage Unit
DSWV			Director(ate) of Special Weapons & Vehicles
DT		Div Tps	Divisional Troops
DT			Double Triple [Bailey Bridge]
DTB		Dvr Trg Bn	Driver Training Bn [RASC]
DTD			Department of Tank Design
DTE		D&TE	Depot & Training Establishment
DTG			Date Time Group
DTI			Director of Tactical Investigation
DTP		Dir of Tk Prod	Director(ate) of Tank Production
DTW			Driver Training Wing
DU			Dental Unit
DUKW			D=1942, U=Utility, K=All-Wheel Drive, W=dual rear axles
DUKW TU			DUKW Training Unit
DVN			Devon [Home Guard]
DVP			Drowned Vehicle Park
dvr	*	Dvr	Driver
Dvr Mech			Driver Mechanic
Dvr Op		D/O	Driver Operator
DVS			Director(ate) of Veterinary Services
DW		Derm Wg	Dermatological Wing
D Welfare			Director(ate) of Welfare
DWC			Dental War Committee
DWR			Duke of Wellington's Regiment (West Riding)
DWS			Director(ate) of Warlike Stores
DWS			Director(ate) of Womens Services
DY		Derby Yeo	Derbyshire Yeomanry
DZ	*		Dropping Zone
E			East
E 1 (etc)			Experimental model No 1 (etc)
E LANCS			East Lancashire Regiment
E YORKS			East Yorkshire Regiment (Duke of York's Own)
EA	*		East Africa(n)
EA			Elevated Aerial/Antenna
EA	*		Enemy Aircaft

Abbreviation		Alternatives	Meaning
EA Boat			Eastern Army Boat
EAA			East African Artillery
EAAC			East African Armoured Corps
EAAOC			East African Army Ordnance Corps
EAASC			East African Army Service Corps
EAC			East Africa Command
EAC			Equipment Assembly Company
EAE			East African Engineers
EAEME			East African Electrical and Mechanical Engineers
EAIG			Experimental Assistant in Gunnery
EAM			Emergency Ammunition Magazine
EAS			Engineer Assault Squadron
EBE			Experimental Bridging Establishment
EBW			Engineer Base Workshop
EC Coy			Excavator Company [RE]
EC(IA)			Emergency Commission [Indian Army]
ECAC			Executive Committee of the Army Council
ECC			Emergency Crew Control
ech	*	Ech	Echelon
ECT			Electro-Convulsion Therapy
ECTC			Emergency Cooking Training Centre [ATS]
ED			Efficiency Decoration (Territorial)
EDE			Experimental Demolition Establishment
EE			English Electric
EEF			Egyptian Expeditionary Force
EEW		EE Wkshp	Engineer Equipment Workshop
EF	*		Expeditionary Force
EFC			Equivalent Full Charge [gunnery]
EFC			Expeditionary Force Canteen
EFI			Expeditionary Forces Institute
EFTS			Elementary Flying Training School
EFU			Entomological Field Unit
eg	*		For example [Exempli Gratia]
EGM			Empire Gallantry Medal

Abbreviation		Alternatives	Meaning
EHG			Edinburgh [Home Guard]
EI			Equitation Instructor
EL			East Lancashire [Home Guard]
EL			East Lothian [Home Guard]
ELD			Electric Light Director
elev			Elevation
ELS			Emergency Landing Strip
ELY			Isle of Ely [Home Guard]
E & M			Electrical & Mechanical
EME	*		Electrical Mechanical Engineer
E & MEO		EME	Electrical & Mechanical Engineering Officer
EMER			Electrical & Mechanical Engineering Regulations
EMF		emf	Electro-Motive Force
emgy			Emergency
Emgy Bty			Emergency Battery [RA]
EMI			Electrical & Musical Industries
EMO			Embarkation Medical Officer
emp		Empl	Employ/ed/ment
EMS			Emergency Medical Services
EMSH			Emergency Medical Services Hospital
En		en	Enemy
engr	*	Engr	Engineer
ENSA			Entertainments National Service Association
EO			Engineering Officer
EOP			Emergency Observation Post
EP			Embarkation Point
EP			Embussing Point
EP			Entraining Point
EP			Extreme Pressure
EPI			Expected Point of Impact
EPIP			European Privates Indian Pattern [tent]
eqpt	*	Eqpt	Equipment
ER			East Riding of Yorkshire [Home Guard]
ER			Emergency Reserve
ER		Eqpt Regs	Equipment Regulations

Abbreviation		Alternatives	Meaning
ERE			Extra-Regimentally Employed
ERY			East Riding Yeomanry
ES			Effective Strength
ESA			Expense Stores Account
ESB			Experimental Selection Board
ESBD			Engineer Stores Base Depot
ESD			Embarkation Supply Depot
ESD			Engineer Stores Depot
ESM			Experimental Sergeant Major [RA]
ESO	*		Embarkation Staff Officer
ES(P)C			Engineer Stores (Port) Section
est	*	Estb	Establish/ed/ment
ESU			Electro-Static Unit
ESU			Elementary Selection Unit
ESX			Essex [Home Guard]
ET			Early Treatment [of VD]
ETA			Estimated Time of Arrival
Etc		&c	Etcetera
ETD			Estimated Time of Departure
ETE			Experimental Tunnelling Establishment
ETO			European Theatre of Operations
EUDL			Equivalent Uniformly Distributed Load
evac	*	ev	Evacuate/d/tion
EVL			Emergency Vaccine Laboratory
EW			Early Warning
EW			Experimental Wing
EWBB			Extra Widened Bailey Bridge
EWS			Eastern Warfare School
Ex			Exercise
excl	*	Excl	Exclude/d/ing or Exclusive
EY			Ermengency Use [rifle adapted for rifle grenade training]
F			Fahrenheit
F			Fife [Home Guard]
FA			Field Artillery
FAD			Forward Ammunition Depot
Fahr			Fahrenheit
FAMO			Forward Air Maintenance Organization

Abbreviation		Alternatives	Meaning
FAMTO			First Aid Motor Transport Outfit [vehicle spares and consumables]
FANY			First Aid Nursing Yeomanry
FAP			Flank Aiming Point
FAP			Forward Ammunition Point
farr			Farrier
FAS			Forward Area Sight [AA]
FAT			Field Ambulance Transport
FAT			Field Artillery Tractor
FB			Field Battalion
FB			Field Branch
FB			Fire Brigade
FB			Floating Bay [bridging]
FBE	*		Folding Boat Equipment
FBPE	*		Folding Boat Pontoon Equipment
FC			Fire Command
FC			Forward Control
FCB			Ferro-Cement Barge
FCM			Field Court Martial
FCNL			French Committee of National Liberation (Comité français de Libération nationale)
FCP			Forward Control Post
FCTC			Field Cookery Training Centre
fd	*	Fd; Fld	Field
FD			Full Dress
F & D			Flint & Denbighshire [Home Guard]
FDAO			Field Dental Anaesthetic Outfit
fd bchy	*		Field Butchery and Cold Storage Depot
fd bky	*	Fd Bky	Field Bakery
Fd Cash Off		FCO	Field Cash Office
FDC			Field Dental Centre
Fd Coy			Field Company
FDCO			Field Dental Casting Outfit
Fd Hyg			Field Hygiene
FD Lab		FDL	Field Dental Laboratory
Fd Pk			Field Park
Fd Pk Coy			Field Park Company
Fd Pk Sqn			Field Park Sqn

Abbreviation		Alternatives	Meaning
Fd San			Field Sanitation
Fd San Sect			Field Sanitation Section [RAMC]
Fd Sqn			Field Squadron
Fd Svy			Field Survey
FDF			Fiji Defence Force
FDL		FD Lab	Field Dental Laboratory
FDL	*		Forward Defended Locality
FDO			Field Dental Outfit
FDS	*		Field Dressing Station
FDS		Fwd Del Sqn	Forward Delivery Squadron
FDT			Fire Direction Table
FDU		Fd DU	Field Dental Unit
FDU			Fortress Destruction Unit
FDW			Field Defence Works
FF	*		Field Force
FF	*		Fire-Fighting
FF			Free French
FF			Frontier Force
F&F		F and F	Field and Fortress (or Fixed)
FF Coy			Fire-Fighting Company
FFC			Fuse Factor Correction [ammunition]
FFD			First Field Dressing
FFE			Fire For Effect
FFF			Free French Forces
FFI			Field Force Institute
FFI			Forces Françaises de l'Intérieur (French Forces of the Interior)
FFI			Free From Infection
FFY		F&FY	Fife and Forfar Yeomanry
FG			Fort George [station monogram]
FGCM	*		Field General Court Marshal
FGH			Fort Garry Horse [Canada]
FH			Face Hardened [armour]
FH Sect		Fd Hyg Sect	Field Hygiene Section [RAMC]
FHQ			Fighting Headquarters
FI			Decimal point [in morse signalling]
FI			Financial Instruction
FI			Firing Interval

Abbreviation		Alternatives	Meaning
FID			Fuse Instantaneous Detonating [ammunition]
Fig			Figure
FL		F/L	First Light
FL			Foreign Legion [French]
Flk		Fk	Flank
flt	*		Flight
Fm		fm	Farm
FM			Field Marshal
FM			Frequency Modulation/Modulated
FMA	*		Forward Maintenance Area
FMB			Fast Motor Boat
FMC			Field Maintenance Centre [RASC]
FMC			Formation Maintenance Company
fmn	*	Fmn	Formation
FMR			Field Miniature Range
FMSVF			Federated Malay States Volunteer Force
FMU			Field Medical Unit
FO			Fire Order [RA]
FOB			Forward Observer Bombardment
FOBU			Forward Observation & Bombardment Unit
F of M			Figure of Merit
FOO	*		Forward Observation Officer
FOP			Flat Oil Paint
For Coy		Forest Coy	Forestry Company
Foresters			Sherwood Foresters (Notts and Derby Regiment)
FoS			Fall of Shot
FoS			Foreman of Signals
FoSQMS			Foreman of Signals Quartermaster Sergeant
FoSSM			Foreman of Signals Sergeant Major
FP			Field Punishment [officially abolished in 1923]
F/P			Forfeiture of Pay
FPO		Fd PO	Field Post Office
fps		fs	Feet Per Second
FQMS			Farrier Quartermaster Serjeant or Sergeant

Abbreviation		Alternatives	Meaning
FRD		Fd RD	Field Remount Depot
freq	*		Frequency
FS	*	F Sy; Fd Sy	Field Security
FS	*		Field Service
FS			Flash Spotting
F&S			Flash and Sound
FSC		Fd Svy Coy	Field Survey Coy [RE]
FSD			Field Supply Depot
FSM			Farrier Serjeant Major [RAVC]
FSMD			Field Survey Map Depot
FSMO			Field Service Marching Order
FSP			Field Security Police
FSP			Flash Spotting Post
F sp	*	FS	Flash Spotting
FSPB	*		Field Service Pocket Book
FSPBP			Field Service Pocket Book Pamphlet
FSR			Field Service Ration(s)
FSR			Field Service Regulations
FSRS			Field Survey Reproduction Section
FSS			Field Sanitary Section [RAMC]
FSS			Field Security Section
FSS	*		Fixed Signal Service
FSU	*		Field Surgical Unit [RAMC]
FT			Field Trial
FT			Flintshire [Home Guard]
ft	*	Ft	Foot/Feet
FT			Fuze Time
ft3/min			Cubic feet per minute
FTC			Field Test Centre
FTF			Flame Thrower Fuel
FTO			Forward Tank Officer
FTR			Field Training Recommendation
FTR		FT Regt	Field Training Regiment [RA]
Ftr			Fitter
FTU	*		Field Transfusion Unit [RAMC]
FTU			Forward Treatment Unit [RAMC, malaria]
FUP			Forming Up Place
fus	*		Fusilier(s)
FVD			Fighting Vehicles Division

Abbreviation		Alternatives	Meaning
FVDD			Fighting Vehicles Design Department
FVPE			Fighting Vehicles Proving Establishment [From 1942]
FVS			Fighting Vehicle School
fwd	*	Fwd	Forward/ed
FWD			Front Wheel Drive
Fwd Del Sqn		FDS	Forward Delivery Squadron
G			City of Glasgow [Home Guard]
GA			General Assembly
GAC			Gun Angle Control
GAD		Gds Armd Div	Guards Armoured Division
GAHW			Guards Armoured Holding Wing
gal	*	gall	Gallon
GAP			Gun Aiming Point [RA]
GATW		Gds Armd Trg Wing	Guards Armoured Training Wing
GBE			Knight Grand Cross of the Most Excellent Order of the British Empire
GBPU			Guards Brigade Postal Unit
GBS			Ground Bullets Speed [infantry training mnemonic]
GC			George Cross
GC			Gold Coast
GC			Guides Cavalry [India]
GC			Gun Cotton
GC Coy		GCC	General Construction Company [RE]
GCCS			Government Code and Cipher School
GCB			Knight Grand Cross of the Most Honourable Order of the Bath
GCIE			Knight Grand Commander of the Most Eminent Order of the Indian Empire
GCM	*		General Court Martial
GCMG			Knight Grand Cross of the Most Distinguished Order of St Michael and St George
GD			General Duties
GD		Gd Def	Ground Defence

Abbreviation		Alternatives	Meaning
gd	*	Gd	Guard
GD		Guards Dep	Guards Depot
GDA			Gun Defended Area
GDC			Gun Detachment Commander
GDF			Gibraltar Defence Force
GDO			General Duty Officer
Gds			Guards
gdsm	*	Gdsm	Guardsman/men
GE			Garrison Engineer
Gel			Gelatine
gen	*	Gen	General
Gen Hosp			General Hospital
Gen Tpt Coy			General Transport Company
GEP		GE Pk	General Equipment Park
GF			Gun Fire
GGHG			Governor General's Horse Guards [Canada]
GH			Gardner's Horse [India]
GH			General Hospital
GHQ	*		General Headquarters
GHQ Liaison Regt			General Headquarters Liaison Regiment
GIB			Gibraltar [station monogram]
GIB			Greek Independent Brigade
GL			General List
GL			Gun-Laying
GLASGOW H		GH	Glasgow Highlanders
GLN			Glamorganshire [Home Guard]
GLOSTERS			Gloucestershire Regiment
GLR			Gun-Laying Radar
GLS			Gloucestershire [Home Guard]
GM			George Medal
GM		G-M	Gun Metal
GM		Gnr Mech	Gunner Mechanic
GMB			Greek Mountain Brigade
GMC			General Motors Corporation
GMT			General Military Training
GMT			Greenwich Mean Time
GNF			Guns Now Firing
gnr	*	Gnr	Gunner

Abbreviation		Alternatives	Meaning
Gnr Mech			Gunner Mechanic
Gnr Op			Gunner Operator
GO			Gas Operated
GO			General Order
GO			Gridded Oblique [air photography]
G(O)			General staff (Operations)
GOC			General Officer Commanding
GOCinC			General Officer Commander in Chief
GOP			Gun Observation Post
GOR			Gun Operations Room [AA]
GORDONS			Gordon Highlanders
Govr			Governor
Govt			Government
GP			General Principles
GP			General Purpose
gp	*		Group
GPD			Glider Pilot Depot
GPH			Gallons Per Hour
GPI			General Paralysis of the Insane
GPO			Gun Position Officer [RA]
GPOA		GPO Ack	Gun Position Officer's Assistant [RA]
GPR			Glider Pilot Regiment
GPS			General Production Section
GPT			General Pack Transport?
GPW			Glider Pilot Wing
GPWWC			German Prisoners of War Work Camp
GQG			Le Grand Quartier General [French]
GR			General Roster
GR			George Rex
GR			Graves Registration
GR			Gurkha Rifles
GR&EU		Graves R&E	Graves Registration & Enquiries Unit
GREF			General Reserve Engineering Force
Gren			Grenade(s)
GREN GDS		GG: G Gds	Grenadier Guards
GRM			Government Rubber Monovinylacetylene

Abbreviation		Alternatives	Meaning
grn	*	Grn	Garrison
GRO	*		General Routine Order(s)
GRTD			General Reinforcement Training Depot
GS	*		General Service
GS	*		General Staff
GS			General Stores
G(P)			General Staff (Plans)
G(SD)			General Staff (Staff Duties)
GS Pol			General Staff Policy
GSC		GS Corps	General Service Corps [from February 1942]
GSCD&TC			General Service Corps Depot & Training Centre
GSGS			Geographical Section, General Staff
GSI			General Staff India
GSM			Garrison Serjeant Major
GSO I/2/3		GI/II/III	General Staff Officer Grade 1 (Lt Col) Grade 2 (Maj) Grade 3 (Capt)
GSP (NA)			Garrison Services Pool (North Africa)
GST			German Summer Time
GSW			Gun Shot Wound
GT		Gen Tpt	General Transport
GT		G/T	Gun Tower
GT			Gun-Target (line) [artillery]
GT coy	*	GT Coy	General Transport Company
GTB			Guards Training Battalion
GTE			Gunnery Training Equipment
GTS			Glider Training School
GV			Gentian Violet
H			Hampshire & Isle of Wight [Home Guard]
H		H/	Honorary [rank or appointment]
(H)			Home [as opposed to Overseas]
HA		H/A	High Angle [artillery]
H&A			Honours and Awards
HAA	*		Heavy Anti-Aircraft
HAC			Honourable Artillery Company
HAC			Humber Armoured Car
HAD			Hot Air Disinfestor

Abbreviation		Alternatives	Meaning
HAG			Heavy Artillery Group
HALLAMS		Hallams	Hallamshire [Bn TA]
HAMPS		Hamps	Hampshire Regiment
HAT			Home Ambulance Train
HAVR			Havildar [Indian Army]
HB			Hostile Battery
HC			High Capacity
HCAA			Honorary Catering Advisor to the Army
H Cav		HCAV; Hcav	Household Cavalry
HCD			High Current Density
HCE			Hexa Chlora Ethane [Ammunition]
HCR			Household Cavalry Regiment
Hd			Head
HD			Highland Division
HD			Hirings Directorate
HD			Home Details
HD			Horse Drawn
HD			Holland
HD			Lincolnshire [Home Guard]
HDO			Home Dental Outfit
HDS			Huntingdonshire [Home Guard]
HDT			Horse-Drawn Transport
HE	*		High Explosive
HE			Home Establishment
HEAP			High Explosive Armour Piercing
HEAT		HE/AT	High Explosive Anti-Tank
HEDA			High Explosive Delayed Action
HEDELAY			High Explosive with Delay fuse
HEGRAZ			High Explosive with Graze fuse
HERTS		Herts	Hertfordshire
HES		HE(S)	High Explosive Substitute
HESH			High Explosive Squash Head
HETF			High Explosive Time Fuse
hex			Hexagon
HF	*		Harassing Fire
HF	*		High Frequency
HF			Home Forces
HF			Hostile Fire
HFD			Herefordshire [Home Guard]

Abbreviation		Alternatives	Meaning
HFTC			Highland Fieldcraft Training Centre
HG			Home Guard
HG&TA			Home Guard & Territorial Army
HGCU			Heavy Glider Conversion Unit
HH			Hodson's Horse [India]
H Hr			H-Hour
HIS			Home Issues Section
HKMC			Hong Kong Mule Corps
HKR			Hong Kong Regiment
HKSRA			Hong Kong & Singapore Royal Artillery
HKVDC			Hong Kong Volunteer Defence Corps
HLC			Harbour Launch Company
Hldg		Hg	Holding
HLI			Highland Light Infantry (City of Glasgow Regiment)
HLIC			Highland Light Infantry of Canada
HM			His/Her Majesty
HMG			Heavy Machine Gun
HMP			High Melting Point
HMSO			His Majesty's Stationery Office
HO			Heavy Oil
HO		H/O	Hostilities Only
HOC			Holding Operational Commando
Hon			Honour/s/able
Hor			Horse/d/s
hosp	*	Hosp	Hospital
how	*	How	Howitzer
HP		hp	Half-Pay
HP	*	hp	High Power
HP	*	hp	Horse Power
HP			Hospital Pattern [tent]
HP			Hyde Park [station monogram]
HQ	*	H/Qtrs	Headquarters
HQ&RSD			Headquarters & Regulating Station Detachment [RAOC]
HQTERE			Headquarters Tunnelling Engineers RE
HQVG			Headquarters Vehicle Group

Abbreviation		Alternatives	Meaning
hr	*		Hour(s)
HRM			Higher Rate Messing
HRS RASC			Heavy Repair Shop Royal Army Service Corps
HS			High Speed
HS			Home Service
HS			Home service only [medical category, from late 1944]
HS			Hospital Ship
HSC			Humber Scout Car
HSR			Home Service Ration
HSSG		HQ SSG	Headquarters Special Services Group
HT	*		High Tension
HT	*		Horsed Transport
HTS			Hertfordshire [Home Guard]
HTS			High Tension Steel
HU			Holding Unit
HV			High Velocity
hy	*	Hvy	Heavy
Hy AA			Heavy Anti-Aircraft
hyd			Hydraulic
hyg	*		Hygiene
IA			Immediate Action
IA			Indian Army
IA			Indian Artillery
IAB			Indian Armoured Division
IAC			Indian Armoured Corps
IAD			Intermediate Ammunition Depot
IAE			Inspectorate of Army Equipment
IAF HQ			Indian Army Force Headquarters
IAO			Indian Army Order
IAOS			Inspector(ate) of Army Ordnance Services
IAPC			Indian Auxiliary Pioneer Corps
IAS			Indian Amphibian School
IASC			Indian Army Service Corps
IAT			Inflammation of Areolar Tissue
IB		Inf Bde	Infantry Brigade
IBBG			Independent Belgian Brigade Group

Abbreviation		Alternatives	Meaning
IC	*		In charge of
IC			Intelligence Corps
IC			Inter-Communication
IC	*		Internal Combustion
I/C		i/c	In Command
ICA			Inter-Communication Amplifier
ICD			Intelligence Corps Depot
ICE			Internal Combustion Engine
ICI			Imperial Chemical Industries
ICSC			Indian Continuous Service Cadre
ICTC			Infantry Carrier Training Centre
IDC			Imperial Defence College
idc			Post-nominal: Passed Imperial Defence College
Idn		Ind	India(n)
IE		I/E	Illegal Enlistment
IE			Indian Engineers
IE			Interior Economy
I(E)			Instructor (Educational) [AEC]
ie	*		Namely or That is to say [id est]
IEME			Indian Electrical & Mechanical Engineers
IF			Intermediate Frequency
IFV			Inspector(ate) of Fighting Vehicles
IG			Instructor in Gunnery
IG		Ir Gds	Irish Guards
IG			Iron Galvanized
IGB		Indpt Gds Bde	Independent Guards Brigade
IGH			Indian General Hospital
ign		Ign	Ignition
IGSC		ISGSC	Inter-service Ground Strip Code
IGT			Inspector General of Training
IHWS			Infantry Heavy Weapons School
IJP			Initial Joint Plan
IK			Installation Kit
Illum		Ill	Illuminating/ion
ILO			Intelligence Liaison Officer
IM			Intra-Muscular
IMA			Indian Mountain Artillery
IMB			Indian Mountain Battery

Abbreviation	*	Alternatives	Meaning
IMD			Indian Medical Department
IMH			Indian Military Hospital
IMI			Repeat your whole transmission [in morse signalling]
Imm			Immediate
IMS			Indian Medical Service(s)
IMTC			Infantry Mortar Training Centre
in	*		Inch
IN			Nairnshire Bn, Inverness [Home Guard]
inc		Inc	Incendiary
incl	*		Include/d/ing or Inclusive
Incr			Increment
Ind	*		India/n
Ind		Indr	Indirect
Ind Fd Amb			Indian Field Ambulance
indep	*	Indpt; Indep	Independent
Indpt Bde			Independent Brigade
Indpt MG Coy			Independent Machine-Gun Company
Indpt Para Coy			Independent Parachute Company (Pathfinders)
inf	*		Infantry
Inf Bde			Infantry Brigade
Inf Bde Gp			Infantry Brigade Group
Inf Div			Infantry Division
infm	*		Inform/ed/ation
Info		info; infm	Information
INNISKILLINGS		Innisks	Royal Inniskilling Fusiliers
inst			Instant [ie this month]
instr	*	Instr	Instruct/ed/tion ort Instructor
int	*	Intel	Intelligence
INT QSA			What is my signal strength? [in signal message]
intercom		I/C	Intercommunication
Intsum		Int Sum	Intelligence Summary
INV			Invernesshire [Home Guard]
IO	*		Intelligence Officer
IoC		IOC	Inns of Court Yeomanry
IOD			Indian Ordnance Depot/ Department

Abbreviation		Alternatives	Meaning
IOM			Isle of Man [Home Guard]
IOO	*		Inspecting Ordnance Officer [RAOC]
IOR			Indian Other Rank(s)
IOTCNA			Intelligence Officer Training Centre North Africa
IP			Indian Pattern
IPBG		Indpt Para Bde Gp	Independent Parachute Brigade Group
IPWC			Inspector of Prisoner of War Camps
IR			Immediate Report
IR			Immediate Reserve
IR		I/R	Infra-Red
IRASC			Inspector Royal Army Service Corps
IRTD			Infantry Reinforcement Training Depot
IRV			India Rubber Vulcanised [wire]
IS		Int Sum	Intelligence Summary
IS	*		Internal Security
ISO			Companion of the Imperial Service Order
ISRB			Inter Services Research Bureau
ISSAEE			Inter-Service Small Arms Experimental Establishment
ISTC			Infantry Specialist Training Centre
ISTDC		ISTD	Inter-Service Training & Development Centre
It		Itn	Italian
IT		I.T.	Izod Test
I-Tank		ITk: I-Tk; IT	Infantry Tank
ITB			Indian Tank Brigade
ITBU			Indian Field Broadcasting Unit
ITC			Infantry Training Centre
ITC			Intelligence Training Centre
ITC&ACF			Inspector Training Corps & Army Cadet Force
ITD			Infantry Training Depot
ITS			Initial Training School
ITT			Infantry-Tank Telephone
ITT			Inspector(ate) of Technical Training

Abbreviation		Alternatives	Meaning
ITW			Infantry Troops Workshop [REME]
ITW			Initial Training Wing
IU			International Unit [vitamins]
IV			Intra-Venous
IV			Issue Voucher
IWBB			Improvised Widened Bailey Bridge
IWT	*		Inland Water Transport
IWTG			Inland Water Transport Group
IWTLAW			Inland Water Transport Light Aid Workshop
IWTOC			Inland Water Transport Operating Company
IWTOG			Inland Water Transport Operating Group
JA			Judge Advocate
JAG			Judge Advocate General
Jap			Japan(ese)
JBG			Jewish Brigade Group
JCA			Jamaica [station monogram]
JCA			Junior Civil Assistant
JD			Judging Distance
JD			Junction Distribution
JDB			Junction Distribution Box [radio]
JEW			Jewish
JG			Jungle Green
JIBG			Jewish Infantry Brigade Group
JNCO			Junior Non-Commissioned Officer
Jnr			Junior
JOMP/AP			Joint Outline Maintenance Project/ Administrative Plan
JP			Joint Planning
JPS			Joint Planning Staff
JRB			Joint Recruiting Board
JRC			Junction Remote Control [radio]
JSC		jsc	Junior Staff Course
JSS			Junior Staff School
JTC			Junior Training Corps
junc	*		Junction
JUO			Junior Under Officer [Royal Military College]
JWPS			Joint War Production Staff

Abbreviation		Alternatives	Meaning
K			Kesteven Bn, Lincolnshire [Home Guard]
K			Send your message [in morse signalling]
KACR			Kenyan Armoured Car Regiment
KAR			King's African Rifles
KB		Kino Br	Kinema Branch
KBE			Knight Commander of the Most Excellent Order of the British Empire
Kc		KC	Kilocycles
Kc/s			Kilocycles per second
KCB			Knight Commander of the Most Honourable Order of the Bath
KCIE			Knight Commander of the Most Eminent Order of the Indian Empire
KCMG			Knight Commander of the Most Distinguished Order of St Michael and St George
KD			Khaki Drill
KDG			King's Dragoon Guards
KEO			3rd King Edward's Own (Probyn's Horse) [Indian Army]
KFS			Knife, Fork and Spoon
KGOBS&M			King George's Own Bengal Sappers & Miners [India]
KGVO			King George Vth's Own
KHC			King's Honorary Chaplain
KHP			King's Honorary Physician
KHS			King's Honorary Surgeon
KIA		KiA	Killed in Action
KINGS		Kings	King's Regiment (Liverpool)
KINGS OWN		Kings Own	King's Own Royal Regiment (Lancaster)
KM		Km: km	Kilometer
KO			Knocked Out
KOH			King's Own Hussars
KOMR			King's Own Malta Regiment
KOSB			King's Own Scottish Borderers
KOYLI			King's Own Yorkshire Light Infantry

Abbreviation		Alternatives	Meaning
KR			Kenya Regiment
KR			King's Regulations
KRD			Kinema Repair Detachment [RAOC]
KRIH			King's Royal Irish Hussars
KRRC			King's Royal Rifle Corps
KSLI			King's Shropshire Light Infantry
KT			Kent [Home Guard]
KZ			Killing Zone
L			Light
L			Lindsey Bn, Lincolnshire [Home Guard]
L/			Local [rank]. EG L/Cpl = local corporal
LA			Local Auditor
LAA	*		Light Anti-Aircraft
LAA SL Bty			Light Anti-Aircraft & Searchlight Battery [RA]
LAA SL Regt			Light Anti-Aircraft & Searchlight Regiment [RA]
lab	*		Laboratory
lab	*		Labour
LAD	*		Light Aid Detachment
L/AWD			Land/Air Warfare Department
LB			Landing Bay [bridging]
lb	*	Lb	Pound [weight]
L bdr	*	LBdr	Lance Bombardier [RA]
lbf/ft			Pound-force per foot
lbf/in2			Pound-force per square inch
LBG			Large Box Girder [bridge]
LBH			Lothian & Borders Horse
LBY			Lothian & Borders Yeomanry
LC			Landing Craft
LC Coy			Light Composite Company
LCA			Landing Craft Assault
LCC			Load Carrying Capacity
LCF			Landing Craft Flak
LCG(L)			Landing Craft Gun (Large)
LCH			Landing Craft Headquarters
LCI			Landing Craft Infantry

Abbreviation		Alternatives	Meaning
LCI(L)			Landing Craft Infantry (Large)
LCI(M)			Landing Craft Infantry (Mortar)
LCI(R)			Landing Craft Infantry (Rocket)
LCI(S)			Landing Craft Infantry (Small)
LCM			Landing Craft Mechanized
LCN			Landing Craft Navigation
LCOCU			Landing Craft Obstacle Clearance Unit
LCOH		LCoH; L/CoH	Lance Corporal of Horse
L cpl	*	LCpl	Landing Craft Personnel
LCP(L)			Landing Craft Personnel (Large)
LCP(L)(S)			Landing Craft Personnel (Large) (Smoke)
LCP(SY)			Landing Craft Personnel (Survey)
LCpl		L/Cpl (see text); L/C	Lance Corporal
LCS(L)			Landing Craft Support (Large)
LCS(M)			Landing Craft Support (Medium)
LCS(S)			Landing Craft Support (Small)
LCT			Landing Craft Tank
LCT(A)			Landing Craft Tank (Armoured)
LCT(CB)			Landing Craft Tank (Concrete Buster)
LCT(HE)			Landing Craft Tank (High Explosive)
LCT(R)			Landing Craft Tank (Rocket)
LCV			Light Command Vehicle (Royal Artillery)
LCVP			Landing Craft Vehicle Personnel
ldg	*		Landing
ldr		Ldr	Leader
ldr		Ldr	Loader
LDRD			London District Reception Depot
Ld SH			Lord Strathcona's Horse [Canada]
LDV			Local Defence Volunteers
LDY			Leicester & Derbyshire Yeomanry
LE			Low Explosive
LE			Lower Establishment
LEI			Leicestershire [Home Guard]
LEICS		Leics	Leicestershire Regiment
LF			Lancashire [Home Guard]

Abbreviation		Alternatives	Meaning
LF			Lancashire Fusiliers
LF			Low Frequency
LFA			Land Forces Adriatic
LFA		Lt Fd Amb	Light Field Ambulance [RAMC]
LF&ML(G)			Land Forces & Military Liaison (Greece)
LG			Lewis Gun
LG			London Gazette
Lgr			Leaguer
lh		l/h: LH	Left Hand [side]
LIAP			Leave in Addition to Python
Lieut		Lt	Lieutenant
LILOP			Leave in Lieu of Python
LINCOLNS		Lincolns	Lincolnshire Regiment
LIR			London Irish Rifles
LK			Lanarkshire [Home Guard]
LL		L/L	Last Light
LL			Live Load [bridging]
LMAB			London Munitions Assignment Board
LMC			Leyland Motor Company
LMG			Light Machine Gun
LMG	*		Light Machine Gun
LMS			Line Maintenance Section
LMSR			London Midland & Scottish Railways
LO	*		Liaison Officer
LO			Local Oscillator
LoC	*	LofC	Line(s) of Communication
Loc		loc	Location, Locating
LoCA			Lines of Communication Area
LOCS-A			Lines of Communication Sub-Area
LoE			Limit of Exploitation
LofC			List of Changes
LON			County of London [Home Guard]
LOND R		Lond R	London Regiment
LonDist		LONDIST	London District
LOOB		LOB	Left Out Of Battle
lor	*		Lorried or Lorryborne
LOS			Liaison Officer's School

Abbreviation		Alternatives	Meaning
LoS			Line of Sight
LOVATS		Lovats	Lovat Scouts
LOYALS		Loyals	Loyal Regiment (North Lancashire)
LP			Local Purchase
LP			Low Power
LPO			Local Purchase Officer
LR			Lancashire [Home Guard]
L&R			Left & Right
LRB			London Rifle Brigade
LRDG			Long Range Desert Group
LRM			Lower Rate Messing
LRP			Long Range Penetration
LRPG			Long Range Penetration Group
LRS			Light Repair Section
LS			Land Service
LS			Landing Strip
LS		Leg Staff	Legal Staff
LS		Liv Scot	Liverpool Scottish
LS		Lond Scot	London Scottish
L&S			Light and Sound
LSCTC			Light Scout Car Training Centre
LSD		lsd	Pounds, Shilling & Pence
LSGC			Long Service & Good Conduct [medal or pay]
LSH			Landing Ship Headquarters
LSH			Lord Strathcona's Horse
LSI			Landing Ship Infantry
L sjt		L sgt; LSjt; L/S (see text)	Lance Sergeant
LSP			Legal Staff Pool
LSR			Light Service Respirator
LST			Landing Ship Tank
lt	*	Lt	Lieutenant
lt	*	Lt	Light
LT	*	L/T	Line Telephony or Telegraphy
LT			Local Time
LT	*		Low Tension
Lt Col			Lieutenant Colonel
Lt Fd Hyg Sec			Light Field Hygiene Section
Lt Gen			Lieutenant General

Abbreviation		Alternatives	Meaning
Lt Rep			Light Repair
Lt Ry			Light Railway
Lt Tk		Lt Tank	Light Tank
LTC		L&TC	Leave & Transit Camp
LTIN			Landing Table Index Number
LU			Laundry Unit
Lub			Lubricant(s)
LV			Low Velocity
LVO			Lieutenant of the Royal Victorian Order
LVT			Landing Vehicle Tracked
LW			Liverpool Welsh
LWRA			Leave with Ration Allowance
LZ	*		Landing Zone
M			Married
M		(M)	Medical
M			Merioneth & Montgomery [Home Guard]
M		m	Meter
M			Mixed
M			Movements
MA	*		Military Assistant
MA	*		Military Attache
MAAA			Maritime Anti-Aircraft Artillery
MAAD			Manual of Anti-Aircraft Defence
MAAF			Mediterranean Allied Air Force(s)
MAAR			Maritime Anti-Aircraft Regiment [RA]
MAC			Malta Auxiliary Corps
MAC	*		Motor Ambulance Convoy
mag	*		Magazine
mag	*		Magnetic
maint	*		Maintain/ed or Maintenance
Maint Coy			Maintenance Company
MAIU			Mediterranean Army Interrogation Unit
maj	*	Maj	Major
Mal			Malaria
MAN			Lancashire [Home Guard]
MANCH		Manch	Manchester Regiment

Abbreviation		Alternatives	Meaning
MAP			Ministry of Aircraft Production
MARM		M/H AC	Marmon Herrington Armoured Car
MARU			Mobile Ammunition Repair Unit
MATS			Medical/Ammunition/Transport/ Supplies [planning mnemonic]
max			Maximum
M&B			Make & Break
MB Coy			Motor Boat Company
MBE			Member of the Most Excellent Order of the British Empire
MBES			Miscellaneous Bridging Equipment Set
MBS			Model Bridge Set
M Bn			Motor Battalion
MBU			Mobile Bath Unit
MC			Machine Carbine
MC			Map Code
MC			Message Centre
MC			Military Cross
MC			Mobilization Centre
MC	*	M/C: m/c	Motorcycle [Note: motorcyclist = DR]
MC	*		Movement Control
MC		Mule Coy	Mule Company
M/c		Mc	Megacycles
mc/g			Machining
Mc/s		mc/s	Megacycles per second
MCA			Military Command Athens
MCAF			Movement Control Allied Forces
MCC			Malaria Control Company
MCC			Mobilization Control Centre
MCC			Mobilization Control Centre
MCC			Motor Coach Company [RASC]
MCD		Mil Con Dep	Military Convalescence Depot
MCG		MC Gp	Movement Control Group [RE]
m & cl			Medal & Clasp
MCO			Movement Control Officer
MCP			Movement Control Pool [RE]
MCS		MCofS	Military College of Science
MCS			Multi Channel Section

Abbreviation		Alternatives	Meaning
MCU			Malaria Control Unit
MCW			Modulated Continuous Wave
MD			Military Depot
MDC			Mobile Defence Company
MDC			Motor Driver Company [ATS/ WTS]
MDCU			Military Disembarkation Camp Unit
MDD			Military Docks Directorate
MDO			Military Docks Officer
MDPU			Mobile Dental Prosthetics Unit
MDS			Main Dressing Station [RAMC]
MDT			Mobile Dental Team
MDU			Mobile Dental Unit [dental caravan]
ME			Middle East
ME			Military Engineering
ME			Military Establishment
MEC			Middle East Command
MEF			Middle East Force(s)
ME(T)U			Mechanical Equipment (Transportation) Group
MESH			Middle East School of Hygiene
METC			Middle East Training Centre
MEAL			Mission for Economic Affairs London [USA]
mech	*		Mechanic/al or Mechanized
Mechol			Mechanised Column
med	*		Medical
med	*		Medium
Med Coy			Medical Company
Med Ord			Medical Orderly
Med Pln		Med Pl	Medical Platoon
Med Regt			Medium Regiment [RA]
Med Sect			Medical Section
Med Tk			Medium Tank
MEE			Mechanization Experimental Establishment [1934–1941]
MEF			Middle East Force(s)
MELF			Middle East Land Force(s)
Memo		memo	Memorandum

Abbreviation		Alternatives	Meaning
MES			Mechanical Equipment Section
MESC			Middle East School of Cookery
MESC			Middle East Staff College [Haifa, from 1943]
MESC			Middle East Supply Centre
MESH			Middle East School of Hygiene
MESS			Middle East Staff School [Haifa, to 1943]
MET			Mechanized Transport
Met			Meteorological
met	*	Meteor	Meteorology/ical
METC			Middle East Training Centre
METH			Methodist
METP			Middle East Training Pamphlet
mf			Microfarad
MFDU			Mobile Field Dental Unit [ADC]
MFE			Manual of Field Engineering
MFH			Military Families Hospital
MFL			Malaria Field Laboratory
MFO	*		Military Forwarding Organization/ Officer
MFP			Ministry of Fuel and Power
MFPS	*		Mobile Field Photographic Section
MFS		MF Sch	Motor Fitters School
MFU			Mobile Flotation Unit
MFV			Motor Fishing Vessel
MFW			Manual of Field Works
MFW			Military Foreman of Works
MG	*		Machine Gun
MG			Master Gunner
MG Bn			Machine-Gun Battalion
MGA			Major General Administration
MGAT			Major General Armoured Training
MGB			Medium Girder Bridge
MGGS			Major General General Staff
MGO			Master General of the Ordnance
MGRA			Major General Royal Artillery
MGRA			Master Gunner Royal Artillery
MGRAT			Major General Royal Artillery Training

Abbreviation		Alternatives	Meaning
MGRE			Major General Royal Engineers
MGTC			Machine Gun Training Centre
M/H			Medium/Heavy
MHK			Military Hospital Kowloon
MHL		Mob Hy Lab	Mobile Hygiene Laboratory
MHR			Military Hospitals Reserve
M&HTR			Medium & Heavy Training Regiment [RA]
MHz			Mega Hertz
MI			Military Intelligence
MI Room			Medical Inspection Room
mi2h (etc)	*	MI2H	Miles in 2 Hours
MIA			Missing in Action
MiD		Mid; MD	Mentioned in Despatches
MIDDX		Middx	Middlesex Regiment
mih	*	MIH	Miles in Hour
mil	*		Military
Mil			Militia
min			Minimum
min	*		Minute(s)
minefd	*		Minefield
MIRS			Military Intelligence Research Section
misc			Miscellaneous
mk	*	Mk	Mark
ML			Midlothian [Home Guard]
ML			Mobile Laundry
ML			Muzzle Loading
ML&FDU		Mob Laundry & DU	Mobile Laundry and Forward Decontamination Unit
MLBU	*		Mobile Laundry and Bath Unit
MLDU			Mobile Laundry and Decontamination Unit
MLO			Military Landing Officer
mls			Miles
MM			Mercantile Marine
MM			Military Medal
MM		Mil Msn	Military Mission
mm		m/m	Millimeter
M/M			Motor Mechanic

Abbreviation		Alternatives	Meaning
MMA			Military Manoeuvres Acts 1897 and 1911
MMC			Military Manoeuvres Commission
MMFL			Mobile Malaria Field Laboratory
MMG			Motor Machine Gun
MML			Manual of Military Law [1929]
MMP		MoMP	Manual of Military Publications
MMR			Mass Miniature Radiography
MNBDO			Mobile Naval Base Defence Organization
MNO			Mental Nursing Orderly [RAMC]
MNU			Mobile Neurosurgical Unit
MO	*		Medical Officer
MOB			Military Oil Barge
mob	*		Mobile/Mobilise/Mobilisation
Mob Bact Lab		MBL	Mobile Bacteriological Laboratory
Mob Hyg Lab			Mobile Hygiene Laboratory
Mob Mal Coy		MMC	Mobile Malaria Company
MoE			Memoranda of Examination
MoF			Method of Filling [ammunition]
MOF			Ministry of Food
MOH			Medical Officer of Health
MOH		MoH	Ministry of Health
MOI			Ministry of Information
MOL			Ministry of Labour
MOM		MoM	Ministry of Munitions
MON			Monmouthshire [Home Guard]
MONS		Mons	Monmouthshire
Mor		MOR	Mortar
MORU			Military Operational Research Unit
MOS		MoS; MofS	Ministry of Supply
MOSC			Ministry of Supply Council
MOU			Mobile Opthalmic Unit
mot	*	Mot	Motor/ized
Motor Bn			Motorized Battalion
mov	*		Movement
Mov & Tn			Movements & Transport
MOVCO			Movement Control Organization
MOW			Ministry of Works
MOWP			Ministry of Works Pattern [hut]

Abbreviation		Alternatives	Meaning
MOWT			Ministry of Works Transport
MP			Madras Pioneers [Indian Army]
MP	*		Meeting Point
MP	*		Military Police
MP		Min P: MofP; Min of Prod	Minister of Production
MPB			Mean Point of Burst [ammunition]
MPC			Ministerial Priority Committee
MPCA			Mechanized Petrol Cooking Apparatus
MPDB			Military Prison & Detention Barracks
MPDTU			Military Police Dog Training Unit
MPFC			Mobile Petrol Filling Centre [RASC]
mpg			Miles Per Gallon
MPH			Military Psychiatric Hospital
mph	*	MPH	Miles per Hour
MPI		mpi	Mean Point of Impact
MPP			Military Printing Press
MP(P)C		MPPC	Medical Personnel (Priority) Committee
MPRC			Military Personnel Research Committee
MPSC			Military Provost Staff Corps
MPU			Message Pick(ing) Up
MQMS			Mechanic Quartermaster Sergeant/ Serjeant
MR			Malay Regiment
MR		mr; map ref	Map Reference
MR		Mat Regs	Materiel Regulations
M&R			Maintenance & Repair
MRA			Maritime Royal Artillery
MRC			Medical Research Council
MRC			Mixed Reinforcement Camp
MRD			Materials Resources Department [Ministry of Supply]
MRRA		Mar Regt RA	Maritime Regiment Royal Artillery
MRS			Medical Research Section
MRY			Moray [Home Guard]
MS		M/S	Mild Steel

Abbreviation		Alternatives	Meaning
MS			Military Secretary
MS			Mounted Service
m/s		ms	Manuscript
msg	*	Msg	Message
MSL			Mean Sea Level
MSM			Mechanist Serjeant Major [RASC]
Msn			Mission
MSR			Main Supply Route
MSR			Minimum Safe Range
MSWTC		M&SWTC	Mountain & Snow Warfare Training Centre
MT			Malignant Tertian [malaria]
MT		M/T	Mechanical Transport [often but incorrectly also "Mechanized/ Motorized/Motor"]
MT 68 etc			MT Petrol [the number denotes Octane. Varieties were: 68, 70, 75, 80, 85 & 87]
MT Coy			Mule Transport Company
MT(L)			Military Training (Liaison)
MT80			80 octane leaded petrol
MTA			Mauritius Territorial Artillery
MTB			Militia Training Battalion [RASC]
MTB			Motor Training Battalion
MTC			Mechanized Transport Corps
MTD			Motor Transport Depot [RASC]
mtd	*		Mounted
MTF			Malta Territorial Force
mtg			Mounting
MTIB			Motor Transport Inspection Branch [RASC]
mtn	*	Mtn	Mountain
MTO			Military Testing Officer
MTO			Motor Transport Officer
MTP	*		Military Training Pamphlet
MTP(I)		MTPI	Military Training Pamphlet (India)
MTSD			Mechanical Transport Stores Depor [RASC]
MTT			Mechanical Transport Training
MTTC			Mechanised Transport Training Centre

Abbreviation		Alternatives	Meaning
MTTD			Mechanical Transport Training Depot [RE]
MU			Maintenance Unit
Musn			Musician
MV			Medium Velocity
MV			Motor Vehicle
MV			Motor Vessel
MV			Muzzle Velocity
M&V			Meat & Vegetable
M&V			Meat & Vegetables [rations]
MVO			Member of the Royal Victorian Order
MVS			Mobile Veterinary Section
MWEE			Mechanical Warfare Experimental Establishment [1928–1934]
MWT		MofWT; MOWT	Ministry of War Transport
MWTT			Mountain Warfare Training Team
Mx		MX	Middlesex
MX			Middlesex [Home Guard]
Mx Yeo			Middlesex Yeomanry
MYN			Mines [ammunition]
N			North
NA			North Africa
NAAFI			Naval Army & Air Force Institute
NAS			North American Supply
NB			Note well [nota bene]
NB Hsrs		NB Hussars	New Brunswick Hussars [Canada]
NC			Nitro-Cellulose [ammunition]
NC			Non-Conformist
NC			Normal Charge [ammunition]
N/C		NC	Not Confirmed
NCAC			North China Army Command
NCC			Non-Combatant Corps
NCI			Napthalene Creosote Iodoform [powder, anti-lice]
NCO	*		Non-Commissioned Officer
NCO TB			Non-Commissioned Officer Training Battalion [R Signals]
ND			Northumberland [Home Guard]
NDC			National Defence Company

Abbreviation		Alternatives	Meaning
NE			Non-Effective
NE			North East
neg			Negative
NEO			Naval Embarkation Officer
NES			Non-Effective Strength
NF			Royal Northumberland Fusiliers
Nfld	*		Newfoundland
NFS			National Fire Service
NG			Nitroglycerine [explosive]
NHA			Not Hearing Aircraft [signal message]
NI			Northern Ireland
NICD			Northern Ireland Coast Defences
NID			Northern Ireland District
NIH		NiH	North Irish Horse
NIV			Not in Vocabulary [stores & spares]
NK			Norfolk [Home Guard]
N/K		NK	Not Known
Nl MA			Netherlands Military Administration
NMA		M&A	Nuffield Mechanization & Aero
NMR			Natal Mounted Rifles [South Africa]
NMS			No Movement Seen
NN			Northamptonshire [Home Guard]
NNSH			North Nova Scotia Highlanders [Canada]
NO			Nursing Orderly [RAMC]
No		no	Number
NOIC			Nursing Officer In Charge
NOK		NoK	Next Of Kin
NORFOLK		Norfolk; R Norfolk	Royal Norfolk Regiment
NORTHAMPTONS		Northamptons	Northamptonshire Regiment
NPAM			Non-Permanent Active Militia [Canada]
NR			Northern Rhodesia
NR			Not Recorded
NR			Not/Non Registered
NRR			Northern Rhodesia Regiment

Abbreviation		Alternatives	Meaning
NRY			North Riding of Yorkshire [Home Guard]
NS			National Service
NS			North Staffordshire [Home Guard]
NS			Nursing Sister
N/S		n/s	Nearside [ie passenger side/side closest to kerb]
NS(AF)A			National Service (Armed Forces) Act
NSA			National Service Act(s)
NSFF			National Shell Filling Factory
NSH		NS Hldrs	Nova Scotia Highlanders [Canada]
N STAFFS		N Staffs	North Staffordshire Regiment
NTM		ntm	Notice to Move
NTR			Nothing to Report
NTS			Nottinghamshire [Home Guard]
NW			North West
NWE			North West Europe
NWEF			North Western Expeditionary Force
NWEF			Norway Expeditionary Force
NWF		N(W)F	National (War) Formulary
NY			Nyasaland
NYD			Not Yet Diagnosed
N Yeo		NY	Northamptonshire Yeomanry
NYDG			Not Yet Diagnosed Gas
NYDN			Not Yet Diagnosed Neurological/ Nervous
NZ	*		New Zealand
NZASC			New Zealand Army Service Corps
NZE			New Zealand Engineers
NZEF			New Zealand Expeditionary Force
NZMLO			New Zealand Military Liaison Office
NZWWSA			New Zealand Women's War Service Auxiliary
O		(O)	Operations
O			Orders
(O)			Overseas [as opposed to Home]
OBD			Oil Bound Distemper
OBD	*		Ordnance Beach Detachment

Abbreviation		Alternatives	Meaning
OBE			Officer of the Most Excellent Order of the British Empire
Obj			Objective
Obs		obsn	Observe, observation
Obst			Obstacle
OC			Observer Corps
OC	*		Officer Commanding
OC			Orthopaedic Centre [RAMC]
Ocdt		O/Cdt; Ocdt	Officer Cadet
OCRASC			Officer Commanding Royal Army Service Corps
oct			Octane
OCTG			Officer Cadet Training Group
OCTU			Officer Cadet Training Unit
OD			Oil Dressed [ammunition packaging]
OD			Olive Drab
OD			Ordnance Depot
OD			Outside Diameter
ODP			Outdoor Distemper Paint
OETA			Occupied Enemy Territory Administration
OF			Ordnance Factory
OFC			Operator Fire Control
Off			Offensive
offr	*	Offr	Officer
OFP		Ord Fd Pk	Ordnance Field Park
OG			Olive Green
O Gp			Orders Group
OH			Overhead
OHC			Overhead Cam
OHC			Overhead Cover
OHMS			On His Majesty's Service
OHP			Overhead Protection
OHV			Overhead Valve
OI			Operational Instruction
OIC	*		Officer-in-Charge (of)
OK			Oerlikon
OLQ			Officer-Like Qualities
OM			Officers' Mess

Abbreviation		Alternatives	Meaning
OM			Order of Merit
OMCS			Officers' Mess Cook's School
OME			Ordnance Mechanical Engineer [RAOC]
OMW			Ordnance Manual of War [RAOC]
OO			Officer Only [to read message]
OO	*	Op O	Operation Order
OO			Orderly Officer
OO	*		Ordnance Officer
OO(1-4)			Ordnance Officer 1st – 4th Class [RAOC, Col, Lt Col, Maj, Capt & Subalterns)
OOB			Order of Battle
OOM			Order of March
OP			Immediate priority [in signal message]
OP	*		Observation Post
op	*		Operate/d/tion/tional or Operator
OP			Operational Plan
OPA			Observation Post Officer's Assistant
OPO			Observation Post Officer
Ops			Operations
Ops Room			Operations Room
OPU			Officer Producing Unit
OR			Orderly Room
OR	*		Other Rank(s)
ORA			Operating Rooom Assistant [RAMC]
ORBAT			Order of Battle
ORC			Orderly Room Clerk
ORC			Other Ranks' Club
ord	*	Ord	Ordnance
Ord Ammn Coy			Ordnance Ammunition Company
Ord Fd Pk		OFP	Ordnance Field Park
org	*		Organize/d/ation
ORK			Orkney [Home Guard]
ORQMS			Orderly Room Quartermaster Sergeant/Serjeant
ORS			Operational Research Section
ORS			Orderly Room Sergeant/Serjeant
ORTU			Other Ranks Training Unit

Abbreviation		Alternatives	Meaning
ORU			Operations Room Unit
OS			Off Side
OS			Officers Shop
OS			Ordnance Services
OS			Ordnance Survey
OS			Overseas [medical category, from late 1944]
O/S		o/s	Offside [ie driver's side/side furthest from kerb]
OSA			Official Secrets Act
OSD			Officer's Service Dress
OSD		OSDEF	Orkney & Shetland Defences
OSNT			Overseas Non-tropical [medical category, from late 1944]
OT			Observer-Target (line) [artillery]
OTC			Officer Training Corps
OTC			Officers' Transit Centre
OTS			Officer Training School
OTS			Officer's Tactical School
OTU			Officer Training Unit?
OU			Most Immediate priority [in signal message]
OU			Official Use
OVP		Ord Veh Pk	Ordnance Vehicle Park
OWL			Operator Wireless & Line
OWP		OBWP	Oil-Bound Water Paint
OX & BUCKS		Oxf & Bucks	Oxfordshire and Buckinghamshire Light Infantry
OXF			Oxfordshire [Home Guard]
oz	*	Oz	Ounce
P			Presbyterian
P			Primary [malaria]
P1O			Part 1 Orders
P2O			Part 2 Orders
P2O			Part Two Orders
PA			Personal Assistant
P/A			Paid Acting [rank]
PAC (NA)		PA Centre	Preventive Ablution Centre [North Africa]
PAD	*		Passive Air Defence
PAD		Pol Armd Div	Polish Armoured Division

Abbreviation		Alternatives	Meaning
PAD			Port Ammunition Depot
PAG			Prince Alfred's Guard [South Africa]
PAGD			Polar Ammon Gelatine Dynamite [ammunition]
PAIC			Persia and Iraq Command
PAIF			Persia and Iraq Force(s)
Pal			Palestine
PALESTINE R		Palestine R; Pal R	Palestine Regiment
Pam		pam	Pamphlet
PAM			Permanent Active Militia [Canada]
para	*		Parachute
PARA		Para Regt	Parachute Regiment
para	*		Paragraph(s)
Para Bde			Parachute Brigade
Para Bde Gp			Parachute Brigade Group
paratps	*	paras	Paratroops
PASC			Polish Army Service Corps
PATS			Palestine Auxiliary Territorial Service
PAVO			11th Prince Albert Victor's Own [Indian Army]
PB			Phosphor-Bronze
PB			Plymouth Brethren
PBE			Paint Bituminous Emulsion
PBI			Poor Bloody Infantry
PBM		PBMR	Principal Beach Master
PBP			Pontoon Bridge Park [RASC]
PBR			Powered Barge, Ramped
PBS			Pre-fabricated Bituminous Surface
PC		P Corps; Pnr Corps	Pioneer Corps [from 1940]
PC			Pitch Circle
PC			Privy Councillor
P&C			Postal & Courier
PCC		PC Coy	Port Construction Company
PCC			Position Correction Chart [RA]
PCDB			Punishment Camp and/or Detention Barracks
PCLU			Pioneer Corps Labour Unit

Abbreviation		Alternatives	Meaning
PCRG			Port Construction & Repair Group
PCU			Power Control Unit
pd			Per Diem (Per Day)
PD			Petrol/eum Depot
PD			Point Detonation/ing [ammunition]
PD			Potential Difference [electricity]
PDC			Physical Development Centre
PDF			Point Detonating Fuse [ammunition]
PDG			Paint Detector Gas
PDGK			Paint Detector Gas Khaki
PE			Peace Establishment
PE			Procurement Executive
PEC			Physical Exhaustion Centre
PEI Hldrs			Prince Edward Island Highlanders [Canada]
PEILH			Prince Edward Island Light Horse [Canada]
PEM			Pembrokeshire [Home Guard]
pen			Penetration
PENT			Pentolite [ammunition]
PESD			Port Examination Service Detachment
pet	*		Petrol(eum)
Pet Dep			Petrol(eum) Depot
PF			Position Finder
pf			Post-nominal: Qualified as Captain Instructor in Coastal Gunnery
PFA			Parachute Field Ambulance [RAMC]
PFU			Prepared For Use [paint]
PGS			Packsaddlery General Service
ph	*	photo	Photograph/ic
PH			Poona Horse [India]
PHD			Priddy's Hard [station monogram]
ph R	*		Photographic Reconnaissabnce
PHOS		phos	Phosphorous [ammunition]
photogrid	*		Vertical Air Photograph, Gridded
PIAT			Projector Infantry Anti-Tank
PII			Part Two Orders
Pipe Maj			Pipe Major

Abbreviation	*	Alternatives	Meaning
PIS			Photographic Interpretation Section
PIU			Photographic Intelligence Unit
PJI			Parachute Jump Instructor
pk	*	Pk	Park
PL			Parts List
PL			Pioneer & Labour
pl		Pn; Pln	Platoon
PL			Princess Louise's Kensington Rifles
PLDG			Princess Louise's Dragoon Guards
PLGD			Plugged [ammunition]
PLM			Parish Lulworth Motley [twin MG mounting]
PLUTO			Pipelines Under The Ocean
pm			Afternoon/Evening [ie the 12 hours after midday]
PM			Primitive Methodist
PM		P/M	Principal Matron
PM	*		Provost Marshal
PMC			President of the Mess Committee
PMG			Packsaddlery Machine Gun
PMLO			Principal Military Landing Officer
PMO			Principal Medical Officer
pmr	*		Paymaster
Pmr in C			Paymaster in Chief
PMT			Primary Military Training
Pn Comd		Pln Comd	Platoon Commander
PNE			Permanently Non-Effective
pnr	*	Pnr	Pioneer
PO	*		Post Office
PO			Potential Officer
poa			Point of Aim
POC		Port Ops Coy	Port Operations Company
POD			Port Ordnance Detachment
POG			Port Operating Group
POL	*		Petrols, Oils & Lubricants
Pol			Poland/Polish
POME			Principal Ordnance Mechanical Officer
POMU (NA)			Pipeline Operating & Maintenance Unit (North Africa)

Abbreviation		Alternatives	Meaning
PoP			Plaster of Paris
Port Ops		PO	Port Operations
POS		PoS	Port of Shipment
pos			Positive
posn	*		Position
POW			Petrol Oil & Water
POW			Prisoner of War
PP	*		Petrol Point
PPA			Popski's Private Army
PPCLI			Princess Patricia's Canadian Light Infantry
PPI			Plan Position Indicator
Ppr			Piper
PPU			Priority of Preparation of Units
PR			Palestine Regiment
PR			Parachute Regiment
pr	*	Pdr	Pounder [method of denoting size of gun]
PR			Punjab Regiment [Indian Army]
PRC			Polish Resettlement Corps
PRH	*		Petrol Railhead
PRI			President of the Regimental Institutes
Pri			Priority
pro	*	Pro	Provost
Pro Coy			Provost Company [CMP]
prob			Probation
prov			Provisional
PRP	*		Petrol Refilling Point
PRS			Paint Research Station
PRTD			Palestinian Recruit Training Depot?
PS			Parachute School
PSA			Percussion Small Arms [ammunition]
PSB			Parachute Selection Board
psc†			Passed Staff College Senior Wing OR passed staff college prior to 1939
psc			Passed Staff College Junior Wing
PSD			Petrol Supply Depot

Abbreviation		Alternatives	Meaning
PSDU			Petroleum Supply Demonstration Unit
PSI			Permanent Staff Instructor
PSL			Pistol Self Loading
PSO			Personnel Selection Officer
PSO			Principal Supply Officer
PSOC			Principal Supply Officer's Committee
PSP			Perforated (or Pierced) Steel Planking
PSS			Personnel Selection Staff
PSTO			Principal Sea Traffic Officer
PSU			Power Supply Unit
PT			Code-sign follows [in signal message]
PT			Physical Training
pt			Pint
pt	*	Pt	Point
PTC			Primary Training Centre
PTCG			Port and Travel Control Group
PTD			Palestine Training Depot
pte	*	Pte	Private
PTG		PT Gp	Pack Transport Group
PTI			Physical Training Instructor
P&TJ			Palestine & Trans-Jordan
Ptl		ptl; pl	Patrol
PTO			Pacific Theatre of Operations
PTO			Principal Technical Officer
PTP			Pioneer Training Pool
PTS			Parachute Training School
PTTC			Petroleum Technical Training Centre
PTW			Primary Training Wing
Pty			Party
PU			Postal Unit
PULHHEEMS			Physical Capacity, Upper Limbs, Locomotion, Hearing (Right & Left), Eyesight (Right & Left), Mental Capacity, Stability (Emotional)
PUO			Pyrexia of Unknown Origin
PUS			Permanent Under Secretary-of-State

Abbreviation		Alternatives	Meaning
PV			Paravane
PW		P-W	Part-Worn
PW			Pay Warrant
PW			Port Workshop [REME]
PW	*	POW	Prisoner of War
PWAS			Polish Women's Auxiliary Service
PWB			Petroleum Warfare Board
PWC(NA)			Prisoner of War Centre (North Africa)
PWD			Petroleum Warfare Department
PWD			Port Workshop Detachment
PWD			Psychological Warfare Division
PWE			Political Warfare Executive
PWV			Prince of Wales's Volunteers
Q			Quartan [malaria]
Q		QM	Quartermaster
QAANB			Queen Alexandra's Army Nursing Board
Q (AE)			QMG Army Equipment Branch [War Office]
QAIMNS			Queen Alexandra's Imperial Military Nursing Service
QAIMNS(R)			Queen Alexandra's Imperial Military Nursing Service (Reserve)
QAMH			Queen Alexandra's Military Hospital
QAMFHNS			Queen Alexandra's Military Forces Hospital Nursing Service
QAMFNS			Queen Alexandra's Married Families Nursing Service [defunct]
QAMNSI			Queen Alexandra's Military Nursing Service India
QC			Quartering Commandant
QE			Quadrant Elevation
QF			Quick Firing
QFSA			Quick Firing Semi-Automatic
QM	*	Q; Qr-Mr	Quartermaster
Q (M)			Quartermaster (Maintenance)
QMG			Quartermaster General
QMS	*		Quartermaster Serjeant/Serjeant
QMH			Queen Mary's Hospital

Abbreviation		Alternatives	Meaning
QOH			Queen's Own Hussars
QOOH			Queen's Own Oxfordshire Hussars
Q (Ops)			QMG Operations Branch [War Office]
QOR of C			The Queen's Own Rifles of Canada
QOWH			Queen's Own Worcestershire Hussars
QQS			Signal strength is... [in signal message]
QQX			Message not to be sent by wireless [in signal message]
QRL			Queen's Royal Lancers
qs			Post-nominal: Qualified – Staff
qt			Quart
Q&T			Quartermastering & Transport?
QUEENS		Queens	Queen's Royal Regiment (West Surrey)
QVOMS&M			Queen Victoria's Own Madras Sappers & Miners [India]
QVR			Queen Victoria's Rifles
QVS			Queen Victoria's School (Dunblane)
QW			Queen's Westminster's
R			Message received [in morse signalling]
R			Regiment
R			Rosshire [Home Guard]
"R"			Repairable [RAOC use]
RA			Ration Allowance
RA			Royal Artillery
RAA			Royal Australian Artillery
RAAC			Rome Allied Area Command
RABD			Royal Artillery Base Depot
RAC			Royal Armoured Corps
RAC OTS			Royal Armoured Corps Officer's Tactical School
RAC Tac Sch			Royal Armoured Corps Tactics School
RAC Trg Sch NA			Royal Armoured Corps Training School North Africa
RACD			Royal Army Clothing Depot
RACD (I)			Royal Armoured Corps Depot (India)

Abbreviation		Alternatives	Meaning
RAChD			Royal Army Chaplains Department
RACTE			Royal Armoured Corps Training Establishment
RadSil			Radio Silence
RAE			Royal Australian Engineers
RAEC			Regular Army Emergency Commission
RAF			Royal Air Force
RAG			Respirator Anti-Gas
RAG		RA Gp	Royal Artillery Group
RAMC			Royal Army Medical Corps
RAM Coll		RAM College	Royal Army Medical College
RAMO			Rear Air Maintenance Organization
RAMTS			Royal Artillery Mechanical Traction School
RAOC			Royal Army Ordnance Corps
RAOCS			Royal Army Ordnance Corps School
RAOS			Regulations for Army Ordnance Services
RAP			Reasonable Anticipation Programme
RAP	*		Regimental Aid Post
RAPC			Royal Army Pay Corps
RAPWI			Recovery of Allied Prisoners of War and Internees
RAR			Rhodesian African Rifles
RARO			Regular Army Reserve of Officers
RASC			Royal Army Service Corps
RASC (C)			Royal Army Service Corps (Ceylon)
RASC TC			Royal Army Service Corps Training Centre
RASCV			Royal Army Service Corps Vessel
Rat		Rats	Ration/s
RATD			Royal Artillery Training Depot
RATE			Royal Artillery Training Establishment
RAVC			Royal Army Veterinary Corps
RAVS			Royal Army Veterinary School
RB			Rifle Brigade

Abbreviation		Alternatives	Meaning
R&B			Renfrewshire & Buteshire [Home Guard]
R BERKS		R Berks	Royal Berkshire Regiment
RC			Reception Camp
RC		Red C	Reduced Charge [ammunition]
RC			Reporting Centre
RC			Roman Catholic
RC Coy		Rd Constr Coy	Road Construction Company [RE]
RCA			Royal Canadian Artillery
RCAMC			Royal Canadian Army Medical Corps
RCASC			Royal Canadian Army Service Corps
RCB			Regular Commissions Board
RCC		Ry Constr Coy	Railway Construction Company [RE]
RCCS			Royal Canadian Corps of Signals
RCD			Royal Canadian Dragoons
RCE			Royal Canadian Engineers
RCEME			Royal Canadian Electrical and Mechanical Engineers
RCHA			Royal Canadian Horse Artillery
RCL			Ramped Cargo Lighter
RCL			Recoiless
RCM			Radio Counter-Measures
RCM			Regimental Corporal Major
RCMG			Railway Construction & Maintenance Group
RCOC			Royal Canadian Ordnance Corps
RCR			Royal Canadian Regiment
RCS			Royal Canadian Signals
RD			Research Department
RD			Research Directorate
rd	*		Road(s)
Rd			Round(s)
RDF			Radio Direction Finding
RDH			9th Royal Deccan Horse [Indian Army]
RDI	*		Relief Driver Increment
RDL			Radio Detection & Location
RDLR			Regiment De La Rey [South Africa]

Abbreviation		Alternatives	Meaning
RDS	*		Returned Stores Depot
RDS			Road Delivery Service
RDT			Road Delivery Transport?
RDW			Regiment De Wet [South Africa]
RDW			Research Department Woolwich
RDX			Research Department Explosive
RDX/BX			Research Department Explosive/ Beeswax
RE			Royal Engineers
Rec	*	Recy	Recover/ed/y
Recce Gp	*		Reconnaissance
Recce Gp		R Gp	Reconnaissance Group
recd			Received
RED			Reduced propellant [ammunition]
ref	*		Reference
Refit			Refitting
reg	*		Regulate/d/ing or Regulation(s)
regt	*		Regiment
Rel			Relief
RE(M)			Royal Engineers (Movements)
REME			Royal Electrical & Mechanical Engineers [from 19 May 42]
REN			Renfrewshire [Home Guard]
reorg	*		Re-organization
rep	*		Represent/ed/ative
Repat			Repatriate/ion/ing
res	*	Res	Reserve
RESB			Royal Engineer and Signal Board
Restd			Restricted
RE(T)			Royal Engineers (Transportation)
Rev			Reveille
Revs			Revolutions
RF		R/F	Radio Frequency
RF			Rim Fire [ammunition]
RF			Royal Fusiliers
rfn	*		Rifleman
rft	*	rfmt	Reinforcement
Rft Gp			Reinforcement Group
rft HU	*		Reinforcement Holding Unit
rft SU	*		Reinforcement Sub-Unit

Abbreviation		Alternatives	Meaning
RFU			Reinforcement Unit
RG&CF			Royal Gun & Carriage Factory
RGA			Royal Greek Army
RGH			Royal Gloucestershire Hussars
RGRS		Rgrs	Rangers
RH	*	Rh; rh	Railhead
rh		r/h: RH	Right Hand (side)
RH			Royal Hospital (Chelsea)
RHA			Rolled Homogenous Armour
RHA	*		Royal Horse Artillery
RHC			The Black Watch (Royal Highlanders of Canada)
RHH			Royal Herbert Hospital
RHMA	*		Rail or Road Head Maintenance Area
RHQ			Regimental Headquarters
RHU			Reinforcement Holding Unit
RI			Riding Instructor
RIASC			Royal Indian Army Service Corps
RIDG			Royal Inniskilling Dragoon Guards
R IR F			Royal Irish Fusiliers
RIV		R&IV	Receipt & Issue Voucher
RL			Lewis Bn, Rosshire [Home Guard]
RL		R/L	Rear Link
RL		R/L	Reporting Line
RL			Royal Lancers
RLC			Release Leave Certificate
RLI			Rand Light Infantry [South Africa]
RLW			Regiment Louw Wepener [South Africa]
rly	*		Railway
RM			Remount(s)
RM			Royal Marine
RM AA			Royal Marine Anti-Aircraft
RM Cdo			Royal Marine Commando
RMA	*		Rear Maintenance Area
RMA			Royal Malta Artillery
RMA			Royal Military Academy
RMASB			Royal Marine Armoured Support Battery

Abbreviation		Alternatives	Meaning
RMASG			Royal Marine Armoured Support Group
RMASR			Royal Marine Armoured Support Regiment
RMC			Royal Military College
RMD			Radio Maintenance Detachment
RMD			Raw Materials Department [Ministry of Supply]
RMD		R(M)D	Rifle (Motor) Depot
RMD		RM Div	Royal Marine Division
RMO			Regimental Medical Officer
RMR			Royal Montreal Regiment [Canada]
RMS			(Duke of York's) Royal Military School
RMS			Root Mean Square
RMSA			Regulations for the Medical Services of the Army
RMSM			Royal Military School of Music
RMT Coy			Reserve Mechanized Transport Company
RN			Royal Navy
RNA			Royal Netherlands Army
RNB			Royal Netherlands Brigade
RNC			Royal Natal Carbineers [South Africa]
RO			Record Office
RO			Release Order
RO			Retired Officer
RO	*		Routine Order
ROC			Royal Observer Corps
ROD			Regional Ordnance Depot
ROF			Royal Ordnance Factory
ROG			Railway Operating Group [RE]
ROO	*		Rail or Road Head Ordnance Officer
ROS			Returned Ordnance Stores
RP	*		Refilling Point
RP			Regimental Paymaster
RP	*		Regimental Police(man)
RP		Rel pt	Release Point
RP		R/P	Rocket Projectile

Abbreviation		Alternatives	Meaning
RP	*		Rules of Procedure
RPC			Remount Purchasing Commission
rpg			Rounds Per Gun (per minute)
rpgpd		RPGPD	Rounds Per Gun Per Day
RPM		rpm	Revolutions Per Minute
RPS			Regiment President Steyn [South Africa]
rpt			Report
rptd	*		Repeated
RQB			Report required by... [signal message]
RQMS	*		Regimental Quartermaster Sergeant/Serjeant
RR			Radnorshire [Home Guard]
RR			Rhodesia Regiment
RR			Rocking Roller [bridging]
R-R		RR	Rolls-Royce
RRC			Royal Red Cross
RRC			Royal Rifles of Canada
RRTC		RR Trg Coy	Recruits Reception & Training Coy
RS			Recovery Station [RAOC]
RS			Regulating Station
RS			Returned Stores
RS			Royal Scots
RS Coy		RSC	Railway Survey Company [RE]
RS Coy		RSC	Returned Stores Company
RSAF			Royal Small Arms Factory
RSE			Reserve Storage Egypt [Petroleum]
RSF			Royal Scots Fusiliers
R SIGS		CRS; R Signals	Corps of Royal Signals
RSJ			Reinforced Steel Joist
RSM	*		Regimental Sergeant/Serjeant Major
RSO			Regimental Signals Officer
RSO			Regimental Survey Officer
RSP			Road Staging Post
R Sup O	*		Rail or Road Head Supply Officer
R SUSSEX		R Sussex	Royal Sussex Regiment
RSWD			Regiment South Western District [South Africa]
RT	*	R/T	Radio Telephony

Abbreviation		Alternatives	Meaning
RTA			Regimental Technical Adjutant
RTC		Ry TC	Railway Training Centre
RTC		R&TC	Research and Training Centre
RTC			Royal Tank Corps
RTD&S			Reinforcement Training Depot & School
Rte			Route
R Tks		RTR; R Tanks	Royal Tank Regiment
Rtn			Ration(s)
Rtn			Return
RTO	*		Railway Traffic Officer
RTU			Returned to Unit
RTW			Road Tanker Wagon?
RU			Reception Unit
RU			Rutland [Home Guard]
RUR			Royal Ulster Rifles
RUSI			Royal United Services Institute
RV			Receipt Voucher
RV	*		Rendezvous
RVH			Royal Victoria Hospital
RVHDTE		RVHD&TE	Reserve Veterinary Hospital Depot and Training Establishment
RVP			Returned Vehicles Park
RW			Rehabilitation Wing
RW	*		Royal Warrant [for Pay and Promotion]
RWAFF			Royal West African Frontier Force
RWD			Rear Wheel Drive
RWF			Royal Welsh Fusiliers
RWG			Railway Workshop Group [RE]
RWK			Queen's Own Royal West Kent Regiment
RWP			Regiment Western Province [South Africa]
RWR			Royal Winnipeg Rifles [Canada]
Ry		Rwy; Rly	Railway
Ry Cons Coy			Railway Construction Company
Ry Evac Sec		RES	Railway Evacuation Section [REME]
Ry Surv Coy			Railway Survey Company

Abbreviation		Alternatives	Meaning
RYF			Royal Yugoslav Forces
RYPA			Roll Yaw Pitch Apparatus
R22eR			Le Royal 22eme Regiment [Canada]
S			South
"S"			Serviceable [RAOC use]
SA		S/A	Semi-Automatic
SA	*		Small Arms
SA	*		South Africa(n)
SAA			Small Arms Ammunition
SAAA			School of Anti-Aircraft Artillery
SAAC		SA/AC	Scientific Adviser to the Army Council
SAAD			School of Anti-Aircraft Defence
SAAD			South African Armoured Division
SAAF			South African Air Force
SAAR			South African Artillery Regiment
SAARF			Special Allied Airborne Rescue Force
SAASC			South African Army Service Corps
SAC			Standing Advisory Committee
SACEUR			Supreme Allied Commander Europe
SACMP			South African Corps of Military Police
SACSEA			Supreme Allied Commander South East Asia
SAD			Single Axle Drive
SADE			Special Armour Development Establishment
SAE			Society of Automotive Engineers
SAEC			South African Engineer Corps
SAIC			South African Instructional Corps
Sal		Salv	Salvage(d)
SAMC			South African Medical Corps
San			Sanitary/Sanitation
SAOC			South African Ordnance Corps
SAP			Semi-Armour Piercing
SAPC			South African Pay Corps
SAS		SA Sch	Small Arms School
SAS			Special Air Service

Abbreviation		Alternatives	Meaning
SASC			Small Arms School Corps
SASC			South African Signals Corps
SASch			Small Arms School
SASR			Special Air Service Regiment
SAT		SA Trg	Small Arms Training
SAVC			South African Veterinary Corps
SB			Scottish Borders [Home Guard]
SB			Smooth Bore
SB	*		Stretcher Bearer
SB			Supply Board
SBC			Standard Bayonet Cap
SBG	*		Small Box Girder [bridge]
SBO			Senior British Officer
SBR			Small Box Respirator
SBRO			Service Boot Repair Organization
SBS			Special Boat Section
SBU			Special Boat Unit
SC		S/C; Sc Car	Scout Car
SC			Select Committee
SC			Solventless Cordite [ammunition]
SC			Staff Captain
SC		S Coll	Staff College
SC			Super Charge [ammunition]
SC			Superintending Clerk
SCC			Salvage Collecting Centre
SCC			Somaliland Camel Corps
SCC			Standard Camouflage Colour
SCD			Stores & Clothing Depot
SCDPR			Sub-Committee on Defence Policy & Requirements
SCF			Senior Chaplain to the Forces
Sch			School
Sch of A			School of Artillery
Sch of AA Arty		SAAA	School of Anti-Aircraft Artillery
Sch of AR		SAR	School of Aircraft Recognition
Sch of Army Co-op		Sch of AC	School of Army Co-Operation [RAF]
Sch of EL			School of Electrical Lighting
Sch of Hyg			School of Hygiene
Sch of Inf			School of Infantry

Abbreviation		Alternatives	Meaning
Sch of MA		SMA	School of Military Administration
Sch of ME		SME	School of Military Engineering
Sch of ME & RE Trg Dep			School of Military Engineering & Royal Engineers Training Depot
Sch of Sigs			School of Signals
Sch of Spr Hvy Arty			School of Super Heavy Artillery
SCIU			Specialist Counter-Intelligence Unit
SCM			Squadron Corporal Major
SCN			Shade Card Number
SCNE			Select Committee on National Expenditure
SCOS			Submarine Cable Operating Section
SCpl			Staff Corporal
SCR			Searchlight Control Radar
SCR			Signal Corps Radio (US)
SCT			Standard Camouflage Tint
SCU			Special Communications Unit
SD			Service Dress
SD			Staff Duties
SD			Superintending Draughtsman
Sd		sd.	Signed
SDB			Special Duties Branch
SDD			Special Discharge Depot [ATS, from early 1942, for pregnant servicewomen]
SDF			Sudan Defence Force(s)
SD&G Regt		SD&G Hldrs	Stormont Dundas and Glengarry Highlanders [Canada]
SDMO			Service Dress Marching Order
SDO			Senior Dental Officer
SDO			Senior Design Officer
SDP	*		Supply Dropping Point
SDS			Special Despatch Service
SDU			Special Dental Unit
SE			South East
SEAAC			South-East Asia Air Command
SEAC			South-East Asia Command
SEAC WU			South-East Asia Command Welfare Unit
SEAFORTHS		Seaforths	Seaforth Highlanders
sec	*		Second

Abbreviation		Alternatives	Meaning
sec	*		Section
SEC			Structural Engineering Committee
SECO		SE Comd	South East Command
Sect		Sec	Section
SEE			Signals Experimental Establishment
SEME			School of Electrical & Mechanical Engineering
SEP			Surrendered Enemy Personnel
Ser No			Serial Number
SEWLROM			Special End of War Leave for Regular Officers and Men
SEWT			Signals Exercise Without Troops
SF			Sherwood Foresters Bns, Derbyshire [Home Guard]
SFK			Suffolk [Home Guard]
SFP			Supplementary Fire Party [NFS]
SG		Scots Gds	Scots Guards
SG			Selection Grade
SG			Surgeon General
SGSRD			Stores Group Supply Reserve Depot
Sgt Maj		Sjt Maj	Sergeant/Serjeant Major
SH			14th Prince of Wales' Own Scinde Horse [Indian Army]
SH			Sherbrooke Hussars [Canada]
SHAEF		Shaef	Supreme Headquarters Allied Expeditionary Force
SHAPE		Shape	Supreme Headquarters Allied Powers Europe
SHC			Saddlery Household Cavalry
SHC			Shorncliffe [station monogram]
Sheldrake			Artillery [Radio code]
shelrep	*	shellrep	Shelling Report
SHF			Super High Frequency
SHP			Shrapnel
SHQ			Squadron Headquarters
SHR			Shropshire [Home Guard]
SIB			Special Interview Board
SIB			Special Investigations Branch
sig	*		Signal(s)
sigmn	*		Signalman/men

Abbreviation		Alternatives	Meaning
SIP			Self-Igniting Phosphorous [ammunition]
SIPS			Special Improvised Plough Steel
sitrep	*	Sitrep; Sit Rep	Situation Report
SJAB			St John's Ambulance Brigade
sjt		sgt	Serjeant/Sergeant (see text)
SKR			Stewartry of Kircudbrightshire [Home Guard]
SL	*	S/L	Searchlight
SL			Special List
SL	*		Start Line
S/L			Streamlined [ammunition]
SLA	*		Supply Loading Airfield
S Lancs			South Lancashire Regiment
SLCD			Special Liaison Cypher Detachment
SLL			Searchlight Laying
SLP	*		Supply Landing Point
SM			Secret Memorandum
SMC	*		Sten Machine Carbine
SMG			Sub-Machine Gun
Smk			Smoke
SMLE			Short Magazine Lee-Enfield
SMO	*		Senior Medical Officer
SMS			Store Movement Schedule
SMT			Square Mesh Track
SNCO			Senior Non-Commissioned Officer
SO			Saddlery Officers
SO			Signal Office
SO			Signals Officer
SO	*		Staff Officer
SOC			Senior Officer's College
SOD			Sawn-Off Daimler [armoured car]
SOE			Special Operations Executive
S of D			Superintendent of Design
S of I		Sch of Inst	School of Instruction
SOM			Somerset [Home Guard]
SOM LI		Som LI	Somerset Light Infantry
SOME			Senior Ordnance Mechanical Engineer
SOMTO			Special Operations Mediterranean Theatre of Operations

Abbreviation		Alternatives	Meaning
SOMTS			Scales of MT Stores
SOP			Standing Operating Procedures
SOR			Sector Operations Room [AA]
SORE			Staff Officer Royal Engineers
SOS			Save Our Souls [emergency]
SOS			Senior Officer's School
SOS		sos	Struck Off Strength
SoS War			Secretary of State for War
SO TA			Staff Office(r) Territorial Army
SP	*	S-P	Self-Propelled
SP	*		Start(ing) Point
SP			Stretcher Party
SP			Strike Point [gunnery]
SP			Supply Point
sp	*		Support/ed
Spec			Special(ist)
Spec emp			Specially Employed
Spec Hosp			Specialist Hospital
Spec Invest Sec		SIS	Special Investigation Section
SPFC			Self-Propelled Floating Crane
SPG			Self-Propelled Gun
SPI			Special Instructions [signal message]
SPIRI			Spiritualist
SQ			Super Quick [fuse]
sq in			Square Inch
SQMC			Squadron Quartermaster Corporal
SQMS	*		Squadron Quartermaster Sergeant/ Serjeant
sqn	*	Sqn: sqdn	Squadron
SR			Sound Ranging
SR			Special Reserve (AKA Militia)
SR		Sup Res	Supplementary Reserve
SRD			Supply Railhead Detachment [RAOC]
SRD			Supply Reserve Depot [RAOC]
SRDU			Serviceable Repairable Doubtful Unserviceable [RAOC]
S rg	*		Sound Ranging
SRH	*		Supply Railhead

Abbreviation		Alternatives	Meaning
SRO			Schedule of Reserved Occupations
SRP			Supply Refilling Point
SRTU			Special Reception and Training Unit
SRY			Sherwood Rangers Yeomanry
SS		Service Stn	Service Station [REME]
SS			Ships Staff
SS			Single Single [Bailey Bridge]
SS			Somaliland Scouts
SS			South Staffordshire [Home Guard]
SS			Special Service
SSB			Senior Selection Board
SSB			Special Service Battalion [Commandos]
SSB			Special Service Battalion [South Africa]
SSB			Special Service Brigade
SSBP			Straight Spirit Bituminous Paint
SSC			Sector Searchlight Commander
SSC			Short Service Commission
SSC			Sudan Service Corps
S sjt	*	SSjt; SSgt	Staff Sergeant/Serjeant
SSM	*		Squadron Serjeant/Sergeant Major
SSM	*		Staff Serjeant/Sergeant Major
SSRC			Small Scale Raiding Commando
SSRF			Small Scale Raiding Force
S STAFFS		S Staffs	South Staffordshire Regiment
SSTO			Superintending Sea Traffic Officer
S sup O	*	SSO	Senior Supply Officer
SSV			Short Sea Voyage
ST			Sticky Type
ST		S&T	Supply & Transport
S & T			Supply & Transport
ST Grenade			Sticky' grenade
ST&B Regs			Supply Transport & Barrack Regulations
sta	*		Station
STC			Senior Training Corps
STC			Signals Training Centre
STC			Special Training Centre

Abbreviation		Alternatives	Meaning
STC			Survey Training Centre [RE]
STC KAR			Supply & Transport Corps King's African Rifles
stereo	*		Stereoscope or Stereoscopic
STG			Stirlingshire [Home Guard]
Stmn			Storeman
Stn			Station
STO			Sea Transport Officer
STO			Special Treatment Orderly [RAMC]
STP			Signals Training Pamphlet
str	*		Seater
STR			Signals Training Regiment [RA]
str	*		Strength
Strat R	*	strat R	Strategic Reconnaissance
STT			School of Tank Technology
STT			Special Training Team
STT&MC			Supply, Technical Training and Mobilisation Centre [RASC]
STW			Specialist Training Wing
SU			Saddlery Universal
SU			Salvage Unit
SU			Superposing Unit
SU			Supply Unit [radio]
SU			Sutherland [Home Guard]
Sub-Condr			Sub-Conductor [RAOC
SUCA			Soldier Under Close Arrest
SUFFOLK		Suffolk	Suffolk Regiment
Sunray			Radio code for commander
SUO			Senior Under Officer [Royal Military College]
sup	*		Supply or Supplied
Sup Col			Support Column
Sup Coy			Supply Company
Sup Coy			Support Company
Sup Gp		Sp Gp	Support Group
sup P	*	Sup Pt	Supply Point
Super Hy		Spr Hy	Super Heavy
Supp			Supplement
Supy List			Supernumerary List
Surg			Surgeon/Surgery

Abbreviation		Alternatives	Meaning
SURREYS		SURREY; E Surrey	East Surrey Regiment
SUS			Soldier Under Sentence
SUV			Supply Unit Vibrating [radio]
SV			Side Valve
SV			Super Velocity
SVC			Singapore Volunteer Corps
SVDC			Special Vehicle Design Committee
SVDS			Super Velocity Discarding Sabot
svy	*		Survey
SW			South West
SW		Sw; S/W	Switch
SWA			South West Area
SWB			South Wales Borderers
SWBB			Standard Widened Bailey Bridge
swbd	*		Switchboard
SWC (NA)			Special Wireless Company (North Africa)
SWG			Special Wireless Group
SWG			Starret Wire Gauge
SWI			Special Wireless Intelligence
SWL			Safe Working Load
SWPA			South West Pacific Area
SWR			Steel Wire Rope
SWSC			Senior War Staff Course
SX			Sussex [Home Guard]
Sy			Security
SY			Staffordshire Yeomanry
SY			Surrey [Home Guard]
T		Tpt; (T)	Transport
TA	*		Territorial Army
TA			Territorial Army Reserve of Officers
TAA			Territorial Army Association
TAB			Typhoid, Para-Typhoid A and B [vaccine]
Tac			Tactical
Tac HQ		THQ	Tactical Headquarters
Tac R		tac R	Tactical Reconnaissance [air]
TAF			Tactical Air Force

Abbreviation		Alternatives	Meaning
TANS			Territorial Army Nursing Service
TAR			Territorial Army Reserve
TARO			Territorial Army Reserve of Officers
TAY			Perthshire [Home Guard] (Tayside)
TBRE			Training Battalion Royal Engineers
TC			Tank Corps
TC	*		Traffic Control
TC			Training College
TC			Transit Camp
TC KAR			Transport Corps King's African Rifles
TCC		TC Coy	Troop-Carrying Company [RASC]
TCMT			Training Centre Mechanised Transport [ATS]
TCP			Traffic Control Point
TCP			Troop Command Post
TC&RD		TC & Rec Dep	Training Centre and Reception Depot
TCV	*		Troop-Carrying Vehicle
TD			Temporary Duty
TD			Territorial Decoration
TD			Triple Double [Bailey Bridge]
TDC			Top Dead Centre
TDMR			Tank Delivery & Maintenance Regiment
TDR			Tank Delivery Regiment
TDS			Tank Delivery Squadron
TE			Tangent Elevation
TE			Training Establishment
Tech			Technical
Tech Stmn			Technical Storeman
TelCon			Telephone Communication(s)
Telecom		Tels	Tele-Communications
Temp		Temp; T/	Temporary
TEV			Technical Equiment Vehicle?
TEWT			Tactical Exercise Without Troops
tfc	*		Traffic
tfd			Transferred
TFF			Transjordan Frontier Force

Abbreviation		Alternatives	Meaning
T&G			Tongue & Groove
Tgt		tgt	Target
THI			Time Handed In
THR			Tower Hamlet Rifles
TI			Technical Instruction
Tipper Coy			Tipper Company [RASC]
TIS			Technical Intelligence Summary
TISC			Treasury Inter-Services Committee
TJFF			Trans-Jordan Frontier Force
Tk			Tank(s)
Tk Tptr		T/Tptr	Tank Transporter
TL			Tower of London [station monogram]
TM			Town Major
TMC			Telephone Manufacturing Company
TMC	*		Thompson Machine Carbine
TMH			Tidworth Military Hospital
TMO			Technical Maintenance Officer
TMS			Technical Maintenance Section
Tn	*		Transportation
Tnl Coy			Tunnelling Company [RE]
TNT			Tri-Nitro Toluene [explosive]
TO			Technical Officer
TO			Training Officer
TO	*		Transport Officer
TocH			Talbot House
TOET			Test of Elementary Training
TofF			Time of Flight
TofO		TOO	Time of Origin
TOG			The Old Gang
TOO			Time of Origin
Top		Topo, Topog	Topographic(al)
TOR			Time of Receipt
TOS		tos	Taken On Strength
ToS			Tam O'Shanter
TOS			Telegraph Operating Section
TOT		ToT	Time on Target
TOT			Treffry O Thompson [disinfector]
TOTE			Table of Tools & Equipment

Abbreviation		Alternatives	Meaning
TP			Trade Pattern
TP	*		Traffic Post
tp	*		Troop
TP			Tyre Pressure
Tp Ldr			Troop Leader
TPB			Trade Pattern Bicycle
TPEE			Tropical Proofing Experimental Establishment
tpi			Threads Per Inch [screw thread]
TPL		Tpl	Tropical(ised)
TPO			Tank Position Officer
tpr	*	Tpr	Trooper
tpt	*		Transport
tptd	*		Transported
tptr	*		Transporter
Tptr			Trumpeter
TQMS			Technical Quartermaster Sergeant/ Serjeant
TR			Training Regulations
Transf			Transfusion
trav			Traverse
TRBE			Target Recognition Base Ejection [ammunition]
TRD			Training & Reinforcement Depot
TRE			Telecommunications Research Establishment
trg	*	tg	Training
TRP			Passenger Train
TS		Tech S	Technical Stores
TS			Triple Single [Bailey Bridge]
TS			Tyneside Scottish
T/S			Temporary Service
TSC		Tech S Coy	Technical Stores Company
TSC			Transportation Stores Company [RE]
TSM			Troop Sergeant/Serjeant Major
TSMG			Thompson Sub-Machine Gun
TSR			Transvaal Scottish Regiment [South Africa]
TSS			Tubular Scaffolding Set
TT			Tank Transporter

Abbreviation		Alternatives	Meaning
TT		Tech Trg	Technical Training
TT			Triple Triple [Bailey Bridge]
TTC		TTC RE	Transportation Training Centre Royal Engineers
TTG			Technical Training Group
TTS			Tank Testing Station
TTS			Trade Training School
TU			Training Unit
TULO			Tank Unit Landing Officer
TURCO			Turnaround Control Organization
TVP			Transit Vehicle Park [RAOC]
TW		Tpt Wg	Transport Wing
TWD			Peebleshire [Home Guard]
TWH			Tidworth [station monogram]
"U"			Unserviceable [RAOC use]
U/			Unpaid [rank]
UA			Uniformity Agreement [RE Works Services]
U/A			Unpaid Acting [rank]
UB			United Board [Chaplain]
UC			Universal Call
UCB			Unit Construction Bridge
UCRB			Unit Construction Railway Bridge
UDF			Union Defence Force(s) [South Africa]
UE			Unit Equipment
UE			Unit Establishment
UEO			Unit Education Officer
UHF	*		Ultra High Frequency
UHG			Ulster Home Guard
u/i		U/I	Unidentified
UK			Block letters [in morse signalling]
UK	*		United Kingdom
UKCC			United Kingdom Commercial Corporation
UL			Unattached List [Indian Army]
UL			Unemployed List
UM			Urgent Memorandum
UMI			Unit Maintenance Inspection
UMR			Umvoti Mounted Rifles [South Africa]

Abbreviation		Alternatives	Meaning
UMS			Unit Medical Section
UNC			Unified National Coarse [screw thread]
Unclas			Unclassified
UNF			Unified National Fine [screw thread]
UNRRA			United Nations Relief & Rehabilitation Administration
unspec			Unspecified
UO			Under Officer [Royal Military College]
UP			Universal Pattern
UP		U/P	Unpaid
UP			Unrotated Projectile
UR	*		Unregistered [in signal message]
US		U/S	Unserviceable
USA			United States of America
USL		usl	Unemployed Supernumerary List
USO			Unit Savings Officer
U/T		u/t	Under Training
UTE			User Trials Establishment
UTP			Upper Thames Patrol [Home Guard]
UV	*		Ultra-Violet
UXB			Unexploded Bomb
UXO			Unexploded Ordnance
V			Volt
V		(V)	Volunteer
VA		V-A	Vickers-Armstrong
VAD			Voluntary Aid Detachment
VAOS			Vocabulary of Army Ordnance Stores
VC			Victoria Cross
VCC			Vehicle Collection Centre
VCIGS			Vice Chief of the Imperial General Staff
VCP			Visual Command Post
VD			Vehicle Detachment
VD			Venereal Disease
VDWO			Vehicle Depot Workshop Organization

Abbreviation		Alternatives	Meaning
VE			Commencing signal [in morse signalling]
VE			Verbal Message
VE	*		Victory in Europe
VES			Veterinary Evacuating Station
vet		Vet	Veterinary
VF			Variable Frequency? View Finder?
VF			Vulcan Foundry
VGO			Vehicle Group Organization
VH		Vet Hosp	Veterinary Hospital
VHF			Very High Frequency
VIE			Visual Indicator Equipment [AA]
VIR			Vulcanised India Rubber
VJ			Victory over Japan
VL			Vice Lieutenant [of County]
VLF			Very Low Frequency
VLO			Verticle Line Overlap [air photography]
VM			Vehicle Mechanic
VMSMT			Vocabulary of Miscellaneous Stores for Mechanical Transport
Vol			Volume
Vol			Volunteer/ary
VOR			Vehicle Off Road
VP			Vent Percussion [ammunition]
VP	*		Vital Point
VP			Vulnerable Point
VR			Voluntary Release
V&R		VR	Veterinary & Remount
VRCS			Veterinary & Remount Conducting Section
VRD	*		Vehicle Reception Depot [RASC]
VRD	*		Vehicle Reserve Depot [RASC]
VRS			Vehicle Reception Store
VS	*	V/S	Visual Signalling
VSC			Vocational Selection Centre
VSD			Vehicle Shipment Depot
VT		V/T	Valve Transmitting
V/T		VT	Visual Telegraphy [semaphore]
VT			Visual Training

Abbreviation		Alternatives	Meaning
vtm	*		Vehicles to the Mile
VWD			Vehicle Workshop Detachment
W			Watt
W			West
W/			War [rank, eg W/Sgt]
w/		w	With
(W)			Women
WA			West Africa
WA			Word After [in signal message]
WAA			West African Artillery
WAAC			West African Armoured Corps
WAAF			Women's Auxiliary Air Force
WAASC			West African Army Service Corps
WAC			West Africa Command
WADS			Women's Auxiliary Defence Service
WAE			West African Engineers
WAOC			West African Ordnance Corps
WAR			Warwickshire [Home Guard]
WARWICKS		Warwicks	Royal Warwickshire Regiment
WB			Water Bottle
WB			Water Bowser
WB			Whole Blood
WB			Word Before (signal message)
WB Sect			Waterboring Section [RE]
WC			Western Command
WCP			Water Clarifying Powder
WCR			War Clothing Regulations
WCW		WC&W	Wheels Carriages & Wagons
WD			War Department
WD			Water Duties
WD		WDgns	Westminster Dragoons
WD			White Drill [uniform]
Wd		WD	Wheeled
wd		wdr; w/d	Withdraw(al)
WDC			War Department Constabulary
WDC			Weapon Developmernt Committee
WDF			War Department Fleet
WDF			Western Desert Force
WDLA			War Department Land Agent

Abbreviation		Alternatives	Meaning
WDTS			War Dogs Training School
WE		W/E	War Emergency
WE	*		War Establishment
WE			Web(bing) Equipment
wef	*	WEF	With Effect From
WELCH		Welch	Welch Regiment
WEO			Workshop Executive Officer
WES			War Emergency Standard
WES			Wesleyan
WES			Westmoreland [Home Guard]
WG		Welsh Gds	Welsh Guards
Wg			Wing
WGEP			Wool Grease Emulsion Paint
wh		whld	Wheel(ed)
Wh		whld	Wheel/ed
Whit			Whitworth
WI			West Indies
WI			Women's Institute
WI			Wrought Iron
WIA		WiA	Wounded in Action
WIATS			West Indies Auxiliary Territorial Service
WILTS		Wilts	Wiltshire Regiment
Wks			Works
wksp	*	Wkshp; Wkshop	Workshop
WL	*		Wagon Line [RA]
WL			West Lancashire [Home Guard]
WL			West Lothian [Home Guard]
WLA			Women's Land Army
WLO			Wagon Line Officer [RA]
WLS			Wagon Loading Ship
WM			Ward Maid
WM			White Metal
WMA			Womens's Medical Adviser
WN			Weedon [station monogram]
Wng			Warning
WngO			Warning Order
WNM			Machars Bn, Wigtownshire [Home Guard]
WNR			Rhinns Bn, Wigtownshire [Home Guard]

Abbreviation		Alternatives	Meaning
WNSR			West Nova Scotia Regiment [Canada]
WO			War Office
WO	*		Warrant Officer
WOCS			War Office Controlled Stores
WOHU			War Office Holding Unit
WOI/II/III		WO1; WO2; WO3	Warrant Officer First/Second/Third Class
WOR			Worcestershire [Home Guard]
WORCS		Worcs	Worcestershire Regiment
WOSB			War Office Selection Board
WOTC			War Office Transport Column
WP	*		Water Point
WP			Water Pump
WP			White Phosphorous
WP			Winch Portable
WP			Witness Point [RA]
W&P Coy			Workshop & Park Company [RE]
wpfg	*		Waterprooofing
WPM		wpm	Words Per Minute [Morse]
WR			West Riding of Yorkshire [Home Guard]
WRCNS			Women's Royal Canadian Naval Service
WS	*	W/S; War Subst	War Substantive [rank]
WS	*		Warlike Stores
WS	*		Wireless Set
WSI			War Service Increment [pay]
WSP			Water Sterilising Powder
WSS			Water Supply Set
WT	*		Weapon Training
WT	*	W/T	Wireless Telegraphy
WTC			Wading Trials Centre
WTC		WTk Coy	Water Tank Company [RASC]
WTC			Water Transport Company [RASC]
WTC			Waterborne Training Centre [RASC]
WTS			Wiltshire [Home Guard]
WTS			Womens Transport Service [ATS]
WTU			Water Transport Unit

Abbreviation		Alternatives	Meaning
WTW			Waterborne Training Wing [RASC]
WVEE			Wheeled Vehicle Experimental Establishment
WVS			Women's Voluntary Service
WWCP	*		Walking Wounded Collection Point
WWSA			Women's War Service Auxiliary [NZ]
Wx			Wessex
WY			Warwickshire Yeomanry
W YORKS		W Yorks	West Yorkshire Regiment
X-country			Cross-country
XE			Oblique stroke [in morse signalling]
Xing			Crossing
XPM			Expanded Metal
X&PRS			X-ray & Physiotherapy Repair Section
X rds		X rd; X-Rds	Crossroad(s)
XRU			X-Ray Unit
XSO			X-Ray Service Officer [REME]
YD			Yorkshire Dragoons
yd	*	Yd	Yard(s)
Yeo			Yeomanry
YH			Yorkshire Hussars
YMCA			Young Men's Christian Association
YORKS & LANCS		Yorks & Lancs; Y & L	Yorkshire and Lancashire Regiment
Y rds			Y roads [shape of junction]
YS			Young Soldier
Y-S			Yugo-Slav
YSTC			Young Soldiers Training Centre
YSTU			Young Soldiers Training Unit
Z			Zetland [Home Guard]
ZL			Zero Line
1/2 Track			Half Track
2i/c		2iC	Second in Command
2Lt			Second Lieutenant
4WD			Four Wheel Drive
Ø Hr		Z Hr	Zero Hour
ØØØØ Hrs			Midnight

Part 4

REGIMENTS AND CORPS

The army in WW2 was made-up of a huge number of different units; these were most commonly termed 'regiments', 'battalions', and 'corps', although there was also the occasional use of 'department' or 'service'. Some regiments or battalions referred to themselves as brigades (for historical reasons), and some of the larger infantry regiments could be made-up of more than two dozen individual battalions, whereas some regiments just comprised a single battalion (or equivalent). Some of the units were regular, in that in peacetime they belonged to the regular full-time professional component of the army, whereas others came from the reserve. As well as individual reservists (soldiers who had spent some time in the regular army and were required as part of their contract to be ready to be recalled to the colours in time of emergency), there were a large number of reservist units, the so-called "weekend warriors"; the majority of these were part of the Territorial Army (TA), but others were part of the Supplementary Reserve (SR) or the Militia.[1] Additionally, many other units were formed during the war for "hostilities only".

'Formation' was the word used for army organisations above the unit level. In the operational sphere, these were called: brigades, divisions, corps, armies, and army groups. For administrative training and other reasons, other formation level organisations were known as commands, districts, areas, garrisons etc.

Precedence & Seniority

Precedence and seniority are not always the same thing! Precedence is variously defined in dictionaries as "The condition of being dealt with before other things, or of being considered more important than other things... the order of importance given to people in particular societies, groups, or organizations...the right to precede others in ceremonies or social formalities". It is this last definition that best applies here. To try to simplify a complex topic, in British Army terms, we might consider it like this: if one wanted to compile a list of all the units in the army and make sure that it was in the correct order for a parade, so that the marching troops would parade past the saluting dais in the correct order, then this list would reflect their precedence.

However, related to this but not the same is the thorny issue of seniority. If we consider that seniority relates simply to the date that a unit was founded, then the British Army precedence would look very different. A couple of examples: within the Foot Guards, the Grenadier Guards take precedence over the Coldstream Guards, but members of the latter regiment will argue strongly and forcefully that they are in fact senior because they were founded earlier (1650) than the Grenadiers (1656). The 22nd Dragoons were only formed in 1940 as a so-called "war-raised" cavalry regiment, but they claimed heritage dating back to 1716 and took their WW2 precedence immediately after the most junior of the regular cavalry regiments (17/21L), and thus before dozens of units that had already been in continuous existence for over 200 years.

Listed below are all the various units and corps that made-up the British Army during World War 2. This first list shows us the official order of precedence as used during that conflict:

The Life Guards and Royal Horse Guards (in that order)
- Royal Horse Artillery *Note A*
- Regiments of Cavalry of the Line *Note B*
- Regiments of the Royal Armoured Corps *Note B*
- Royal Regiment of Artillery *Notes A, C*
- Corps of Royal Engineers
- Royal Corps of Signals
- Regiments of Foot Guards *Note B*
- Regiments of Infantry of the Line and The Rifle Brigade *Note B*
- Hong Kong – Singapore Royal Artillery
- Royal Malta Artillery
- Royal Army Chaplains' Department
- Royal Army Service Corps (including the Army Catering Corps from March 1941)
- Royal Army Medical Corps
- Royal Army Ordnance Corps
- Army Air Corps
- Royal Electrical and Mechanical Engineers (formed 19 May 1942)
- Royal Army Pay Corps
- Royal Army Veterinary Corps
- Army Educational Corps[2]
- Small Arms School Corps
- Army Dental Corps
- The Corps of Military Police
- Pioneer Corps

Intelligence Corps
Army Physical Training Corps
General Service Corps
Queen Alexandra's Imperial Military Nursing Service
Royal Monmouthshire Royal Engineers (Supplementary Reserve)
Units of the Supplementary Reserve[3]
Militia units
Honourable Artillery Company (TA)
Territorial Army *Note D*
Territorial Army Nursing Service
Auxiliary Territorial Service
Militia units in Bermuda, the Channel Islands and Malta[4]
Training Corps[5]

Notes

A But *only* when "on parade with their guns", when they take "the right of the line and march at the head of the Household Cavalry". On other occasions, such as on operations, they become the senior component of the Royal Regiment of Artillery.[6]

B In the order of precedence shown later.

C Except RHA and the Hong Kong-Singapore RA who appear separately.

D In the same order as for the Regular Army.

Not all the regiments and corps shown here appeared on the original list; for example, the CMP, the MPGS and the SASC are all conspicuous by their absence. They have been inserted in this list in a position of precedence based upon post-war lists. The Army Commandos are also missing from the list.

The information contained in the notes is critical here; for example, the single line above that gives the precedence for the "Regiments of Infantry of the Line and the Rifle Brigade" refers to nearly seventy regular regiments, all of which included at least one TA battalion, plus a couple of dozen other TA regiments that bore their own regimental title and which were not to be found within the regular army – see below. So, in this case, care has to be taken as this precedence only refers to the battalions within the regular army, and the Territorial Army equivalents come much further down the list, but which then follow the same internal order of precedence amongst themselves. However, although this is the official line, what happened during the conflict was that the distinction between regular and reserve units seems to have been largely ignored, and the only criterion applied was where the regiment came in the regular order of seniority.

In some ways, during the conflict this sort of thing didn't matter, because the regular battalions of 1939 soon found themselves taking in reservists, volunteers, and conscripts, all of which watered down to a large degree the fundamental character of these battalions, although in many cases it must be said that a sufficiently large backbone of pre-war regulars remained, and such units always prided themselves on being "regular". Another result of the wartime demand for manpower was that the infantry battalions, firmly county-based or at least regional in terms of most of their peacetime recruits, became less so over the course of the war as recruits were sent where the need arose. And in terms of performance during the war, it was all down to factors such as leadership, training, experience, character, cohesion and esprit de corps – simply being a "regular" battalion as opposed to a TA or war-raised unit was no guarantee of success on the battlefield.

Where the system of precedence *did* matter was in the allocation of units to formations, for example the three infantry battalions required to make up an infantry brigade. In this case, the battalions would always be listed according to their position in the order of precedence (and their vehicles and equipment would be marked accordingly). For example, 25th Infantry Brigade in early May 1940 comprised, in order, 1/7 Queens (a TA unit), 2nd Essex (a regular battalion), and 1st Royal Irish Fusiliers, another regular battalion. If the last battalion was posted elsewhere and a battalion of the Royal Scots took their place, then that battalion would become the senior, and the other two would "shuffle down one place"; such restructuring usually meant that the unit codes (painted on the front and rear of a regiment's vehicles) would all have to be repainted, sometimes across all three units in the whole brigade.

The same thing also happened within armoured brigades; within 29th Armoured Brigade in January 1945, the senior regiment was the 23rd Hussars (a war-raised cavalry regiment who had only formed in 1940), followed by 3rd Battalion Royal Tank Regiment (a regular battalion of the RTR who could trace their origin to 1916), and the junior regiment was 2nd Fife and Forfar Yeomanry (a Territorial Army yeomanry cavalry regiment that had its origins in 1793). The management of precedence and seniority was much simpler within the Royal Armoured Corps than it was within the infantry.

Another unintended complication that illustrates this occurred during World War 2 as the result of a policy taken early in the war to convert a number of infantry battalions into regiments of the Royal Armoured Corps. A good example would be the 9th Battalion of the Gordon Highlanders, a TA unit which in July 1942 changed role from infantry to tanks and became 116 Regiment Royal Armoured Corps. The 9th Battalion was thus suddenly elevated in the order of precedence, and as 116 RAC they found themselves senior to the Royal Artillery, the Royal Engineers, the Foot Guards, and indeed the Gordon Highlanders' own regular 1st Battalion!

We shall now consider how the thorny issues of precedence and seniority were arranged by looking at the arms and corps in the order noted above.

The Royal Armoured Corps

The units that made-up the Royal Armoured Corps (formed April 1939) came from different sources. These were, eventually: the twenty regular cavalry regiments, six "war raised" cavalry regiments, the eight regular, four "regular war-raised", and twelve territorial battalions of the Royal Tank Regiment, a single unit of militia cavalry, some of the Yeomanry cavalry regiments, 32 infantry battalions converted to become regiments of the Royal Armoured Corps, and, from January 1944, the Reconnaissance Corps.[7, 8] Within the RAC, units took precedence in the order shown below.

The two regiments of the Household Cavalry (LG and RHG) were not part of the Royal Armoured Corps, and although they functioned operationally as two (amalgamated) armoured car regiments, they did so under their own arrangements and largely on their own terms. In a similar manner, seven battalions of Foot Guards were converted in the middle of the war from infantry into the armoured role. These were the 2nd and 4th Grenadier Guards, the 1st and 4th Coldstream Guards, the 3rd Scots Guards, the 2nd Irish Guards, and the 2nd Welsh Guards. These retained their independence, did not become part of the RAC, and were operationally employed within the Guards Armoured/Tank brigades or the Guards Armoured Division (GAD).[9]

Full Title	Operational Abbreviation	Alternative (Army List)[10]
HOUSEHOLD CAVALRY		
The Life Guards	LG	L G
Royal Horse Guards (The Blues)	RHG	R H G
CAVALRY OF THE LINE (REGULAR)		
1st King's Dragoon Guards	KDG	K D G
The Queen's Bays		
(2nd Dragoon Guards)	BAYS	The Bays
3rd Carabiniers		
(Prince of Wales's Dragoon Guards)	3 DG	3rd D G
4th/7th Royal Dragoon Guards	4/7 DG	4th/7th D G
5th Royal Inniskilling Dragoon Guards	5 DG	5th Innis D G
1st The Royal Dragoons[11]	ROYALS	The Royals
The Royal Scots Greys (2nd Dragoons)[12]	GREYS	The Greys
3rd The King's Own Hussars	3 H	3rd H
4th Queen's Own Hussars	4 H	4th H
7th Queen's Own Hussars	7 H	7th H
8th King's Royal Irish Hussars	8 KRIH	8th H
9th Queen's Royal Lancers	9 L	9th L
10th Royal Hussars (Prince of Wales's Own)	10 H	10th H

Full Title	Operational Abbreviation	Alternative (Army List)[10]
11th Hussars (Prince Albert's Own)	11 H	11th H
12th Royal Lancers (Prince of Wales's)	12 L	12th L
13th/18th Royal Hussars (Queen Mary's Own)	13/18 H	13th/18th H
14th/20th King's Hussars	14/20 H	14th/20th H
15th/19th The King's Royal Hussars	15/19 H	15th/19th H
16th/5th Lancers	16/5 L	16th/5th L
17th/21st Lancers	17/21 L	17th/21th L
CAVALRY OF THE LINE (WAR-RAISED)		
22nd Dragoons	22 D	22nd Dns
23rd Hussars	23 H	23rd H
24th Lancers	24 L	24th L
25th Dragoons	25 DGNS	25th Dns
26th Hussars	26 H	26th H
27th Lancers	27 L	27th L

ROYAL TANK REGIMENT (REGULAR, TA & WAR-RAISED)

Royal Tank Regiment[13]	R Tks	R T R

THE RECONNAISSANCE CORPS

Reconnaissance Corps		RECCE CORPS

THE MILITIA

North Irish Horse[14]		NIH

THE TERRITORIAL ARMY YEOMANRY CAVALRY

Royal Wiltshire Yeomanry (TA)		R WILTS YEO
Warwickshire Yeomanry (TA)		WARWICK YEO
Yorkshire Hussars (TA)		YORKS H
Nottinghamshire Yeomanry (TA)/ Sherwood Rangers Yeomanry		SRY
Staffordshire Yeomanry (TA)		STAFFS YEO
Yorkshire Dragoons (TA)		YORKS DGNS
Derbyshire Yeomanry (TA)		DERBY YEO
Royal Gloucestershire Hussars (TA)		RGH
Lothians and Border Yeomanry (TA)/ Lothians and Border Horse		LBY/LBH
Fife & Forfar Yeomanry (TA)		FFY
2nd City of London Yeomanry (Westminster Dragoons) (TA)		W DGNS

County of London Yeomanry (Sharpshooters) (TA)[15]	SHARPSHOOTERS
Northamptonshire Yeomanry (TA)	N YEO
East Riding Yeomanry (TA)	E RIDING YEO
Inns of Court Regiment (TA)	INNS OF COURT

Non-RAC Yeomanry Units

It should be noted that by no means all of the former Yeomanry (territorial cavalry) units found themselves employed in the armoured role. Between the wars, 33 former Yeomanry cavalry regiments had found themselves converted to become part of the Royal Artillery, and another three became units within the Royal Corps of Signals (The Cheshire Yeomanry, North Somerset Yeomanry, and the 1st County of London Yeomanry/Middlesex Yeomanry). The units that became part of the Royal Artillery were as follows (shown in order of yeomanry precedence):

Shropshire Yeomanry
Ayrshire Yeomanry
Leicester Yeomanry
Duke of Lancaster's Own Yeomanry
Lanarkshire Yeomanry
Northumberland Yeomanry
South Notts Hussars
Denbighshire Yeomanry
Westmoreland and Cumberland Yeomanry
Pembroke Yeomanry
Royal East Kent Yeomanry
Hampshire Yeomanry
Buckinghamshire Yeomanry
Dorset Yeomanry
Hertfordshire Yeomanry
Berkshire Yeomanry
Devon Yeomanry
Suffolk Yeomanry
North Devon Yeomanry
Worcestershire Yeomanry (Queen's Own Worcestershire Hussars)
West Kent (Queen's Own) Yeomanry
West Somerset Yeomanry
Oxfordshire Yeomanry (Queen's Own Oxfordshire Hussars)
Glasgow Yeomanry (Queen's Own Royal Glasgow Yeomanry)
Lancashire Hussars
Surrey Yeomanry (Queen Mary's Regiment)
Norfolk Yeomanry (King's Own Royal Regiment)
Sussex Yeomanry
Glamorgan Yeomanry
City of London Yeomanry (Rough Riders)

Bedfordshire Yeomanry
Essex Yeomanry
Scottish Horse

In the best British army manner, this meant that all of these regiments of yeomanry had an order of precedence within the arm or corps that they now belonged to, in the RAC, RA, or RCS, but another separate order of precedence that only applied *within* the yeomanry. For example, the Shropshire Yeomanry had become an RA unit, and as such were junior in army terms to all the Yeomanry units now within the RAC, but in purely yeomanry terms, were in fact the sixth most senior yeomanry regiment, taking their place immediately after the Staffordshire Yeomanry. The details of this precedence were to be found within the Army List. When these yeomanry units became part of their new corps, it was accepted that the former titles would be incorporated within their new unit designations. For example, 55th (West Somerset Yeomanry) Field Regiment RA, or 64th (Queen's Own Royal Glasgow Yeomanry) Anti-Tank Regiment RA.

In the Army List, after the yeomanry cavalry came another category within the TA, that of Scouts. Only one regiment was included, The Lovat Scouts. These were, in some arcane manner, combined within the Scottish Horse (the most junior of the yeomanry), from 1940.

The Royal Regiment of Artillery

The "Royal Regiment" as it is often referred to (usually by its own members) was in effect a corps (the senior) of the army and was a huge organisation that consisted of a large number of component parts.[16] The distinction between the different types of unit (based upon the nature of equipment they operated and their specific role) was often of little interest to the rest of the army – they were all just "gunners" – but it was extremely important to the members of this very large corps; one estimate is that there were nearly one thousand RA regiments of many different types during the war, and at its maximum strength the corps employed about 800,000 men. In order of precedence within the corps, the constituent parts were:

Royal Horse Artillery. Sixteen field regiments of artillery were designated as RHA. This was simply a result of history, as the RHA had been formed to provide mobile artillery support for the cavalry in the Napoleonic period. RHA Regiments, reflecting these origins, often became self-propelled regiments in order to support armoured formations.

Royal Artillery. The majority of the units within the Royal Regiment of Artillery were classified as RA. A number of different types of regiments (at least 31) existed at various times, as shown below. Because of this sub-division, it is possible to use the term "RA" in two different ways: firstly, as shorthand to refer to the entire Royal Regiment of Artillery, and secondly, to refer only to the RA regiments within the Royal Regiment of Artillery.

Hong Kong-Singapore Royal Artillery. One gun regiment and three LAA regiments were formed; these were effectively lost and no longer active following the surrender of the garrison.

Royal Malta Artillery. Already in existence pre-WW2, the RMA operated both coastal and anti-aircraft guns during the conflict, as well as forming a searchlight battery.

Honourable Artillery Company. The HAC were the senior unit within the Territorial Army, and as such, were given their own place in the order of precedence to reflect this.

It should be stressed that this "simple" order of precedence only applied within the corps itself, and that in overall army terms, these component parts were regarded as separate units, each with their position of precedence, as already shown.

As noted, the RA operated many different types of regiments, their titles reflecting their role and main equipment. These titles were not static and would be changed as and when a unit changed role, for example from field regiment to air landing regiment, although in most cases the same regimental number would be retained. The list below is in alphabetical order and does not reflect any order of precedence.[17]

Air Landing (Light and Anti-Tank)
Air Observation Post (Squadrons)
Anti-Aircraft (Light, Heavy, Maritime & Z)[18]
Anti-Tank
Coastal
Defence
Field
Field Radar
Garrison
Heavy
Heavy (Coast)
Infantry[19]
Jungle Field
Light
Light Anti-Aircraft/Anti-Tank
Medium
Mixed[20]
Mortar[21]
Mountain
Pack
Parachute (Field, Light, Light A/T & LAA)
Searchlight
Super Heavy
Super Heavy Railway
Survey
Training

Examples of the naming conventions used by the RA are as follows:

Abbreviation	Full Title
3 (etc) RHA	3rd Regiment Royal Horse Artillery[22]
91 Fd Regt RA	91st Field Regiment Royal Artillery
5 Med Regt RA	5th Medium Regiment Royal Artillery
32 Hvy Regt RA	32nd Heavy Regiment Royal Artillery
51 LAA Regt RA	51st Light Anti-Aircraft Regiment Royal Artillery
3 Svy Regt RA	3rd Survey Regiment Royal Artillery
6 HAA Regt RA	6th Heavy Anti-Aircraft Regiment Royal Artillery
102 ATk Regt RA	102nd Anti-Tank Regiment Royal Artillery
7 Mtn Regt RA	7th Mountain Regiment Royal Artillery

Within the RA, the regiments could be grouped in two ways; numerically regardless of role (eg 1, 2, 3 etc), or by role, in effect grouping all of the field regiments together (in numerical order), followed by the medium, then the heavy etc. It was common practice for the regiments to be referred to by their number, spoken as digits, for example, "Two Five Field Regiment", or "Five Four Medium Regiment", rather than by ordinal numbers, 25th, 54th etc. Batteries within the regiments each carried their own numerical designations and often included an honorific battery title in brackets.[23] For example, in February 1941 6 RHA comprised three batteries: N Battery (The Eagle Troop), O Battery (The Rocket Troop) and P Battery (The Dragon Troop).

The Corps of Royal Engineers

Unlike most other units, the basic element of the Royal Engineers was the company/squadron.[24] Within an operational division (of any type) it was usual to have three field companies/squadrons, allowing one to be attached to each of the three brigades within the division.[25] For example, in late 1939, 51st (Highland) Division were supported by 236, 237 and 238 Field Companies RE. Additionally, each division would have a field park company/squadron, which held more stores and equipment and provided specialised support. In some instances, a division would also be allocated additional RE sub-units, for example a bridging platoon.

Other, more specialised RE units were in existence at battalion/regimental, company/squadron, troop, or detachment level, and on operations, these would usually be controlled by the divisional Commander Royal Engineers (CRE) or the Commander Corps Royal Engineers (CCRE), or even held and controlled at Army or Army Group level. As a corps the RE were responsible for the following tasks:

Airborne/Parachute and Airlanding support engineering
Airfield construction

Armoured engineering
Bomb Disposal
Camouflage
Chemical & Gas warfare & protection (including Heavy Mortars)[26]
Counter-Mobility (eg laying minefields, creating roadblocks and other obstacles, cratering, digging anti-tank ditches, laying barbed wire etc)
Construction including camps and other infrastructure
Mobility (eg clearing minefields, road-building and improvement, drainage, and bridging & rafting)
Forestry
Fortress
Infrastructure support
Inland Water Transport (IWT)
Lines of Communication support
Movement Control
Port and Dock operations
Postal & Courier services
Railway services
Survey, Topography, Printing & Mapping
Tunnelling and Quarrying
Water supplies[27]

It can be seen that the "sappers" were responsible for an enormous range of activities in direct and indirect support of the army in the field. The list of trades within the corps was therefore seemingly endless, including soldiers employed as pioneers, draughtsmen, machinists (metal), boilermaker's mate and washout men, storemen, electricians, plumbers, clerks, checkers movement control, general dutymen, steelwork erectors, wiremen, welders, painter and decorators, bricklayers, and steam raisers. Because of the very specialised nature of their work and equipment, the RE retained responsibility for servicing, maintenance and repair of much of their own equipment, even after the formation of REME in 1942.

The Royal Corps of Signals

Because the Royal Corps of Signals (frequently but erroneously noted as the Corps of Royal Signals and/or CRS) was created from an arm of the Royal Engineers in July 1920; the corps took its precedence immediately after the RE from whence they had sprung. The corps was responsible for the provision of all communications systems (less postal, which remained an RE responsibility), which included the maintenance of all, and operation of some, radio and other communications systems, including line, telephone networks, cipher operations, and despatch services.[28] The corps was also responsible for the correct setting of time – not the Royal Artillery!

Many units of the Royal Signals were therefore small, often at the company/squadron level or below, sections and detachments probably being the most common. Regiments generally existed to provide training functions, not field roles.

The Foot Guards

The five regiments of foot guards were all infantry and fielded multiple battalions during the conflict. Because of their status as household troops to the sovereign, they always took precedence before the other line infantry battalions. Within the Brigade of Guards (as they were known collectively), their own precedence was as follows:

Full Title	Operational Abbreviation	Alternative (Army List)
The Grenadier Guards	GREN GDS	Gren G'ds
The Coldstream Guards	COLDM GDS	C G'ds
The Scots Guards	SG	S G'ds
The Irish Guards	IG	I G'ds
The Welsh Guards	WG	W G'ds

The Infantry of The Line and Light Infantry Battalions

Regiments of infantry were originally called by the name of their commanding officer, and then later given numbers to reflect both their precedence and seniority. In 1881, the Childers Reforms named the regiments to reflect their new territorial/county affiliations, which confirmed their precedence as well as giving them titles which, although often modified over the years, were largely recognisable during WW2. This applied to all the (non-Guards) infantry battalions; these were referred to as line infantry (those that had once fought their battles by standing in line shoulder to shoulder), or those known as rifle or light infantry units, whose origins came from the experiments in using skirmishing units of rifle or light infantry during the American and Napoleonic wars. In some usage, line infantry simply meant all the non-guards infantry battalions, regardless of their origins.

All of the infantry regiments (including the foot guards) had multiple battalions, themselves numbered.[29] For example, 1st Battalion The Royal Scots, 3rd Battalion The Buffs, or 5th Battalion The Rifle Brigade. In the case of battalions originally belonging to the Territorial Army, the numbering system could be different: at the start of the war many of the territorial battalions were ordered to form a duplicate or second (also known as second-line) battalion from within. For example, the 5th Bn Queens became the 1/5th Queens and its second or duplicate battalion was the 2/5th Queens. In practice, after a couple of years of war there was little to distinguish between regular, first-line, or second-line battalions; what counted was leadership, training, combat experience, and esprit de corps.

Listed below are these regiments, in order of precedence, as well as their official abbreviations (used in operational staff work) and their alternative abbreviation (used within the Army List publication):

Full Title	Operational Abbreviation	Alternative (Army List)
The Royal Scots (The Royal Regiment)	RS	R Scots
The Queen's Royal Regiment (West Surrey)	QUEENS	The Queen's R
The Royal East Kent Regiment	BUFFS	Buffs
The King's Own Royal Regiment (Lancaster)	KINGS OWN	King's Own R
Royal Northumberland Fusiliers	NF	R North'd Fus
The Royal Warwickshire Regiment	WARWICKS	R War R
The Royal Fusiliers (City of London Regiment)	RF	R Fus
The King's Regiment (Liverpool)	KINGS	The King's R
The Royal Norfolk Regiment	NORFOLK	R Norfolk R
The Lincolnshire Regiment	LINCOLNS	Lincoln R
The Devonshire Regiment	DEVONS	Devon R
The Suffolk Regiment	SUFFOLK	Suffolk R
The Somerset Light Infantry (Prince Albert's)	SOM LI	Somerset LI
The West Yorkshire Regiment (The Prince of Wales's Own)	W YORKS	W York R
The East Yorkshire Regiment (Duke of York's Own)	E YORKS	E York R
The Bedfordshire and Hertfordshire Regiment	BEDS & HERTS	Bedfs & Herts R
The Leicestershire Regiment	LEICS	Leicester R
The Green Howards (Alexandra, Princess of Wales's Own Yorkshire Regiment)	GREEN HOWARDS	Green Howards
The Lancashire Fusiliers	LF	Lan Fus
The Royal Scots Fusiliers	RSF	R S Fus
The Cheshire Regiment	CHESHIRE	Cheshire R
The Royal Welch Fusiliers	RWF	R W Fus
The South Wales Borderers	SWB	S Wales Bord
The King's Own Scottish Borderers	KOSB	K O S B
The Cameronians (Scottish Rifles)	CAMERONIANS	Cameronians
The Royal Inniskilling Fusiliers	INNISKILLINGS	Inniskilling Fus
The Gloucestershire Regiment	GLOSTERS	Gloster R
The Worcestershire Regiment	WORCS	Worc R

Full Title	Operational Abbreviation	Alternative (Army List)
The East Lancashire Regiment	E LANCS	E Lan R
The East Surrey Regiment	SURREYS	E Surrey R
The Duke of Cornwall's Light Infantry	DCLI	D C L I
The Duke of Wellington's Regiment (West Riding)	DWR	D W R
The Border Regiment	BORDER	Border R
The Royal Sussex Regiment	R SUSSEX	R Sussex R
The Hampshire Regiment	HAMPS	Hampshire R
The South Staffordshire Regiment	S STAFFS	S Stafford R
The Dorsetshire Regiment	DORSET	Dorset R
The South Lancashire Regiment		
(The Prince of Wales's Volunteers)	S LANCS	S Lan R
The Welch Regiment	WELCH	Welch R
The Black Watch	BLACK WATCH	Black Watch
The Oxfordshire and Buckinghamshire Light Infantry	OX & BUCKS	Oxf & Bucks LI
The Essex Regiment	ESSEX	Essex R
The Sherwood Foresters (Notts and Derby Regiment)	FORESTERS	Foresters
The Loyal Regiment (North Lancashire)	LOYALS	Loyal R
The Northamptonshire Regiment	NORTHAMPTONS	North'n R
The Royal Berkshire Regiment (Princess Charlotte of Wales's)	R BERKS	R Berks R
*The Royal Marines (when serving under the Army Act, eg not serving under the Naval Discipline Act)[30]		
The Queen's Own Royal West Kent Regiment	RWK	R W K
The King's Own Yorkshire Light Infantry	KOYLI	K O Y L I
The King's Shropshire Light Infantry	KSLI	K S L I
The Middlesex Regiment (Duke of Cambridge's Own)	MIDDX	Midd'x R
The King's Royal Rifle Corps	KRRC	K R R C
The Wiltshire Regiment (Duke of Edinburgh's)	WILTS	Wilts R
The Manchester Regiment	MANCH	Manch R
The North Staffordshire Regiment (Prince of Wales's)	N STAFFS	N Stafford R
The Yorkshire and Lancashire Regiment	YORKS & LANCS	Y & L R

Full Title	Operational Abbreviation	Alternative (Army List)
The Durham Light Infantry	DLI	Durham L I
The Highland Light Infantry (City of Glasgow Regiment)	HLI	H L I
The Seaforth Highlanders (The Duke of Albany's)	SEAFORTHS	Seaforth
The Gordon Highlanders	GORDONS	Gordons
The Queen's Own Cameron Highlanders	CAMERONS	Camerons
The Royal Ulster Rifles	RUR	R U Rif
The Royal Irish Fusiliers (Princess Victoria's)	R IR F	R Ir Fus
The Argyll & Sutherland Highlanders	A&SH	A & S H
The Rifle Brigade (Prince Consort's Own)	RB	Rifle Bde
The Lowland Regiment	LOWLAND	Lowland R
The Highland Regiment	HIGHLAND REGT	Highland R

Territorial Infantry Battalions

All of these regular infantry battalions (less the Guards) had one or more territorial battalions which used the same title as the regular unit. In addition, a number of the regular battalions had one or more affiliated territorial battalions which used a different (historical) title, wearing their own cap badge and unit embellishments, but which were "under the wing" of the regular unit for some administrative and training purposes; these are listed below. The operational abbreviated titles, where different to the parent regiment, are shown in capitals.[31]

Regular Battalion	Affiliated TA Battalion(S)	Abbreviated Title
The Bedfordshire and Hertfordshire Regiment	1st & 2nd Bns Hertfordshire Regt (TA)	HERTS
Black Watch	1st Bn Tyneside Scottish (TA)	TYNE SCOT
Queen's Own Cameron Highlanders	1st & 2nd Bns Liverpool Scottish (TA)	LIVPL SCOT
Gordon Highlanders	1st – 3rd Bns London Scottish (TA)	LOND SCOT
Highland Light Infantry (City of Glasgow Regiment)	1st & 2nd Bns Glasgow Highlanders (TA)	GLAS H
King's Regiment (Liverpool)	Liverpool Welsh	
King's Royal Rifle Corps	1st & 2nd Bns Queen Victoria's Rifles 1st & 2nd Bns Rangers 1st & 2nd Bns Queen's Westminsters	

Regular Battalion	Affiliated TA Battalion(S)	Abbreviated Title
King's Shropshire Light Infantry	1st & 2nd Bns Herefordshire Regt (TA)	HEREFORD
Middlesex Regiment (Duke of Cambridge's Own)	1st & 2nd Bns Princess Louise's Kensington Rifles	KENSINGTONS
Oxfordshire and Buckinghamshire Light Infantry	1st & 2nd Bns Buckinghamshire (TA)	BUCKS
Rifle Brigade (Prince Consort's Own	1st & 2nd Bns London Rifle Brigade 1st – 3rd Bns Tower Hamlet Rifles	
Royal Ulster Rifles	1st & 2nd Bns London Irish Rifles (TA)	LIR
Suffolk Regiment	1st & 2nd Bns Cambridgeshire Regt (TA)	CAMB
South Wales Borderers	Brecknockshire Bn (TA) 1st – 4th Bns Monmouthshire Regt (TA)	BRECKNOCK MON
Yorkshire and Lancashire Regiment	Hallamshire Bn (TA)	HALLAMS

The Remaining Corps and Services:

The Army Air Corps (AAC)

The AAC was founded on 21st December 1941 and was a combatant corps comprising two (later three) new large regiments that had been founded because of the new conditions of World War 2. These were, in order of precedence, the Glider Pilot Regiment, the Parachute Regiment, and from March 1944, the Special Air Service Regiment. The AAC, although not a deployable formation or headquarters in its own right, was in every sense one of the combatant arms of the army as all three components existed solely to conduct frontline – and frequently behind the frontline – operations. The corps was disbanded in 1949 before being reformed in 1957.

The Royal Army Chaplains' Department (RAChD)

The department provided chaplaincy and pastoral services to the army. It was an all-officer volunteer unit, recruiting only from already ordained ministers; the majority of these were "war only" posts, intended to fill the huge need for chaplains in a much-expanded army. Most units of regimental/battalion size were authorised to have one chaplain on strength, who was invariably referred to as "Padre". Although the majority of chaplains were from the Church of England (Anglo-Protestant), a substantial percentage came from other faiths, including Roman Catholic, Church of Scotland, Presbyterian, as well as Jewish, Baptist, and others. All non-CofE chaplains were identified by initials after their rank to indicate their faith. As well as their religious duties, many chaplains also provided a welfare function, acting as an "independent listener" to give soldiers someone to turn to in hour of need. As such, many (but not all) believed that they remained men of God foremost and officers second, and so occupied a privileged position, managing to be both within and outside the chain of command at the same time. On operations many chaplains performed acts of great gallantry; they were also responsible for the collection and temporary burial of the dead. In some units, chaplains insisted that they be the only person to collect and administer to the dead, in order to shield soldiers, as far as possible, from seeing the often-mutilated remains of their friends and comrades.

Although the rank insignia worn by chaplains used the same system as other commissioned officers, their rank was based on a graduated system of *Chaplains to the Forces*. The highest appointment was the Chaplain General to the Forces (CGF), the equivalent of a Major General. The largest formations and commands etc might be provided with a Deputy Chaplain General to the Forces (DCGF), who was a Grade 1 or CF1, the equivalent of a Colonel. Intermediate formations would have a Chaplain to the Forces Grade 2 (CF2), the equivalent of Lieutenant Colonel. Above unit level, Divisions would typically employ a Chaplain to the Forces Grade 3 (CF3), the equivalent of a Major. Chaplain to the Forces Grade 4 (CF4) was the equivalent of a Captain, and by far the most numerous rank held within the department; almost all unit Padres were CF4.

The Royal Army Service Corps (RASC)

Responsible for aspects of both supply and transport (ST), the RASC was another enormous corps with diverse responsibilities. In terms of supply, to delineate it from functions of the RAOC, it was generally responsible for expendable stores (such as fuel, rations and fodder), rather than items of a more permanent (accountable) nature which were the responsibility of the RAOC. In terms of transport, in the inter-war years it had managed the transition from a largely horsed to an almost entirely wheeled transport organisation, although during WW2 it did once again become responsible for some horse, donkey, and mule transport in various theatres. Its basic element was the company, and these were generally on the establishment of, and controlled by, divisions and larger formations, although brigade companies were not unknown.

Like the RE, RAOC and REME, the RASC was a very large organisation with a huge remit; as well as the motor transport function always associated with this corps, the RASC was also responsible for a great number of other aspects of supply and transportation, including:

Air Despatch
Ambulance transport
Ammunition (storage and supply)
Animal fodder

Barrack services
Firefighting services
Food & rations (including operating bakeries, butcheries and cold storage depots)
Fuel, oils and lubricants (storage & distribution)
Stationery and publications (general service)
Transport (excluding those under the responsibility of the RE)
Tipper operations
Water transportation

Additionally, it also took under its wing the Army Catering Corps (ACC) when it was founded in 1941 – a clear example of a "corps within a corps".[32] It was also responsible for the Entertainment National Service Association (ENSA), delivering (supposedly!) morale-lifting entertainment for the troops, and also NAAFI and its deployable arm, EFI.[33] Listed amongst the trades within the corps were butcher, coppersmith, blacksmith and turners, as well as drivers and mechanics.

The Royal Army Medical Corps (RAMC)

The RAMC had performed exceptionally well during WW1, and it was to the country's credit that this aspect of military service was highly valued. During WW2, nearly 20,000 officers and soldiers served in the corps, not only as doctors and surgeons, but also as medical assistants and orderlies, laboratory technicians, radiographers, and in the management of specialist medical equipment and supplies, including pharmaceuticals. At the tactical level, the basic unit supporting formations was the field ambulance, although individual RAMC doctors would be found attached to all major units as their Regimental Medical Officer (RMO), assisted by a small party of soldiers, normally belonging to the unit; these included stretcher bearers and orderlies. The casualty reception and evacuation systems were based on the experience gained during WW1, and always attempted to give the most appropriate treatment as close to the location of wounding as possible, with the intention of quickly treating lightly wounded soldiers in order to rapidly return them to their units, or to efficiently evacuate more seriously wounded personnel to surgical units and/or hospitals. As well as field surgical units (FSU) and general and base hospitals, forward detachments of the RAMC included field dressing stations (FDS) and casualty clearing stations (CCS).

Another often overlooked but important aspect of the corps' duties was hygiene and sanitation, including the testing of water to make sure that it was potable; this was the responsibility of numerous NCO-led field hygiene sections. Anti-malarial control units were to be found in tropical areas, as well as specialist detachments dealing with such unpleasant ailments as venereal disease (one assumes that few wanted to be posted to No 1 Combined VD Treatment Centre), scabies and other diseases and infestations. Field transfusion units, convalescent depots, dermatology, psychiatric, ophthalmological, radiological and orthopaedic services (amongst others) were also provided, with many specialists in these fields being commissioned into the corps for the duration of the conflict to provide the expertise required. It was also one of the very few corps to include women within its ranks, as from March 1942 the first of hundreds of qualified female doctors became medical officers for the duration, although not in frontline units; the intention was to free up the younger, fitter male officers for service in field force units. By 1944 female doctors made up 3.6% of the total. By May 1945, there were around 11,400 medical officers of both sexes serving in the corps, 75% of whom were employed either as RMOs or in field units such as field hospitals, casualty clearing stations, and field ambulances.[34]

The Royal Army Ordnance Corps (RAOC)

Between the wars, the RAOC in the United Kingdom maintained half a dozen large specialist depots for the storage of different commodities, including vehicles, weapons, clothing, and even paint. In 1937, a new and huge Central Ordnance Depot (COD) was opened on the site of a First World War ammunition factory at Chilwell, Nottingham, which became used mainly for the storage of the expanding fleet of vehicles. At this time the corps was actively investigating the latest and most scientific methods of conducting its business and was revising many of its old practices (some of which predated the Boer War), based on the latest civilian techniques and systems for storage and distribution. Another COD at Branston in Staffordshire, previously a machine-gun factory, was opened in 1938, and this became the main depot for the supply of clothing and associated ancillaries, such as material, boots and boot laces, buttons, wellington boots, and later, the famous demob suits. By September 1939, five CODs were in operation and being run by the RAOC: these two, plus the older sites at Didcot, Weedon and Woolwich, as well as the Central Ammunition Depot (CAD) at Bramley. During WW2 the huge expansion of the army meant that many other depots on this scale were needed, including the enormous COD at Bicester (specifically to support Operation OVERLORD), and others at Donnington and Greenford, plus CADs at Monkton Farleigh/Corsham, Nesscliffe, Kineton, and Longtown.

From these hubs the RAOC managed a complicated network of ordnance depots, sub-depots, parks and sub-units, responsible for the receipt of tens of thousands of items of war stores; the corps looked after their subsequent storage and then supply to the troops. Until the formation of REME in late 1942, the RAOC was largely responsible for the maintenance and repair of the majority of vehicles in the army, which included an extensive workshop organisation, both in the rear areas and closer to the front lines. Even after these functions had mainly passed to the REME, the RAOC continued to be responsible for an astonishing range of aspects of both supply and repair, including the following:

Accommodation stores
Ammunition and explosives (technical aspects)
Clothing and personal equipment

Equipment & vehicle repair (until formation of REME in 1942)
General Service (GS) and miscellaneous stores
Kinematography
Medical, dental & veterinary stores
Mobile Laundry and Bath Units
Painting
Salvage
Supplies (non-expendable stores)
Spares and spare parts
Small arms and non-RA weapons
Tools

The majority of RAOC troops therefore formed part of a huge and remarkably efficient network that existed solely to keep the army supplied and maintained, in close cooperation with the RASC and later REME. Its units and sub-units could therefore vary in size from a small detachment under an NCO, to huge workshops, ordinance field parks and depots, staffed by hundreds or even thousands of personnel.

The Royal Electrical and Mechanical Engineers (REME)

REME was created by Royal Warrant on 1st October 1942. The corps was created because of the expanding need for technical tradesmen and units to support the maintenance and repair of vehicles, weapons, and other equipment. Upon formation, REME took responsibility for such tasks for the majority of the army, although some specialist items remained the responsibility of individual corps and services, particularly within the RE, R Signals and RASC, who maintained their own tradesmen for this purpose.[35] The members of the new corps came from a variety of cap badges, including RASC, RAOC and RE. In forming the new corps, the RAOC lost about 60% of its strength; on formation, REME was about 1% ex-RE, 4% ex-RASC, and 95% ex-RAOC.[36] It should be noted that not all tradesmen immediately became members of REME, with many remaining badged as RAC, RA, RE and R Signals until the early 1950s.

The REME repair organisation in the field during WW2 was based upon dividing the repair of equipment into progressive stages known as echelons (or lines). At each stage, REME units operated either as part of an existing formation or unit (First echelon), or as self-contained REME units commanded by a REME officer (the other three). The main method used to decide which echelon should do the repair was the time that such a repair would take. In general terms, the more difficult or complex a repair, the further back it would take place. The four "stages of repair" were as follows:

First (1st) echelon. Work at this level was limited to fairly minor repairs, replacements and adjustments, which could be quickly completed within unit lines. The first echelon was also responsible for immediate (battlefield) vehicle recovery. The term Light Aid Detachment (LAD) was (and is) used to indicate a small mobile sub-unit operating at this level, designed to support a mechanized unit (eg armoured), and which did not possess full workshop facilities.[37]

Second (2nd) echelon. Within this echelon, most repairs were conducted at a workshop by the replacement of assemblies, although other repairs could be undertaken, provided they could be completed using the equipment and personnel available in the workshop and within a defined period of time.

Third (3rd) echelon. Within this echelon, assemblies that had been removed at second echelon were repaired, usually by replacing the defective components with new, reconditioned, or, in some cases salvaged, parts. Third echelon work also included the replacement of those assemblies which could not be removed or repaired at second echelon, because of the time, special tools, or technical ability required.

Fourth (4th) echelon. All other repairs, the most complex, were completed in fourth echelon, limited only by time, workshop facilities, availability of spare parts and personnel, as well as by consideration of the economic effectiveness of such repairs. One Base Workshop to conduct such repairs was usually provided for each Army (or equivalent).[38]

The Royal Army Veterinary Corps (RAVC)

The process of mechanisation between the wars saw the RAVC reduce in size hugely. By the start of World War 2 the corps numbered less than 200 personnel. However, the scale of the conflict and an unforeseen need to provide horse, mule, donkey (and sometimes camel) transportation in difficult (especially mountainous) terrain, as well as the need to look after the army's guard and explosive-search dogs, lead to an expansion, until by the end of the conflict there were over 500 officers and nearly 4000 other ranks.[39] The majority of the officers were trained veterinary surgeons, whilst the other ranks provided clerical supporting services and veterinary assistance, meaning farriers and the like. The corps also assumed responsibility for what was known as remount services, in other words the replacement of transportation animals. The corps depot, also known as No 1 Reserve Veterinary Hospital Depot and Training Establishment, was moved from Woolwich in 1939 to Doncaster racecourse, where it remained for the rest of the war.

The Small Arms School Corps (SASC)

One of the smaller corps of the army, the SASC were responsible for the efficient handling and operation of small arms, usually defined as weapons below 1" in calibre, although this somewhat limited definition expanded to include such items as infantry anti-tank weapons and light mortars; the Royal Artillery remained overall responsible for larger guns and howitzers. As well as responsibility for devising the most effective and safe drills for operating these weapons, the corps was also responsible for the provision of courses of instruction for unit weapon training instructors. Because of its unhealthy proximity to occupied Europe, the corps moved from its traditional home at Hythe in Kent to Pendine in South Wales in the autumn of 1940 for the duration of the war.

The Military Provost Staff Corps (MPSC)

The MPSC were the military's professional custodians in military prisons and detention barracks. Effectively a non-combatant corps, the MPSC was almost invisible to the most of the army, save those who found themselves undergoing periods of military detention.[40] The MPSC was not responsible for the running of prisoner of war camps, which had their own department within the War Office.

The Army Educational Corps (AEC)

Education in the British Army was seen as somewhat distinct from general military training, which remained the remit of the general staff as well as the individual corps and services. The AEC was only established in June 1920, following experience gained in WW1. Initially, the majority of the members of the AEC were sergeants, who were either qualified teachers or university graduates. During the conflict, the corps was able to expand into a number of other areas, including assisting with regular current affairs (CA) sessions, designed to explain to troops why the war was being fought. Towards the very end of the war, the corps became heavily involved in the provision of educational and technical courses to prepare millions of men for their return to civilian occupations.

The Army Dental Corps (ADC)

Working closely with, but sometimes independently of, the RAMC, the ADC looked after the army's dental health. The majority of the officers were trained dentists, with other ranks providing the necessary technical, clerical, and administrative support. The need for dental services that could operate close to the front line led to the establishment of multiple small mobile field dental units (MFDU), and further to the rear, dental centres and dental laboratories were also used.

The Corps of Military Police (CMP)

The CMP was formed in February 1926 by the amalgamation of the military mounted and foot police. Between 1939 and 1945 the size of the corps increased twelve-fold, from around 4000 to over 50,000. As well as their standard "red cap" provost responsibilities (meaning general policing), from 1941 the CMP were also responsible for vulnerable point (VP) protection – looking after the security and access control of specific important locations and establishments, with its members wearing Oxford blue cloth covers on their service dress caps. The CMP was also responsible for traffic control, a huge undertaking, and also field security and special investigations – a special investigation branch (SIB) was formed to investigate the most serious or complicated crimes. Numerous field security sections (FSS) were deployed; personnel in these units wore Lincoln green cap covers and referred to themselves either as "green caps" or as field security police (FSP), to differentiate themselves from the unloved red caps.[41] In July 1940, the field security units were absorbed into the Intelligence Corps. The senior military policeman in the army was known as the provost marshal (PM), with assistant provost marshals (APM) deployed in support of formations and other commands.[42]

The Royal Army Pay Corps (RAPC)

All officers and soldiers in the army were paid (unless serving a period of detention without pay), and an extremely complex system of allowances was also in operation; both of these functions required the attentions of specialists, and this was provided by the RAPC. All officers within the corps were qualified as paymasters and NCOs as cashiers, with their appointment depending upon their rank, seniority, and of course ability. These paymasters and cashiers operated from hundreds of field, area, and base cash offices, attached to formations and commands. As well as pay and allowances, these cash offices also oversaw the financial transactions conducted by field post offices, service canteens, NAAFI/EFI and the like. By the end of the war, the RAPC was some 20,000 strong, assisted by 13,000 women from the ATS and over 6,000 civilian assistants.

The Pioneer Corps (PNR Corps)

The corps was only formed in 1939, although its predecessor during WW1, the Labour Corps, had once had a strength of over one third of a million men. In October 1939, the Auxiliary Military Pioneer Corps (AMPC) was constituted, and on 22nd November 1940 it was renamed as the Pioneer Corps. Possibly the least glamorous corps in the army order of battle, the Pioneer Corps was seen as a general source of labour for those who needed unskilled or semi-skilled manpower. This could be loading and unloading trucks, ships, and railway coaches, or assisting with construction tasks, especially the provision of manual labour and digging, as well as general carrying ("porterage") tasks. In addition to unskilled labour, pioneer units often became proficient in any number of light engineering and construction tasks and were capable of building defensive works and gun emplacements, as well as assisting with repairing railways, building airfields, and constructing wire entanglements and even dummy minefields. The basic unit was the company, and these were numbered from 1 to (at least) 979; some were armed, others unarmed.[43] The corps was also responsible for a number of non-combatant corps companies, as well as bath and laundry units. A critical task performed by many members of the corps in the lead up to D-Day was assisting in the waterproofing of vehicles for the invasion. During the Normandy landings, 23 pioneer companies with nearly 7,000 personnel landed, making clear the importance of the responsibilities of the pioneers in an active theatre. By the end of the war, the corps numbered around 180,000 British personnel, with another 400,000 in the affiliated corps from the Commonwealth and elsewhere.

The Intelligence Corps (INT Corps)

Despite the successful inclusion of intelligence staff during the First World War, at the end of that conflict the British Army did away with the units and personnel tasked with that most important function. When the BEF deployed to France in 1939, it therefore did so without the support of a professional intelligence branch. It was not until 19th July 1940, under the terms of AO 112/40, that an Intelligence Corps was returned to the order of battle. By the end of the war, it numbered nearly 10,000 personnel, of which around 30% were officers. Unusually, personnel wanting to be officers in the corps and going through the OCTU commissioning route could not volunteer; rather, they were individually identified during training by a branch of Military Intelligence from the War Office and offered the corps. The basic building block of the corps was the field security section (FSS), which usually operated at divisional level. As well as the general intelligence work required to assess the enemy's strength and intentions, the corps was also involved in photographic interpretation and signals intercept, as well as providing many linguists for interrogations and in-country liaison etc. Because of its clear relationship to security, censorship policy was also within the remit of the Intelligence Corps.

The Army Physical Training Corps (APTC)

Another small corps, the APTC was responsible for setting the standards for, and delivering, physical training and education throughout the army. In practice, the majority of physical education within units was given by assistant physical training instructors who had undergone short courses run by the APTC.

The General Service Corps (GSC)

Only formed in February 1942, from July of that year all recruits into the army wore the GSC cap badge when they underwent the first few (usually six) weeks of their initial military training, and before they were posted to their subsequent regiment or corps for specialist training and re-badged as a result. Additionally, some other personnel, mainly officers, with specialist skills and who appeared on either the Special List or the General List (parts of the Army List) were allocated to the GSC permanently.

The Queen Alexandra's Imperial Military Nursing Service (QAIMNS)

The QAIMNS was an all-officer, all-female corps. Before 1926, these nurses had enjoyed some of the privileges of officer status, but it was not until that year that they were granted the equivalent rank with army officers, although they still did not hold a King's Commission...yet.[44] Entrants to the corps came in as already qualified and registered nurses; it was not until 1950 that non-commissioned nurses were admitted into the corps. At the start of World War 2 there were fewer than 700 regular nurses in the service;

the first contingent of six sailed to France with the BEF one week after the outbreak of the war. In order to increase the size of the service, the members of the Territorial Auxiliary Nursing Service (TANS), the TA element, were mobilized and in effect drafted into the corps, although the Army List continue to administer them as though they were a separate entity for the remainder of the conflict.

They subsequently served in almost all theatres of war, providing the nursing services in RAMC hospitals, but some found themselves operating much further forward, particularly in casualty clearing stations. On the last day of April 1941, the King gave somewhat belated approval for the members of the corps to wear their relative rank badges on their uniforms. In September 1941, emergency (war-time only) commissions were granted, and a request for permanent commissions for the regulars was submitted. Strangely, it was not until January 1944 that the nurses were officially authorised to wear khaki battle dress (as much because of the problems of obtaining the correct material in wartime as of dealing with the practicalities of working close to the frontline in an active combat zone); until then the striking but unsuitable grey ward dress (with scarlet capes) was frequently worn, topped with a steel helmet where necessary.

The corps was led by the Matron-in-Chief (a brigadier equivalent), a couple of Chief Principal Matrons (colonels), backed up by a few Principal Matrons (lieutenant colonels) about three dozen Matrons (majors, on the scale of one per hospital), although the vast majority were the Sisters-in Charge, assistant Matrons and Sisters with ten years' service (all captains), as well as all other Sisters (lieutenants). The collective noun 'nursing officers' was introduced for the cohort as a whole. On 1 September 1945 the total number of nursing officers of all ranks stood at 11,024.

The Auxiliary Territorial Service (ATS)

With war looming, in September 1938 it was decided to form a noncombatant all-female component of the Territorial Army, known as the ATS.[45] From 10th April 1941, members of the service were granted full military status, officers held the King's Commission, and by September some 65,000 women were in ATS service.[46] When wartime conscription was extended in December 1941, almost all (unmarried) women conscripted into the army joined the ATS. Roles undertaken included secretarial and clerical support, telephony, catering, stewarding, administration, storage and supply, provost, and transport drivers, including motorcycles and ambulances. Additionally, many members served with anti-aircraft units in the air defence of Great Britain; they were involved in the operation of searchlights and barrage balloons and could act as plotters, operate radar, or set fuzes on the ammunition, but were not allowed to actually fire the guns! By the end of the war around a quarter of a million women had served in the ATS, including Honorary 2nd Subaltern HRH The Princess Elizabeth, who was gazetted on 24th February 1945.[47]

And Finally...

Listed below are just a sample of the many and varied miscellaneous army units, sub-units and detachments needed to support the field army during a global conflict, including those from the wider Commonwealth. None of these possess the cachet attached to a combat unit, but all had their part to play. Unfortunately, for the identification of such units, the War Office lists of these generally failed to indicate which corps they belonged to, probably believing at the time that this information was self-evident. In some cases, their ownership can be inferred, but with many it remains open to interpretation.

1 Indian Military Dairy Farm
No 1 Ethiopian Camel Unit
No 5 Travelling Recruiting Centre (Syria)
3 Mobile Duplicating Section
No 23 Indian Cattle Conducting Section
94 Compressed Gas Depot
101 Tyre Resoling Unit
104 Officers' Mess Cooks School
207 Independent Oxygen & Acetylene Generating Company
English Language Instruction Pool (Polish Forces)
Inspectorate of Penal Establishments Middle East
Meat Inspection Pool RAVC
POW Censorship Unit
The Typewriter Depot & Pool
Wheat Collection Scheme Syria (Spears Mission MEF)

Part 5

RANKS

Ranks and Appointments

The army system of ranks was well established but was made complicated by different terminology used by different regiments, corps and arms. Appointments, on the other hand, related to an actual post or position given to an individual, which was often allied to a specific rank. For example, a battalion or regiment would invariably be commanded by a lieutenant colonel.[1] His regimental sergeant major (appointment) would be held by a warrant officer class I (rank).

British Army ranks were subdivided into two main categories: firstly, other ranks (OR), which included private soldiers (those holding no rank), non-commissioned officers (NCO, lance corporals or equivalent up to staff sergeant or equivalent), and warrant officers (WO); and secondly, commissioned officers (from second lieutenant up to field marshal).[2]

Within the ranks of commissioned officers, captains and below were known as subalterns, majors to colonels were classified as field officers, and brigadiers up to field marshals were classified as general officers.[3] The basic ranks were as follows:

Rank	Category	Sub-category
Private	OR	
Lance Corporal	OR	NCO
Corporal	OR	NCO
Lance Sergeant	OR	NCO
Sergeant	OR	NCO
Staff Sergeant	OR	NCO
Warrant Officer III	OR	WO
Warrant Officer II	OR	WO
Warrant Officer I	OR	WO

Rank		
Second Lieutenant[4]	OFFICER	SUBALTERN
(First) Lieutenant	OFFICER	SUBALTERN
Captain	OFFICER	SUBALTERN
Major	OFFICER	FIELD OFFICER
Lieutenant Colonel	OFFICER	FIELD OFFICER
Colonel	OFFICER	FIELD OFFICER
Brigadier	OFFICER	GENERAL OFFICER
Major General	OFFICER	GENERAL OFFICER
Lieutenant General	OFFICER	GENERAL OFFICER
General	OFFICER	GENERAL OFFICER
Field Marshal	OFFICER	GENERAL OFFICER

However, this is not the end of the story, as many different regiments amended the ranks shown above and use their own terminology, particularly for the non-commissioned ranks. A private soldier could therefore also be called a trooper, gunner, sapper, signalman, guardsman, fusilier, kingsman, rifleman, driver, craftsman, musician, bugler, drummer, or piper, dependent on his regiment or corps and his specific job. A lance corporal in the Royal Artillery would be known as a lance bombardier, and a (full) corporal in the same corps would be known as a bombardier.[5] Lance Sergeant was a strange rank, in that the paid rank of the holder would be corporal, but three stripes would be worn; in effect, the holder would wear the three stripes of a sergeant and carry out the same job whilst being paid as a corporal, and in terms of seniority fell between the two. To make things as difficult as possible, even the spelling of certain ranks varied throughout the army. In the majority of cases in the period, the rank of serjeant was spelt with a J, although increasingly, the alternative spelling of sergeant came into use; there was no obvious rhyme or reason to this, other than certain regiments prefer to do things one way and others in a different way – this statement neatly sums up the British Army!

In the infantry the rank of staff sergeant was not used, with colour sergeant being used in its place. Above the rank of staff/colour sergeant were three classes of Warrant Officer. Warrant Officer III was something of an anomaly, as the rank was only introduced in October 1938 in an attempt to use warrant officers to fill some junior officers' appointments at troop or platoon level. These appointments were platoon sergeant major (in place of a platoon commander in the infantry), troop sergeant major (in place of a troop leader in the RAC), and section sergeant major in place of a section leader in some other corps. The experiment was not successful, and the rank was suspended by ACI 804 of 1940. Those WOIII still serving retained that rank were promoted or were discharged, so that the numbers holding the rank gradually diminished as the war progressed. Warrant Officers were referred to as "Sir" by other ranks below them (so a WOIII would call a

WOII "Sir") but were called either "sergeant major" or "mister (plus their surname)" by officers.

The Household Cavalry had historically not used the rank of sergeant (apparently believing that the root of the word equated to that of servant) and instead called all of their non-commissioned ranks corporals. Instead of a (full) corporal, the rank of lance corporal of horse was used. The equivalent of sergeant was corporal of horse; the equivalent of staff sergeant was staff corporal, and sergeant majors were known as corporal majors.[6]

Both other ranks and officers were able to be temporarily placed into positions requiring a rank higher than that which they officially held. There were various versions of this. The first was known as *local* (in which the holder could only use the rank within the organisation in which he was employed, and therefore if, for example, he was sent away to go on a course, he would (should) revert to his normal substantive rank. *Acting rank* was in many ways seen as a stepping stone to a promotion to substantive rank, and if granted could be used by the holder even if he went away from his own unit; acting rank was used for personnel "called upon to perform the duties of a rank or appointment higher than their substantive rank". Another option was *temporary rank* (more usually applied to officers than ORs), and granted only after holding acting rank for a specified period of time (three months up to and including lieutenant colonels, six months for colonels, and one year for major generals and above).[7] Once temporary rank was granted, the holder automatically became war substantive at one level below, so a lieutenant becoming a temporary major automatically became W/S captain.

Substantive rank was what the ambitious soldier or officer aspired to, as this made the rank permanent and official in every respect. Pay for the rank came automatically with the latter promotion, but with the others, it would have to be stated whether the rank worn was paid or unpaid. So, for example, two soldiers could both be acting corporals, but one could be paid as that rank and the other unpaid.[8] This difference would be known to the clerical and administrative system but would not be obvious just by looking at the soldiers; the rank they wore on their sleeves would look exactly the same and their levels of responsibility would be the same. The other facet of this system of local, acting, temporary, and substantive rank related to the disciplinary procedures should they be accused of an offence. Local and acting ranks were much easier to remove than temporary and particularly substantive ranks; the Army Act specified the circumstances and offences for which rank could be removed, and by whom.[9] As already noted, appointments were different to ranks, although they were related in that most appointments were intended to be filled by a specified rank. For example, the regimental adjutant (appointment) was normally filled by a captain (rank). A divisional commander (appointment) would usually be a major general (rank). In order to meet these requirements therefore, the use of local, acting and temporary ranks was a very useful tool in wartime when the army was expanding rapidly, and particularly when untried and relatively junior replacements had to be found quickly.

Brevet rank was an unusual system and only applied to officers. All officers belonged to a seniority roll within their own regiment or corps, recorded in the Army List. This seniority was based upon such things as their commissioning date, length of service, and subsequent promotions. Regular officers in particular would know exactly where they stood in relation to their peers. But the demands of wartime meant that such seniority could be – and often was – ignored, in order to fast-track those officers seen as the most suitable for higher appointments. It was not unknown for a major general commanding a division to hold the substantive rank of lieutenant colonel. Complicating this process was a decades-old system known as brevet promotion. This was a method of rewarding extraordinary or outstanding service, by granting the officer the right to wear the rank and use the privileges of a rank above their substantive one; it is probable this applied mostly to majors being granted the rank of brevet lieutenant colonel. Although not affecting their seniority as such, the holding of brevet rank would obviously be advantageous when their superiors were looking for officers to promote, and as such was a useful stepping stone, which often led to them being confirmed in the higher rank. It did lead to some anomalies: for example, a unit commanded by a temporary lieutenant colonel could have as its second-in-command a major holding the rank of brevet lieutenant colonel. There can be no doubt that frictions could sometimes be caused by this system, but on the whole, it would appear that everyone understood the "rules of the game".[10]

Rank and other Badges

The whole system of badges used by the British Army during World War 2 is immensely complicated and worthy of the many detailed volumes that have been devoted to the subject. What follows here is a brief overview.

With regard to the officers' rank badges, the placement was generally on each shoulder epaulette with a one-inch space between each emblem. Stars (almost universally referred to as 'pips') measured one inch by one inch, and crowns 1½ inches by 1½ inches. Most units used cloth (worsted) emblems while others preferred metal, and the size and colour could vary. For example, rifle regiments used black insignia, and the Household Cavalry and Foot Guards used their own ornate versions of emblems particular to each regiment. When the British Expeditionary Force deployed to France in late 1939 and early 1940 wearing the new battle dress, few additional emblems were allowed to be worn. One of the lessons picked up from the returning soldiers post-Dunkirk was that it was very difficult not only to identify officers but also individual units, regiments, and corps; this could – and did – cause unnecessary confusion on the battlefield. Therefore, from September 1940 a system of coloured felt shapes were adopted to provide an outline or backing for officers' rank badges. These measured approximately

¼ of an inch larger than the pip or crown, and different colours were used for different regiments and corps as follows:

Colour	Used By
Red	General Staff, RA, CMP, RAOC, Pioneer Corps
Yellow	RAC, RASC, RAPC, ACC
Scarlet	Line Infantry, General List
Cherry	RAMC
Blue	RE, RCS, REME
Cambridge Blue	AAC (inc GPR, Para Regt), AEC
Green	Recce Corps, ADC, Intelligence Corps
Black	APTC
Black on Rifle Green	Rifle regiments
Black on Red	KRRC
Black on Purple	RAChD

Other ranks' rank badges were normally worn on the upper arm or the forearm. The system for lance corporals, corporals, sergeants, and staff sergeants (and equivalents) was based on a number of chevrons usually referred to as stripes. (In the RAOC catalogue of uniform items, these were officially referred to as "Chevrons Worsted SD", and were further broken down as "1-bar, 2-bar, and 3-bar".) A lance corporal wore one, a corporal two, a sergeant three, and a staff sergeant used three stripes with a crown above. Warrant officers wore their ranks on the forearm, with a WOIII wearing a plain crown, a WOII a crown surrounded by a wreath of laurel leaves, and a WOI the royal coat of arms. WOIs carrying out certain appointments, for example a conductor in the RAOC or a regimental sergeant major in the foot guards, wore particularly elaborate versions of these. For full details of all other badges, including cap and collar badges, formation signs, and specific trades and qualification badges, the appropriate authoritative books should be consulted.

From September 1940 a system of curved, coloured shoulder titles was also adopted for use by all ranks (not just the officers), and these were worn at the top of each sleeve immediately under the epaulette seam. Again, these varied in colour according to the unit involved. For example, the RAC used ROYAL ARMOURED CORPS in red lettering on a yellow background, and the RA used ROYAL ARTILLERY in red on a blue background. Most line infantry regiments and battalions used white on a scarlet backing. It should be noted that the abbreviations used on the shoulder straps were often different to the official abbreviations used in correspondence and noted above. Some units managed to get away with using different colour combinations, usually citing historical significance; for example Rifles units could use grey, yellow or black lettering on a rifle green backing.

Finally, another method of identifying a regiment or corps came in the form of small cloth 'Arm of Service' strips which were also introduced in late 1940 and worn by all ranks on the arms. These were single or multi-coloured strips, two inches long and half an inch deep, and they were worn on both sleeves of battle dress and KD, immediately below the formation badge; the colours chosen often had historical links and were generally allied to the coloured cloth backings used for officers' rank badges.

Anomalies

The Auxiliary Territorial Service used a non-standard rank system unique to itself. This reflected its unusual status as a female service. Many of the staunchly conservative senior ranks were against any form of parity with their male counterparts and insisted that this be reflected in the way that the ATS was structured. As a result, the rank structure for officers was similar, but not identical to, the male part of the army, as the table below demonstrates. Privates and the NCO and WO ranks were the same as the male equivalent, although many official documents referred to the non-commissioned elements as "auxiliaries", rather than as "other ranks".

The ATS was officially part of the Territorial Army, and members received less pay than male soldiers, approximately 2/3 of the full rate (and 4/5 of the male ration allowance!). It was not until April 1941 that the ATS was given full military status, meaning that its members would be subject to normal military discipline, and existing regulations were rewritten to reflect this amendment; it was from this point that female officers now held the King's Commission. The only other parts of the army with women serving in their ranks were the Queen Alexandra's Imperial Military Nursing Service (QAIMNS, a wholly-female corps), a few hundred medical and dental officers (RAMC and ADC, from 1941), and all the members of the Women's Transport Service, aka the First Aid Nursing Yeomanry or FANY; all of these corps wore the normal military ranks.

Although in terms of date of formation FANY was senior to the ATS, during WW2 the much larger ATS effectively subsumed the FANY. In September 1938, FANY personnel had formed the Motor Driver Companies of the ATS, then known as the Women's Transport Service. Within the WTS, Officer Cadet and Second Lieutenant were known as Cadet Ensign and Ensign respectively. Lieutenant and Captain used those titles, however, Major, Lieutenant Colonel and Colonel were called Commander, Staff Commander and Commandant respectively. Why? It's a good question…

The equivalent of ATS commissioned officer's ranks both before and after the June 1941 amendment were as follows:[11]

Ats Rank (From Jun 41)	Abbreviation	Pre-1941	Army Equivalent
Chief Controller	(C contr)	Chief Controller	Major General
Senior Controller	(S contr)	Senior Controller	Brigadier
Controller	(Contr)	Controller	Colonel

Ats Rank (From Jun 41)	Abbreviation	Pre-1941	Army Equivalent
Chief Commander	(C comd)	Chief Commandant	Lieutenant Colonel
Senior Commander	(S comd)	Senior Commandant	Major
Junior Commander	(J comd)	Company Commander	Captain
Subaltern	(Sub)	Deputy Company Commander	Lieutenant
Second Subaltern	(2 sub)	Company Assistant	2nd Lieutenant

Despite the different terminology, the same rank insignia was worn on uniforms as for male officers. In the 1945 Army List of ATS commissioned officers, there is only one Chief Controller, two Senior Controllers, and eighteen Controllers. No other ranks are listed other than Second Subaltern. Therefore, it seems that all the appointments between Chief Commander and Subaltern were filled by 2nd Subalterns in Local, Acting or Temporary ranks.

Part 6

BATTLE HONOURS

The awarding of battle honours had been around for nearly 300 years before World War 2, a means of recognising both the presence and contribution of a particular regiment in a specific battle or campaign. By WW2 the accumulation of battle honours was much prized and was seen as one of the main methods of gaining prestige, and a means of comparing the valour of a regiment with that of its neighbours and competitors. The system, like the awarding of medals and decorations, is full of problems and is often open to question. The first battle honour awarded to army regiments was that of TANGIER and was dated between 1662 and 1680. Almost immediately, this was controversial, as hindsight tells us that it was not in fact a battle at all, but rather an occupation and garrison affair, with only a few rather minor skirmishes rather than real battles. Only five regiments gained the honour (one of cavalry, two guards and two of line infantry) but the precedent was set. The system remains full of anomalies; for example, a battle honour could be gained by a single battalion of an infantry regiment comprising over a dozen battalions, but the whole of that regiment would in effect be awarded the same honour and be entitled to have it emblazoned upon their regimental colours. If a battle was decreed to be worthy of an honour, a single or detached company present at the action could also be awarded the self-same honour as if it were a larger unit, but this was not consistently applied. The Corps and Services were not entitled to accumulate battle honours – it was only the cavalry/yeomanry/armour, the infantry (including territorials and militia), and the Royal Marines who could. The Royal Artillery famously claim a single honour – UBIQUE – meaning *everywhere*, and although there is a large degree of truth in this, there are of course also many instances or battles where the "royal regiment" were not present; the same applies to the Royal Engineers.

When deciding exactly what should constitute an individual campaign or battle worthy of a formal honour, as opposed to a small engagement or skirmish, was always subjective. During WW2, even as the conflict was going on, it was clear to many that battle honours would be gained and awarded, but no-one could probably have foreseen the amount of time it would take for the official list to be published; it was not until late 1957 that confirmation was given of the names of the honours, and which units would receive them. Some individual campaigns seem to have been allocated a disproportionate number of honours: the most obvious example is that 67 were awarded for First Army operations in North Africa between 17th November 1942 and 30th April 1943 (a rate of one honour for every 2½ days of fighting), where the whole North African campaign fought by Eighth Army and its predecessors from 12th June 1940 to 9th May 1943 gained 83, a rate of one for every thirteen days of combat. It is hard to see why this was so.

Some of the campaign battle honours awarded included dozens of regiments; EL ALAMEIN was given to 42 British units, and NORTH WEST EUROPE 1944-45 went to no fewer than 92. Many other examples were awarded to a single regiment or battalion. During the course of World War 2, 589 battle honours were awarded to British army units. Listed here are all those which were awarded to at least one British unit – honours awarded only to Indian, Canadian (including Newfoundland & Labrador), Australian, New Zealand, African, South African and/or other nationalities have been excluded.[1] They are listed by active theatre and then chronology (date of the action or first day of action). Although they do not of themselves give a complete history of the British Army during World War 2, they are a useful guide to the geography, chronology, and intensity of that conflict.

NORWAY 1940 (21 Apr 1940 to 27 Dec 41)	
NORWAY 1940	21 Apr – 26 May 40
VIST	21 – 22 Apr 40
KVAM	25 – 26 Apr 40
OTTA	28 Apr 40
STIEN	17 – 18 May 40
POTHUS	25 – 26 May 40
VAAGSO	27 Dec 41
NORTH – WEST EUROPE 1940 – 1942 (10 May 1940 to 19 Aug 42)	
NORTH WEST EUROPE 1940 – 42	19 May 40 – 19 Aug 42
THE DYLE	10 – 16 May 40
SAAR	13 May 40
WITHDRAWAL TO THE ESCAUT	17 – 19 May 40
DEFENCE OF THE ESCAUT	19 – 22 May 40
DEFENCE OF ARRAS	19 – 24 May 40
AMIENS 1940	20 May 40
ARRAS COUNTERATTACK	21 May 40
BOULOGNE 1940	22 – 25 May 40
CALAIS 1940	22 – 26 May 40

FRENCH FRONTIER 1940	23 – 27 May 40
ST OMER – LA BASSEE	23 – 29 May 40
THE SOMME 1940	24 May – 5 Jun 40
YPRES – COMINES CANAL	26 – 28 May 40
DUNKIRK 1940	26 May – 3 Jun 40
CASSEL	27 – 29 May 40
FORET DE NIEPPE	27 – 28 May 40
WORMHOUDT	28 May 40
WITHDRAWAL TO THE SEINE	6 – 10 Jun 40
WITHDRAWAL TO CHERBOURG	9 – 18 Jun 40
ST VALERY-EN-CAUX	10 – 12 Jun 40
BRUNEVAL	27 – 28 Feb 42
ST NAZAIRE	27 – 28 Mar 42
DIEPPE	19 Aug 42
MALTA (11 Jun 1940 to 20 Nov 42)	
MALTA 1940 – 42	11 Jun 40 – 20 Nov 42
BRITISH SOMALILAND (4 Aug 40 to 17 Aug 40)	
BRITISH SOMALILAND 1940	4 – 17 Aug 40
BARKASAN	17 Aug 40
ABYSSINIA (10 Jan 41 to 28 Nov 41)	
ABYSSINIA 1940 – 41	13 Jun 40 – 28 Nov 41
JEBEL DALEIS	10 Jan 41
JEBEL SHIBA	21 – 23 Jan 41
GOGNI	26 Jan 41
BARENTU	27 Jan – 2 Feb 41
AGORDAT	28 Jan – 1 Feb 41
KEREN	3 Feb – 31 Mar 41
KARORA – MARSA TACIAL	9 – 10 Feb 41
CUBCUB	23 Feb 41
MESCELIT PASS	1 Mar 41
MOUNT ENGLAHAT	12 – 15 Mar 41
AD TECLESAN	30 – 31 Mar 41
MASSAWA	8 Apr 41
AMBA ALAGI	20 Apr – 16 May 41
GREECE (10 Apr 1941 to 29 Apr 41)	
GREECE 1941	10 – 29 Apr 41
VEVE	10 – 12 Apr 41
PROASTEION	13 Apr 41
IRAQ (2 May 1941 to 31 May 41)	
IRAQ 1941	2 – 31 May 41
DEFENCE OF HABBANIYA	2 – 6 May 41

FALLUJA	19 – 22 May 41
BAGHDAD 1941	28 – 31 May 41
CRETE (20 May 1941 to 1 Jun 41)	
CRETE	20 May – 1 Jun 41
CANEA	20 – 27 May 41
HERAKLION	20 – 29 May 41
RETIMO	20 – 30 May 41
WITHDRAWAL TO SPHAKIA	28 May – 1 Jun 41
SYRIA (9 Jun 1941 to 12 Jul 41)	
SYRIA 1941	7 Jun – 12 Jul 41
THE LITANI	9 – 10 Jun 41
MERJAYUN	9 – 27 Jun 41
PALMYRA	21 Jun – 3 Jul 41
JEBEL MAZAR	10 – 12 Jul 41
NORTH AFRICA – WESTERN DESERT/EIGHTH ARMY (12 Jun 1941 to 9 May 43)	
EGYPTIAN FRONTIER 1940	12 Jun – 12 Sep 40
WITHDRAWAL TO MATRUH	13 – 17 Sep 40
BIR ENBA	19 Nov 40
SIDI BARRANI	8 – 11 Dec 40
BUQ BUQ	11 Dec 40
BARDIA 1941	3 – 5 Jan 41
CAPTURE OF TOBRUK	21 – 22 Jan 41
BEDA FOMM	5 – 8 Feb 41
MERSA EL BREGA	31 Mar 41
AGEDABIA	2 Apr 41
DERNA AERODROME	7 Apr 41
DEFENCE OF TOBRUK	8 Apr – 10 Dec 41
HALFAYA 1941	15 – 27 May 41
SIDI SULEIMAN	15 – 17 Jun 41
TOBRUK 1941	18 Nov – 10 Dec 41
GUBI I	19 Nov 41
GABR SALEH	19 – 21 Nov 41
SIDI REZEGH 1941	19 – 23 Nov 41
TOBRUK SORTIE 1941	21 – 23 Nov 41
OMARA	22 Nov – 2 Dec 41
TALEB EL ESSOM	24 – 25 Nov 41
BELHAMED	25 Nov – 1 Dec 41
GUBI II	4 – 6 Dec 41
RELIEF OF TOBRUK 1941	7 – 10 Dec 41
ALEM HAMZA	14 – 16 Dec 41

CHOR EL SUFAN	27 – 30 Dec 41
MSUS	25 Jan 42
BENGHAZI	27 – 29 Jan 42
CARMUSA	29 Jan – 5 Feb 42
GAZALA	26 May – 21 Jun 42
RETMA	27 May 42
BIR EL IGELA	27 May 42
BIR EL ASLAGH	27 – 31 May 42
BIR HACHEIM	27 May – 11 Jun 42
THE CAULDRON	5 – 6 Jun 42
KNIGHTSBRIDGE	6 – 7 & 11 – 13 Jun 42
HAGLAG ER RAMI	11 – 13 Jun 42
GABR EL FACHRI	14 Jun 42
VIA BALBIA	14 Jun 42
ZT EL MRASSES	15 Jun 42
SIDI REZEGH 1942	17 Jun 42
TOBRUK 1942	20 – 21 Jun 42
MERSA MATRUH	26 – 30 Jun 42
POINT 174	27 Jun 42
MINQAR QAIM	27 – 28 Jun 42
FUKA	28 Jun 42
DEFENCE OF ALAMEIN LINE	1 – 27 Jul 42
DEIR EL SHEIN	1 Jul 42
RUWEISAT	2 – 4 Jul 42
FUKA AIRFIELD	7 Jul 42
POINT 93	11 Jul 42
RUWEISAT RIDGE	14 – 16 Jul 42
ALAM EL HALFA	30 Aug – 7 Sep 42
WEST POINT 23	1 Sep 42
BENGHAZI RAID	13 – 14 Sep 42
DEIR E MUNASSIB	30 Sep 42
EL ALAMEIN	23 Oct – 4 Nov 42
CAPTURE OF HALFAYA PASS 1942	10 – 11 Nov 42
EL AGHEILA	13 – 17 Nov 42
NOFILLA	17 – 18 Dec 42
ADVANCE ON TRIPOLI	15 – 23 Jan 43
MEDENINE	6 Mar 43
ZEMLET EL LEBENE	6 Mar 43
TADJERA KHIR	6 Mar 43
MARETH	16 – 23 Mar 43
WADI ZEUSS EAST	16 – 17 Mar 43

WADI ZIGZAOU	20 – 23 Mar 43
TEBAGA GAP	21 – 30 Mar 43
POINT 201 (ROMAN WALL)	21 – 22 Mar 43
EL HAMMA	27 – 29 Mar 43
MATMATA HILLS	25 – 28 Mar 43
AKARIT	6 – 7 Apr 43
DJEBEL EL MEIDA	6 Apr 43
WADI AKARIT EAST	6 – 7 Apr 43
DJEBEL ROUMANA	6 – 7 Apr 43
SEBKRET EN NOUAL	7 Apr 43
CHEBKET EN NOUIGES	8 Apr 43
DJEBEL EL TELIL	9 Apr 43
ENFIDAVILLE	19 – 29 Apr 43
TAKROUNA	20 – 21 Apr 43
DJEBEL GARCI	20 Apr 43
DJEBEL TEBAGA	8 – 9 May 43
MALAYA & SOUTH EAST ASIA (8 Dec 1941 to 9 Mar 42)	
MALAYA 1941 – 42	8 Dec 41 – 15 Feb 42
SOUTH EAST ASIA 1941 – 42	8 Dec 41 – 9 Mar 42
NORTH MALAYA	8 – 23 Dec 41
HONG KONG	8 – 25 Dec 41
GRIK ROAD	17 – 23 Dec 41
CENTRAL MALAYA	26 Dec 41 – 10 Jan 42
IPOH	26 – 29 Dec 41
KAMPAR	30 Dec 41 – 3 Jan 42
SLIM RIVER	7 Jan 42
JOHORE	14 – 31 Jan 42
THE MUAR	16 – 23 Jan 42
BATU PAHAT	21 – 26 Jan 42
SINGAPORE ISLAND	8 – 15 Feb 42
BURMA (16 Feb 1942 to 15 Aug 45)	
BURMA 1942 – 45	20 Jan 42 – 15 Aug 45
SITTANG 1942	16 – 23 Feb 42
PEGU 1942	6 – 7 Mar 42
TAUKYAN	7 – 8 Mar 42
PAUNGDE	28 – 30 Mar 42
YENANGYAUNG 1942	11 – 19 Apr 42
MONYWA 1942	30 Apr – 2 May 42
RATHEDAUNG	29 Dec 42 – 3 Feb 43
CHINDITS 1943	Jan – Jun 43
DONBAIK	8 Jan – 18 Mar 43

HTIZWE	6 – 16 Mar 43
POINT 201 (ARAKAN)	28 – 29 Mar 43
MAUNGDAW	1 Jan – 31 May 44
NORTH ARAKAN	1 Jan – 12 Jun 44
BUTHIDAUNG	16 Jan – 3 Feb & 5 Mar – 8 Apr 44
THE YU	18 – 20 Jan 44
RAZABIL	19 – 30 Jan & 10 – 17 Mar 44
CHINDITS 1944	Feb – Aug 44
NGAKEYDAUK PASS	4 Feb – 4 Mar 44
DEFENCE OF SINZWEYA	5 – 29 Feb 44
ALETHANGYAW	8 Mar – 15 Apr 44
TAMU ROAD	12 Mar – 4 Apr 44
IMPHAL	12 Mar – 22 Jun 44
MAYU TUNNELS	15 Mar – 20 Apr 44
SAKAWNG	18 – 25 Mar 44
KOHIMA	27 Mar – 22 Jun 44
SHENAM PASS	1 Apr – 22 Jun 44
POINT 551	3 Apr – 22 May 44
DEFENCE OF KOHIMA	4 – 18 Apr 44
NUNGSHIGUM	5 – 13 Apr 44
RELIEF OF KOHIMA	5 – 20 Apr 44
LITAN	12 Apr – 15 May 44
BISHENPUR	14 Apr – 22 Jun 44
KANGLATONGBI	21 Apr – 22 Jun 44
NAGA VILLAGE	4 May – 4 Jun 44
ARADURA	14 May – 6 Jun 44
MAO SONGSANG	15 – 19 Jun 44
UKHRUL	24 Jun – 20 Jul 44
TENGNOUPAL	21 – 28 Jul 44
KENNEDY PEAK	3 Oct – 7 Nov 44
PINWE	11 – 30 Nov 44
THE SHWELL	1 Jan – 12 Feb 45
SHWEBO	6 – 9 Jan 45
MONYWA 1945	7 – 22 Jan 45
KYAUKMYAUNG BRIDGEHEAD	9 Jan – 12 Feb 45
SAGAING	23 Jan – 12 Feb 45
ARAKAN BEACHES	12 Jan – 29 Apr 45
MYEBON	12 – 21 Jan 45
RAMREE	21 Jan – 15 Feb 45
KANGAW	23 Jan – 17 Feb 45
NYAUNGU BRIDGEHEAD	12 – 21 Feb 45

MYINMU BRIDGEHEAD	12 Feb – 7 Mar 45
MANDALAY	12 Feb – 21 Mar 45
MEIKTILA	12 Feb – 30 Mar 45
MYITSON	13 Feb – 9 Mar 45
AVA	13 Feb – 20 Mar 45
LETSE	23 Feb – 10 Apr 45
TAUNGTHA	24 Feb & 14 – 28 Mar 45
TAMANDU	27 Feb – 11 Mar 45
CAPTURE OF MEIKTILA	28 Feb – 2 Mar 45
DEFENCE OF MEIKTILA	3 – 29 Mar 45
KYAUKSE 1945	8 – 21 Mar 45
FORT DUFFERIN	9 – 20 Mar 45
MAYMYO	11 – 12 Mar 45
THE IRRAWADDY	29 Mar – 30 May 45
PYAWBWE	1 – 10 Apr 45
RANGOON ROAD	1 Apr – 6 May 45
MOUNT POPA	2 – 20 Apr 45
YENANGYAUNG 1945	18 – 25 Apr 45
TOUNGOO	22 Apr – 6 May 45
SITTANG 1945	10 May – 15 Aug 45
KAMA	20 – 30 May 45
MADAGASCAR (5 May 1942 to 6 Nov 42)	
MADAGASCAR	5 May 42 – 6 Nov 42
NORTH AFRICA – TUNISIA – FIRST ARMY (17 Nov 1942 to 30 Apr 43)	
DJEBEL ABLOD	17 Nov 42
SOUDIA	24 Nov 42
MEDJEZ EL BAB	25 – 26 Nov 42
TEBOURBA	27 Nov 42
DJEDEIDA	28 – 29 Nov 42
DJEBEL AZZAG 1942	28 – 30 Nov 42
OUDNA	29 Nov – 3 Dec 42
TEBOURBA GAP	1 – 10 Dec 42
LONGSTOP HILL 1942	23 – 25 Dec 42
DJEBEL AZZAG 1943	5 – 7 Jan 43
TWO TREE HILL	13 Jan 43
BOU ARADA	18 – 25 Jan 43
ROBAA VALLEY	31 Jan 43
DJEBEL ALLILIGA	3 – 4 Feb 43
KASSERINE	14 – 25 Feb 43
SBIBA	19 – 22 Feb 43
THALA	20 – 22 Feb 43

EL HADJEBA	26 Feb 43
DJEBEL DJAFFA	26 Feb 43
SIDI NAIR	26 Feb 43
FORT MCGREGOR	26 – 27 Feb 43
STUKA FARM	26 – 28 Feb 43
STEAMROLLER FARM	26 Feb – 1 Mar 43
HUNT'S GAP	27 – 28 Feb 43
MONTAGNE FARM	28 Feb – 2 Mar 43
KEF OUIBA PASS	28 Feb – 4 Mar 43
DJEBEL GUERBA	2 Mar 43
SEDJENANE I	4 Mar 43
TAMERA	5 – 15 Mar 43
MAKNASSY	12 – 31 Mar 43
DJEBEL DAHRA	20 – 24 Mar 43
DJEBEL CHOUCHA	28 Mar 43
KEF EL DEBNA	28 Mar 43
MINE DE SEDJENANE	30 – 31 Mar 43
MERGUEB CHAOUACH	7 Apr 43
DJEBEL EL MAHDI	7 Apr 43
FONDOUK	7 – 11 Apr 43
OUED ZARGA	7 – 15 Apr 43
PICHON	8 Apr 43
DJEBEL BECH CHEKAOUL	9 Apr 43
DJEBEL EL RHORAB	9 Apr 43
FONDOUK PASS	9 Apr 43
DJEBEL RMEL	10 Apr 43
KAIROUAN	10 Apr 43
SIDI ALI	10 Apr 43
BORDJ	11 Apr 43
DJEBEL ANG	14 – 15 Apr 43
DJEBEL TANNGOUCHA	14 – 25 Apr 43
HEIDOUS	15 – 25 Apr 43
BANANA RIDGE	21 Apr 43
DJEBEL KESSKISS	21 Apr 43
DJEBEL DJAFFA PASS	21 – 22 Apr 43
ARGOUB SELIAH	22 Apr 43
BER RABAL	22 Apr 43
EL KOURZIA	22 – 26 Apr 43
GRICH EL OUED	23 Apr 43
MEDJEZ PLAIN	23 – 30 Apr 43
GUERIAT EL ATACH RIDGE	23 – 24 Apr 43

LONGSTOP HILL 1943	23 – 26 Apr 43
PETER'S CORNER	24 Apr 43
SI MEDIENE	25 – 26 Apr 43
DJEBEL KOURNINE	25 – 30 Apr 43
DJEBEL BOU AOUKAZ 1943, I	27 – 28 Apr 43
SI ABDALLAH	27 – 30 Apr 43
GAB GAB GAP	28 – 30 Apr 43
SIDI AHMED	28 – 30 Apr 43
ARGOUB EL MEGAS	30 Apr 43
NORTH AFRICA – TUNISIA – FIRST & EIGHTH ARMIES (5 May 1943 to 12 May 43)	
NORTH AFRICA 1940 – 1943	12 Jun 40 – 12 May 43
DJEBEL BOU AOUKAZ 1943, II	5 – 6 May 43
TUNIS	5 – 12 May 43
MONTARNAUD	6 May 43
RAGOUBET SOUISSI	6 May 43
HAMMAM LIF	8 – 9 May 43
CRETEVILLE PASS	8 – 11 May 43
GROMBALIA	10 May 43
BOU FICHA	11 May 43
SICILY (9 Jul 1943 to 17 Aug 43)	
SICILY 1943	9 Jul – 17 Aug 43
LANDING IN SICILY	9 – 12 Jul 43
SOLARINO	11 – 13 Jul 43
VIZZINI	11 – 14 Jul 43
AUGUSTA	12 – 13 Jul 43
FRANCOFONTE	13 – 15 Jul 43
LENTINI	13 – 18 Jul 43
PRIMOSOLE BRIDGE	13 – 18 Jul 43
SFERRO	15 – 20 Jul 43
SIMETO BRIDGEHEAD	18 – 21 Jul 43
GERBINI	18 – 21 Jul 43
AGIRA	24 – 28 Jul 43
REGALBUTO	29 Jul – 3 Aug 43
ADRANO	29 Jul – 7 Aug 43
SFERRO HILLS	31 Jul – 3 Aug 43
CENTURIPE	31 Jul – 3 Aug 43
PURSUIT TO MESSINA	2 – 17 Aug 43
SALSO CROSSING	4 Aug 43
SIMETO CROSSING	5 Aug 43
MONTE RIVOGLIA	9 Aug 43

MALLETO	12 – 13 Aug 43
ITALY (3 Sep 43 to 22 Apr 45)	
ITALY 1943 – 45	3 Sep 43 – 22 Apr 45
LANDING AT PORTO SAN VENERE	8 Sep 43
TARANTO	9 – 22 Sep 43
ST LUCIA	9 – 18 Sep 43
VIETRI PASS	9 – 16 Sep 43
SALERNO HILLS	9 – 17 Sep 43
SALERNO	9 – 18 Sep 43
BATTIPAGLIA	10 – 18 Sep 43
CAVA DI TIRRENI	22 – 28 Sep 43
CAPTURE OF NAPLES	22 Sep – 1 Oct 43
CAPPEZANO	24 – 25 Sep 43
MONTE STELLA	24 – 26 Sep 43
SCAFATI BRIDGE	28 Sep 43
CARDITO	3 Oct 43
TERMOLI	3 – 6 Oct 43
THE TRIGNO	22 Oct – 5 Nov 43
VOLTURNO CROSSING	12 – 25 Oct 43
MONTE MARO	22 – 23 Oct 43
ROCCHETTA E CROCE	22 – 23 Oct 43
TEANO	28 – 31 Oct 43
SAN SALVO	2 – 3 Nov 43
CALABRITTO	5 Nov – 6 Dec 43
MONTE CAMINO	5 Nov – 9 Dec 43
THE SANGRO	19 Nov – 3 Dec 43
MOZZAGROGNA	27 – 29 Nov 43
FOSSACESIA	30 Nov 43
ROMAGNOLI	30 Nov – 1 Dec 43
ORSOGNA	3 – 24 Dec 43
MORO BRIDGE or IMPOSSIBLE BRIDGE	5 – 13 Dec 43
CALDARI	13 – 14 Dec 43
VILLA GRANDE	22 – 28 Dec 43
COLLE CEDRO	4 – 9 Jan 44
GARIGLIANO CROSSING	17 – 31 Jan 44
MINTURNO	17 – 25 Jan 44
DAMIANO	18 – 30 Jan 44
CASSINO I	20 Jan – 25 Mar 44
ANZIO	22 Jan – 22 May 44
APRILIA	24 – 26 Jan 44
CAMPOLEONE	24 – 31 Jan 44

MONTE TUGA	26 – 30 Jan 44
MONTE ORNITO	2 – 20 Feb 44
CERASOLA	7 – 9 Feb 44
CARROCETO	7 – 10 Feb 44
MONASTERY HILL	15 – 18 Feb 44
CASTLE HILL	15 – 24 Mar44
HANGMAN'S HILL	15 – 25 Mar 44
CASSINO RAILWAY STATION	17 Mar 44
CASSINO II	11 – 18 May 44
MASSA VERTECHI	14 May 44
MASA TAMBOURINI	15 May 44
CASA SINAGOGGA	16 May 44
AQUINO	18 – 24 May 44
HITLER LINE	18 – 24 May 44
LIRI VALLEY	18 – 30 May 44
PIEDIMONTE HILL	20 – 21 May 44
ADVANCE TO THE TIBER	22 May – 4 Jun 44
ROME	22 May – 4 Jun 44
MELIA CROSSING	24 – 25 May 44
MONTE PICCOLO	26 – 28 May 44
ROCCA D'ARCE	27 – 29 May 44
MONTE ROLONDO	6 – 7 Jun 44
FICULLE	15 Jun 44
MONTE GABBIONE	16 – 17 Jun 44
CITTA DELLA PIEVE	16 – 19 Jun 44
RIPA RIDGE	18 – 19 Jun 44
CAPTURE OF PERUGIA	18 – 20 Jun 44
MONTE MALBE	19 – 20 Jun 44
SANFATUCCHIO	20 – 21 Jun 44
TRASIMENE LINE	20 – 30 Jun 44
GABBIANO	1 Jul 44
ANCONA	2 – 18 Jul 44
AREZZO	4 – 17 Jul 44
TUORI	5 Jul 44
MONTONE	5 – 7 Jul 44
MONTE CEDRONE	13 – 18 Jul 44
CITTA DI CASTELLO	16 – 22 Jul 44
ADVANCE TO FLORENCE	17 Jul – 10 Aug 44
MONTE SAN MICHELE	19 Jul 44
CAMPRIANO	20 – 28 Jul 44
MONTE DOMINI	21 – 24 Jul 44

CITERNA	25 – 26 Jul 44
MONTE SCALARI	27 – 30 Jul 44
POGGIO DEL GRILLO	4 – 8 Aug 44
INCONTRO	5 – 8 Aug 44
FIESOLE	25 Aug 44
GOTHIC LINE	25 Aug – 22 Sep 44
MONTEGAUDIO	28 Aug 44
MONTE GRIDOLFO	30 Aug – 2 Sep 44
MONTORSOLI	1 – 5 Sep 44
TAVOLETO	1 – 4 Sep 44
SAN CLEMENTE	3 – 4 Sep 44
CORIANO	3 – 15 Sep 44
PLAN DI CASTELLO	5 – 8 Sep 44
CROCE	5 – 9 Sep 44
GEMMANO RIDGE	5 – 15 Sep 44
MONTE COLOMBO	14 Sep 44
CASA FABBRI RIDGE	14 Sep 44
MONTESCUDO	14 – 17 Sep 44
RIMINI LINE	14 – 21 Sep 44
FRISONI	16 – 18 Sep 44
SAN MARINO	17 – 20 Sep 44
CERIANO RIDGE	17 – 21 Sep 44
MONTEBELLO – SCORTICATA RIDGE	22 – 24 Sep 44
SANTARCANGELO	22 – 24 Sep 44
MONTE REGGIANO	24 Sep – 1 Oct 44
MARRADI	21 – 24 Sep 44
MONTE GAMBERALDI	25 – 29 Sep 44
CATARELTO RIDGE	28 Sep – 3 Oct 44
BATTAGLIA	2 – 12 Oct 44
MONTE CASALINO	2 – 23 Oct 44
MONTE CECO	3 – 17 Oct 44
SAN MARTINO – SOGLIANO	4 – 5 Oct 44
MONTE FARNETO	6 – 7 Oct 44
MONTLIGALIO	7 – 8 Oct 44
CARPINETA	12 – 15 Oct 44
MONTE LA PIEVE	13 – 19 Oct 44
CESENA	15 – 20 Oct 44
MONTE PIANOERENO	17 – 23 Oct 44
MONTE SPADURO	19 – 24 Oct 44
SAVIO BRIDGEHEAD	20 – 23 Oct 44
MONTE CAVALIO	21 – 23 Oct 44

ORSARA	25 – 26 Oct 44
MONTE GRANDE	1 Nov – 12 Dec 44
CAPTURE OF FORTI	7 – 9 Nov 44
CASA FORTIS	9 – 11 Nov 44
COSINA CANAL CROSSING	20 – 23 Nov 44
CASA BETTINI	24 Nov – 1 Dec 44
LAMONE CROSSING	2 – 13 Dec 44
CAPTURE OF RAVENNA	3 – 4 Dec 44
PIDEURA	4 – 7 Dec 44
DEFENCE OF LAMONE BRIDGEHEAD	9 Dec 44
TOSSIGNANO	12 – 16 Dec 44
PERGOLA RIDGE	14 – 16 Dec 44
CONVENTELIO – COMACCHIO	2 – 6 Jan 45
SENIO POCKET	4 – 5 Jan 45
SENIO FLOODBANK	23 Feb – 3 Mar 45
VALLI DI COMACCHIO	1 – 8 Apr 45
THE SENIO	9 – 12 Apr 45
MENATE	10 – 11 Apr 45
SANTERNO CROSSING	11 – 12 Apr 45
FILO	12 – 14 Apr 45
ARGENTA GAP	13 – 30 Apr 45
SILLARO CROSSING	14 – 16 Apr 45
BOLOGNA	14 – 21 Apr 45
MEDECINA	16 Apr 45
GALANA CROSSING	17 – 19 Apr 45
TRAGHETTO	19 – 20 Apr 45
FOSSA CEMBALINA	20 – 21 Apr 45
IDICE BRIDGEHEAD	20 – 21 Apr 45
SAN NICOLO CANAL	21 Apr 45
MIDDLE EAST (3 Oct 1943 to 21 Nov 44)	
MIDDLE EAST 1941 – 44	20 May 41 – 21 Nov 44
COS	3 – 16 Oct 43
LEROS	12 – 16 Nov 43
ADRIATIC	18 Mar – 21 Nov 44
NORTH – WEST EUROPE 1944 – 1945 (6 Jun 1944 to 5 May 1945)	
NORTH WEST EUROPE 1944 – 45	6 Jun 44 – 5 May 45
NORMANDY LANDING	6 Jun 44
PEGASUS BRIDGE	6 Jun 44
MERVILLE BATTERY	6 Jun 44
PORT EN BESSIN	7 – 8 Jun 44
PUTOT EN BESSIN	8 Jun 44

SULLY	8 – 9 Jun 44
VILLERS BOCAGE	8 – 15 Jun 44
CAMBES	9 Jun 44
BREVILLE	10 – 13 Jun 44
TILLY SUR SEULLES	14 – 19 Jun 44
FONTENAY LE PESNIL	25 – 27 Jun 44
THE ODON	25 Jun – 2 Jul 44
CHEUX	26 – 27 Jun 44
TOURMAUVILLE BRIDGE	27 Jun 44
DEFENCE OF RAURAY	29 Jun – 2 Jul 44
CAEN	4 – 18 Jul 44
THE ORNE (BURON)	8 – 9 Jul 44
HILL 112	10 – 11 Jul 44
ESQUAY	15 – 17 Jul 44
NOYERS	15 – 18 Jul 44
CAGNY	18 – 19 Jul 44
TROARN	18 – 21 Jul 44
BOURGUEBUS RIDGE	18 – 23 Jul 44
MALTOT	22 – 23 Jul 44
THE SOULEUVRE	30 Jul – 1 Aug 44
QUARRY HILL	30 Jul – 2 Aug 44
JURQUES	30 Jul – 4 Aug 44
MOUNT PINCON	30 Jul – 9 Aug 44
CATHEOLIES	2 – 5 Aug 44
LE PERIER RIDGE	2 – 8 Aug 44
LA VARINIERE	4 – 9 Aug 44
BRIEUX BRIDGEHEAD	6 – 8 Aug 44
ESTRY	6 – 12 Aug 44
FALAISE ROAD	7 – 9 Aug 44
FALAISE	7 – 22 Aug 44
ST PIERRE LA VIELLE	9 – 16 Aug 44
NOIREAU CROSSING	14 – 17 Aug 44
THE LAISON	14 – 17 Aug 44
SOUTHERN FRANCE	15 – 28 Aug 44
DIVES CROSSING	17 – 20 Aug 44
LA VIE CROSSING	18 – 20 Aug 44
LISIEUX	21 – 23 Aug 44
LA TOUQUES CROSSING	22 – 23 Aug 44
RISLE CROSSING	25 – 27 Aug 44
THE SEINE 1944	25 – 28 Aug 44
FORET DE BRETONNE	28 – 30 Aug 44

AMIENS 1944	31 Aug 44
BRUSSELS	3 Sep 44
ANTWERP	4 – 7 Sep 44
HECHTEL	7 – 12 Sep 44
HEPPEN	8 – 9 Sep 44
GHEEL	8 – 11 Sep 44
NEERPELT	10 Sep 44
LE HAVRE	10 – 12 Sep 44
AART	14 – 20 Sep 44
BOULOGNE 1944	17 – 22 Sep 44
ARNHEM 1944	17 – 26 Sep 44
THE NEDERRIJN	17 – 27 Sep 44
NIJMEGEN	19 – 20 Sep 44
VEGHEL	22 – 23 Sep 44
BEST	22 – 27 Sep 44
ANTWERP – TURNHOUT CANAL	24 – 29 Sep 44
CALAIS 1944	25 Sep – 1 Oct 44
AAM	1 – 4 Oct 44
THE SCHELDT	1 Oct – 8 Nov 44
OPHEUSDEN	5 – 7 Oct 44
VENRAIJ	12 – 18 Oct 44
THE LOWER MAAS	20 Oct – 7 Nov 44
SOUTH BEVELAND	24 – 31 Oct 44
ASTEN/MELJEL	27 Oct – 5 Nov 44
WALCHEREN CAUSEWAY	31 Oct – 4 Nov 44
WESTKAPELLE	1 – 3 Nov 44
FLUSHING	1 – 4 Nov 44
VENLO POCKET	14 Nov – 3 Dec 44
GEILENKIRCHEN	18 – 23 Nov 44
THE OURTHE	3 – 14 Jan 45
THE ROER	16 – 31 Jan 45
ZETTEN	18 – 21 Jan 45
THE REICHSWALD	8 – 13 Feb 45
WAAL FLATS	8 – 15 Feb 45
THE RHINELAND	8 Feb – 10 Mar 45
CLEVE	9 – 11 Feb 45
GOCH	12 – 21 Feb 45
MOYLAND/MOYLAND WOOD	14 – 21 Feb 45
WEEZE	24 Feb – 2 Mar 45
THE HOCHWALD	24 Feb – 4 Mar 45
SCHADDENHOF	27 – 28 Feb 45

XANTEN	8 – 9 Mar 45
THE RHINE	25 Mar – 1 Apr 45
IBBENBUREN	1 – 6 Apr 45
BENTHEIM	2 – 3 Apr 45
TWENTE CANAL	2 – 4 Apr 45
LINGEN	2 – 5 Apr 45
DREIRWALDE	4 – 8 Apr 45
LEESE	5 – 8 Apr 45
THE ALLER	10 – 17 Apr 45
ARNHEM 1945	12 – 14 Apr 45
BRINKUM	13 – 16 Apr 45
UELZEN	14 – 18 Apr 45
BREMEN	18 – 26 Apr 45
ARTLENBERG	29 – 30 Apr 45
GREECE (2 Dec 1944 to 15 Jan 45)	
GREECE 1944 – 45	16 Sep 44 – 15 Jan 45
ATHENS	2 Dec 44 – 15 Jan 45

Part 7

LAND OPERATIONAL CODE NAMES

According to the 1944 pamphlet 'A Glossary of Military Terms', a code word was "a prearranged secret word used to convey instructions or information". During World War One, the German army had begun to use code names to disguise forthcoming operations, the most famous of these being Operation Michael, the last-gasp spring offensive of 1918 The system was then adopted in Britain (before which, code letters, usually in pairs, were used, but this was limited in scale) and at the operational level was controlled by the British Inter-Services Security Board, an organisation responsible for the creation and distribution of lists of code words called the Inter-Service Code-Word Index. This bureaucracy was necessary in order to control the overall allocation and use of code words, to make sure that only authorised code words were used, and to prevent repetition and therefore confusion. Winston Churchill as Prime Minister and Minister of Defence had very clear ideas about the use and selection of such code names, and famously issued a diktat on the subject, which included the following:

> Operations in which large numbers of men may lose their lives ought not to be decided by code-words that imply a boastful and over-confident sentiment, such as TRIUMPHANT or conversely, which are calculated to invest the plan with an air of despondency, such as WOEBETIDE and FLIMSY...They ought not to be names of a frivolous character...They should not be ordinary words often used in other connections...Names of living people – Ministers and Commanders – should be avoided. After all, the world is wide, and intelligent thought will readily supply an unlimited number of names which do not suggest the character of the operation or disparage it in any way, and do not enable some widow or mother to say that her son was killed in an operation called BUNNYHUG or BALLYHOO.

Proper names are good in this field. The heroes of antiquity, figures from Greek and Roman mythology, the constellations and stars, famous racehorses, names of British and American war heroes, could be used, provided they fall within the rules above.

One thing that Churchill might have emphasised more is that the code name must not have anything to do with the operation being conducted; in other words, if discovered, the code name must not give the enemy a clue as to the location or nature of the operation. Generally, the code names listed here meet that requirement, but there is one notable exception: Operation BLACKWATER of mid-August 1944 involved the establishment of a bridgehead over the Noireau river. Some of the codenames listed below are obscure to the point of being unfamiliar even to native English speakers – ANAKIM, BULBASKET, JOCKWORTH or SABINE by way of example. And a few were definitely in the BUNNYHUG or BALLYHOO category of un-warlike or unfortunate names – BEGONIA, CANDYTUFT, CHUCKLE, ERROR, LOST, KITTEN and SAUCY all spring to mind.[1] Others however proclaimed a greater sense of martial purpose: CLAYMORE, MUSKET, PUGILIST, RAPIER and STRIKE.

Possibly the most famous use of code names during the war were those allocated to the five landing areas during the Normandy invasion of 1944. Under the overarching code name of OVERLORD, the areas were called, from West to east, UTAH, OMAHA, GOLD, JUNO and SWORD. According to Montgomery's BGS (Ops), David Belchem, the first two (US) names were allocated at the request of their commanders because of their personal links to the state and the city in Nebraska respectively: UTAH for Major General Joe Collins, and OMAHA for Major General Leonard Gerow. The other three were more prosaic, allocated because Belchem found them in a pamphlet listing words "which I picked from an old army manual which gave a list of short words easily pronounced and understood on the phone or radio by, for example, a Glaswegian talking to a Texan".[2]

In addition to the operational code names listed below, code names could also be allocated in order to provide security for other reasons. For example, when the first M4 Sherman tanks were being shipped to North Africa directly from the USA, they were referred to as SWALLOW. Similarly, locations, places and targets could be allocated code names. For example, during Operation HUSKY (the invasion of Sicily), Sicily itself was known as HORRIFIED, and MESSINA as GUNMETAL. During OVERLORD, Ouistreham was known as BOARDER, and Lion-Sur-Mer was TRIPOD. In 1940, the codename CROMWELL meant that a German invasion of UK was imminent or had actually begun.

The operations listed here are, in the opinion of the author, the most significant ones, or at any rate the ones most likely to be encountered during research. The habit of allocating code names gained enormous currency during the war, with many commanders even at relatively low levels choosing their own code names for fairly localised operations and even patrols.[3]

Name	Date(s)	Location & Purpose
ACCOLADE	Dec 43	Planned invasion of Rhodes and the Dodecanese, Greece
ACCOMPLISH	28 – 29 Apr 43	Eighth Army attack in Tunisia
ACCUMULATOR	12 – 13 Jun 44	Simulated landing in north west France in support of OVERLORD
ACROBAT	Jan 42	Planned attack on Tripoli, Libya
AERIAL	15 – 25 Jun 40	Evacuation of personnel from western France (sometimes ARIEL)
AGREEMENT	13 – 14 Sep 42	Raid on Tobruk, Libya (often incorrectly referred to as DAFFODIL)
ALBUMEN	7 – 8 Jun 42, 4 – 5 Jul 43	SAS raid on airfields in Crete
ALPHABET	May – Jun 40	Evacuation of Narvik, Norway
AMHERST	Apr 45	3 & 4SAS parachute operation in Netherlands
AMPERE	NK	SOE reception party for second Chindit operation, Burma
ANAKIM	Autumn 43	Proposed only, retaking of Burma
ANGLO	31 Aug – 18 Sep 42	SBS raid on Rhodes, Greece
ANIMALS	21 Jun – 11 Jul 44	SOE sabotage in Greece
ANKLET	26 – 27 Dec 41	Commando raid on Lofoten islands, Norway
ANTHROPOD	27 May 42	Assassination of Reinhard Heydrich
ANVIL	44	Named changed to DRAGOON (see below)
APOSTLE	45	Reoccupation of Norway
APPEARANCE	16 Mar – 8 Apr 41	Reoccupation of British Somaliland
AQUATINT	12 – 13 Sep 42	Commando raid on Normandy, France
ARCHERY	27 Dec 41	Commando raid on Vaagso, Norway
ARCHWAY	Mar – May 45	SAS operations in Germany
ARIEL	Jun 40	See AERIAL
ASTONIA	10 – 12 Sep 44	Capture of Le Havre fortress, France
ATLANTIC	18 – 20 Jul 44	Concurrent offensive with GOODWOOD
AVALANCHE	9 Sep 43	Landing at Salerno, Italy
AVONMOUTH	May 40	Landings at Narvik, Norway
AWARD	NK	Proposed SOE operation on Ramree island, Burma
BALDHEAD	1943 – 45	Multiple SOE operations in Andaman islands, Burma
BAOBAB	29 – 31 Jan 44	2 SAS landing in support of SHINGLE, Anzio, Italy

Name	Date(s)	Location & Purpose
BARCLAY	Jul 43	Deception operations in support of HUSKY
BARRISTER	Sep 40	Proposed attack on Dakar, west Africa
BASALT	3 – 4 Oct 42	Commando raid on Sark, Channel Islands
BATTLEAXE	15 – 17 Jun 41	Relief of siege of Tobruk & capture of Cyrenaica, Libya
BAYTOWN	3 Sep 43	Landing at Reggio di Calabria, Italy
BEGONIA	2 – 6 Oct 43	Airborne component (SAS) of JONQUIL
BERESFORD	3 – 4 Sep 42	Part of Alam el Halfa battle
BERGBANG	2 – 12 Sep 44	5 SAS operations versus German LoC east of Meuse river
BERLIN	25/26 Sep 44	Evacuation of troops from Arnhem
BERTRAM	Sep 42	Deception operations in support of LIGHTFOOT
BIGAMY	Sep 42	SAS/LRDG raid on Benghazi and Benina, Libya
BILLET	Nov 43	SOE Liaison with Burmese nationalists
BISHOP	24 Aug 41	Raid on Bandar Shahpur, Persia
BITING	27 – 28 Feb 42	Raid on Bruneval, France
BLACKCOCK	13 – 26 Jan 45	Clearance of Roer triangle
BLACKWATER	1 – 6 Aug 44	Establishment of bridgehead over Noireau river.
BLAST	Jul – Sep 43	Original name for WADHAM
BLOCKBUSTER	22 Feb – 3 Mar 45	Final phase of VERITABLE
BLUECOAT	30 Jul – 7 Aug 44	Exploitation of COBRA (US) in Normandy, France
BOARDMAN	30 Jun – 31 Aug 43	Deception in support of AVALANCHE
BODYGUARD	43 – 44	Deception in support of FORTITUDE, OVERLORD
BOLERO	42 – 44	US troop build-up in UK
BOTTOM	Dec 44	SOE intelligence gathering for advance into Burma
BOXER	Aug 44	Planned airborne assault and capture of Boulogne, France
BRAGANZA	29 – 30 Sep 42	Attack on Deir el Munassib, Libya
BRANCASTER	Jul 44	Proposed SOE operation in Bhamo area, Burma
BRASSARD	17 – 19 Jun 44	Invasion of Elba, Italy

Name	Date(s)	Location & Purpose
BREVITY	15 – 16 May 41	Offensive against Sollum/Capuzzo/ Bardia, Libya
BRIMSTONE	Jul 43	Planned invasion of Sardinia
BRISTLE	3 – 4 Jun 42	Commando raid on Hardelot, France
BROADSWORD	Sep 43	Deception in support of COCKADE
BUCKLAND	9 – 19 Apr 45	Battle of the Argenta Gap, Italy
BUFFALO	Jan 44	Attack through Cisterna as part of SHINGLE,
BULBASKET	6 Jun – 25 Jul 44	SAS operations in support of OVERLORD
BUTTRESS	Jul – Sep 43	Planned amphibious attack in Gulf of Goia, Italy
CANDYTUFT	27 Oct 43	2 SAS raid on German rear areas, Italy
CANNIBAL	22 Dec 42 – 11 May 43	First offensive in the Arakan, Burma
CANTER	16 – 22 Apr 43	Initial breakthrough attempt on Mareth Line, Tunisia
CANUCK	Jan 45	SAS operations with partisans in Northern Italy
CAPABLE	42	Proposed SOE operation in Irrawaddy delta, Burma
CAPITAL	19 Nov 44	Clearance of northern Burma
CARAVAN	13 – 14 Sep 42	LRDG attack on Barce, Libya
CASCADE	41 – 42	Deception operations in western desert
CASTOR	Oct 44	3 Inf Div clearance of Venlo salient, Netherlands
CHARACTER	Feb – Mar 45	SOE/Force 136 operations in Karen Hills, Burma
CHARIOT	28 Mar 42	Raid on St Nazaire, France
CHARNWOOD	8 – 9 Jul 44	Offensive to capture Caen, Normandy
CHESTERFIELD	23 – 24 May 44	Offensive on the Hitler Line, Italy
CHESTNUT	12 Jul 43	SAS raid on northern Sicily
CHETTYFORD	Jan 44	Deception in support of SHINGLE
CHOKER II	Mar 45	Planned airborne seizure of bridgeheads on River Rhine
CHRONOMETER	10 – 15 Jun 41	Assault on Assab, Eritrea
CHUCKLE	2 Dec 44 – 15 Jan 45	Crossing Montone river towards Senio, Italy
CLAWHAMMER	Sep/Oct 42	Planned raid on German communication site near Cherbourg, France
CLAYMORE	4 Mar 41	Commando raid on Lofoten islands, Norway

Name	Date(s)	Location & Purpose
CLIPPER	18 – 22 Nov 44	Offensive to reduce the Geilenkirchen salient, Germany
COCKADE	43	Deception operations STARKEY, WADHAM & TINDALL
COLD COMFORT	17 Feb 45	SAS operation north of Verona, Italy, (AKA ZOMBIE)
COLIN	22 – 30 Oct 44	Offensive towards s-Hertogenbosch/ Breda, Netherlands
COLLAR	24 – 24 Jun 40	(First) Commando raid on NE France
COLOSSUS	10 Feb 42	Airborne raid on Calitri, Italy
COMET	Sep 44	Planned airborne assault on Nederrijn river, Netherlands
COMPASS	Dec 40 – Feb 41	Offensive against Italians in Cyrenaica, Libya
CONCERTINA	43	Proposed re-occupation of Alderney, Channel Islands
CONDOR	43	Proposed re-occupation of Jersey, Channel Islands
CONSTELLATION (1)	43	Proposed re-occupation of the Channel Islands
CONSTELLATION (2)	Oct 44	VIII Corps clearance of Venlo salient, Netherlands
COONEY	8 Jun 44	French Para Bn (4SAS) operations in Brittany
COPPERHEAD	30 Nov 43	Alternative name for deception operation HAMBONE
CORKSCREW	11 Jun 43	Amphibious assault on Pantelleria island, Italy
CORONET	45	Planned part of DOWNFALL
CORTON	Jan – Oct 44	SOE coastal shipping watch from Elphinstone island, Burma
COUNTENANCE	25 – 31 Aug 41	Allied-Soviet invasion of Persia
COUP DE MAIN	6 Jun 44	Glider-borne capture of Caen canal and Orne bridges, Normandy, France
COVERLET	43	Proposed re-occupation of Guernsey, Channel Islands
CRADLE	Dec 44	Proposed SOE operation in Shwebo area, Burma
CROSSWORD	Apr 45	Negotiations for German surrender in Italy
CRUSADER	18 Nov – 30 Dec 41	Relief of siege of Tobruk & capture of Cyrenaica, Libya
CUDGEL	Dec 43 – Mar 44	Second offensive in the Arakan, Burma

Name	Date(s)	Location & Purpose
CULVERIN	44	Planned operations against Sumatra & Malaysia
CYCLE	10 – 13 Jun 40	Evacuation from Le Havre, France
CYGNET	Aug 42	Incomplete SOE reconnaissance of Bergen, Norway
CYMBAL	Mar 43	Proposed SOE anti-shipping operation on Rangoon river
DAFFODIL	Sep 42	See AGREEMENT
DAUNTLESS	Jun 44	See MARTLET
DEFOE	Jul 44	SAS patrols in Normandy
DERRICK	Jul 43	Deception in support of HUSKY
DEVON	3 – 6 Oct 43	Commando landing at Termoli, Italy
DIADEM	11 May – 4 Jun 44	Operations in Liri Valley, Italy
DICKENS	15 – 25 Mar 44	Third battle of Cassino, Italy
DILWYN	43 – 45	Later name for TENDON
DINGSON	5 – 18 Jun 44	4 SAS operation in Brittany, France
DOOMSDAY	May 45	Liberation of Norway
DOVER	25 – 26 Aug 41	Occupation of Abadan, Persia, part of COUNTENANCE
DOWNFALL	45	Planned invasion of Japan
DRACULA	Apr – May45	Capture of Rangoon, Burma
DRAGOON	15 Aug 44	Invasion of Southern France
DREADNOUGHT	Jun 44	Proposed attempt to outflank Caen from the east
DRIFTWOOD	7 – 8 Jan 44	2 SAS attack on railway lines in Italy, in support of SHINGLE
DRYAD	2 – 3 Sep 42	Commando raid on Casquets lighthouse, Channel Islands
DUNHILL	Aug 44	SAS disruption of German operations prior to COBRA (US)
DYNAMO	26 May – 4 Jun 40	Evacuation from northern France (Dunkirk)
ECLIPSE	May 45 –	The occupation of Germany
ENCORE	Feb – Mar 45	Assault on Gothic Line, Italy
ENTERPRISE	29 Apr – 7 May 45	Crossing of Elbe River and advance to Baltic coast
EPSOM	26 – 30 Jun 44	Attempted capture of Caen, France
ERROR	Apr 42	Deception operations in India/Burma
EXPORTER	Jun – Jul 41	Invasion of Syria and Lebanon
EXTEND	42	Landing at Fort Dauphin, Madagascar
EXTENDED CAPITAL	Nov 44 – Mar 45	Development of CAPITAL to include Rangoon

Name	Date(s)	Location & Purpose
FAUST	May 45	Distribution of food to Dutch population
FAUSTIAN	13 – 16 Jul 43	Airborne landing to capture Primosole bridge, Sicily, part of HUSKY
FERDINAND	44	Deception operations in Italy, part of BODYGUARD
FIREBRAND	Sep – Oct 43	Proposed invasion of Corsica
FIRST CULVERIN	44	Operations in Northern Sumatra, not undertaken
FLAVIA	Apr 44	Proposed SOE recce for operation with Chinese agents, southern BURMA
FLIMWELL	Jan 43	Later renamed CAPABLE
FLIPPER	10 – 18 Nov 41	Attack on Rommel's HQ, Libya
FORK	10 May 40	Occupation of Iceland
FORTITUDE	Spring 44	Deception in support of OVERLORD
FORTITUDE NORTH	Spring 44	Deception threat to Norway, part of FORTITUDE
FORTITUDE SOUTH	Spring 44	Deception threat to Pas de Calais, part of FORTITUDE
FOXLEY	44	Plan to assassinate Hitler
FRANKTON	7 – 12 Dec 42	RM commando raid on Bordeaux
FREEBORN	Jun 42	Planned strengthening of defences in Egypt
FRESHMAN	19 Nov 42	Airborne attack on Vermork, Norway
FUSILADE	Sep 44	Assault and occupation of Dieppe, France
FUSTIAN	13 – 16 Jul 43	Airborne assault on Primosole bridge, Sicily
GAFF	25 Jul – 12 Aug 44	Attempted assassination of Field Marshal Rommel
GAIN	16 Jun – 31 Jul 44	1 SAS Operations in Orleans area, France, in support of OVERLORD
GALIA	Dec 44 – Feb 45	SAS operations in north-west Italy
GALLOP	Mar 43	Part of PUGILIST
GANGWAY	Autumn 43	Planned capture of Naples, Italy
GARDEN	17 – 25 Sep 44	Ground component of MARKET-GARDEN, Netherlands
GATWICK	44 – 45	Early version of VERITABLE
GAUNTLET	25 Aug – 3 Sep 41	Combined Operations raid on Spitzbergen, Norway
GLUTTON	10 Jul 43	Cancelled parachute drop in Sicily, part of HUSKY

Name	Date(s)	Location & Purpose
GOBLET	Sep 43	Planned landing at Crotone, Italy
GOLDFLAKE	Spring 45	Move of I Canadian Corps and 5th Infantry Division from Italy to NWE
GOODWOOD	18 – 20 Jul 44	Capture of eastern Caen and Bourguebus ridge, Normandy, France
GRAFFHAM	Feb – Mar 44	Deception operation in support of BODYGUARD
GRAIN	Nov 43	Liaison with Burmese nationalists in Arakan (as part of BILLET)
GRAPESHOT	6 Apr – 2 May 45	Spring offensive, northern Italy
GREENLINE	15 – 17 Jul 44	Preparation for GOODWOOD
GRENADE	23 Feb – 10 Mar 45	US Army crossing of Roer River, Germany
GROUSE	18 Oct 42	Advance party for FRESHMAN
GUILLOTINE	Jul – Aug 42	Reinforcement of Cyprus
GYMNAST	Spring 42	Proposed landings in north-west Africa, early version of TORCH
HAINTON	Mar 44	Original name for HEAVY
HAMBONE	30 Nov 43	Alternative name for deception operation COPPERHEAD
HARDY	27 Jul – 19 Sep 44	SAS disruption of German lines of communication, France
HARLEQUIN	43	Army component of STARKEY
HARLINGTON	Mar 43	Original name for early version of CHARACTER
HATCH	Dec 44	Landing SOE agents in Andaman islands
HEATHER	17 – 26 Feb 45	Clearance of areas near Weeze, Germany
HEAVY	Mar 44	Offensive in Burma in cooperation with indigenous forces
HECTOR	43	Proposed SOE operation in Burma
HENSINGHAM	Jun 44 – Jan 45	SOE operation in Burma
HOTSPUR	Dec 42	SOE kidnapping in Goa
HOUNDSMITH	20 Nov 44	SAS raid on Dijon, France
HOUNDSWORTH	6 Jun – 6 Sep 44	SAS disruption of German lines of communication in support of OVERLORD
HOWARD	6 – 29 Apr 45	SAS reconnaissance into north-west Germany
HUSKY	9 Jul – 17 Aug 43	Invasion of Sicily
HYACINTH	Sep 42	Part of AGREEMENT
IBROX	Spring 45	Planned SAS operation to destroy Snasamoen railway bridge, Norway

Name	Date(s)	Location & Purpose
INFATUATE	Sep 44	Planned airborne assault on Walcheren Island
IRONCLAD	5 May – 6 Nov 42	Invasion of Madagascar
IRONSIDE	44	Deception operations in western France in support of OVERLORD
JAEL	Jul – Oct 43	Deception operation in support of OVERLORD
JANE	18 Sep 42	Landing at Tamatave, Madagascar
JOCKWORTH	15 Aug – 9 Sep 44	3 SAS operations in Villefranche area, France
JONQUIL	Oct 44	2 SAS operation to liberate Allied POWs, Italy
JUBILEE	19 Aug 42	Raid on Dieppe, France
JUNCTION	Jan 45	SOE operation in Arakan, Burma
JUPITER	10 – 11 Jul 44	Recapture of Hill 112, Normandy
JURIST	28 Aug – 3 Sep 45	Capture of Penang, Malaysia
KEYSTONE	Apr 45	SAS operation in Netherlands
KINGFISHER	Autumn 45	Planned rescue of Allied Prisoners of war from Japanese in Borneo
KINGSHEAD	Jul 44	Proposed SOE operation in Burma
KITTEN	20 – 25 Aug 44	Advance from Normandy to the River seine
KROHCOL	8 – 11 Dec 41	Incursion into southern Thailand
LABEL	Jan – Mar 45	SOE insertion into Burma
LADBROKE	9 Jul 43	Glider landing near Syracuse, Sicily, part of HUSKY
LEEK	24 Feb 45	Crossing of Niers river and capture of Weeze, Germany
LEVER	12 – 19 Apr 45	Clearance operation in northern Italy
LIGHTFOOT	23 Oct – 1 Nov 42	First phase of Battle of El Alamein
LIGHTNING	3 – 4 Jan 45	Capture of Akyab island, Burma
LINE	Sep 42	Part of IRONCLAD, advance from Majunga to Tannanarive
LINNET	Sep 44	Planned airborne drop to stop German withdrawal in area of Tournai, France
LINNET II	Sep 44	Planned airborne landing in area of Aachen/Maastricht
LONGCLOTH	8 Feb – late Apr 43	First Chindit incursion into northern Burma
LONGSHANKS/ CREEK	9 Mar 43	SOE attack on shipping in Goa
LOST	22 – 23 Jun 44	SAS operation in Brittany, part of DINGSON

Name	Date(s)	Location & Purpose
LOYTON	12 Aug – 9 Oct 44	SAS target reconnaissance in Vosges mountains, France
LUSTRE	Mar – Apr 41	Movement of troops to Greece
MAHOUT	Jun – Oct 43	SOE operation in Rangoon
MAILFIST	45 – 46	Planned liberation of Singapore
MALLARD	6 Jun 44	Airborne landings in support of OVERLORD
MANDIBLES	40 – 41	Planned occupation of selected Dodecanese islands
MANNA	Apr – May 45	Airdropping of food to Dutch population
MANUAL	Nov 43	Liaison with Burmese nationalists (as part of BILLET)
MAPLE	Jan 44	2 SAS operations in support of SHINGLE
MARKET	17 – 25 Sep 44	Airborne component of MARKET-GARDEN, Netherlands
MARTLET	25 Jun – 1 Jul 44	Capture of Rauray area, Caen, France
MATADOR	Dec 41	Cancelled pre-emptive strike into Thailand
MENACE	23 – 25 Sep 40	Attempt to capture Dakar, French West Africa
MILAN II	45	Planned airborne seizure of bridgeheads on River Rhine
MINCEMEAT	43	Deception operation in support of HUSKY
MINERVA	20 Dec 42	Disastrous recce of Sumatra
MOSES	3 Aug – 5 Oct 44	Continuation from BULBASKET
MUSKET	Nov 42	Contingency plan for assault on Taranto
MUSKETOON	11 – 21 Sep 42	Commando raid on Glornfjord power plant, Norway
MUSTANG	Autumn 43	Contingency plan to capture Naples, Italy
NARCISSUS	10 Jul 43	SAS raid on Sicily
NATION	Nov 43	Liaison with Burmese nationalists (as part of BILLET)
NELSON	Jun 44	Planned SAS operation in France
NEPTUNE	Jun 44	Naval component of OVERLORD
NEWTON	19 Aug – 11 Sep 44	3 SAS patrol operation in Champagne-Burgundy, France
NICETY	15 – 16 Sep 42	Attempt to seize the Jalo oasis., Libya
NOAH II	Aug – Sep 44	SAS harassment of retreating Germans in Belgium

Name	Date(s)	Location & Purpose
NOAH'S ARK	44 – 45	Planned SOE operation to harass German withdrawal from Greece
NORMAN	Summer 43	Planned capture of Sardinia and Corsica
NUNTON	Spring 44	Deception operations in conjunction with DIADEM
NUTCRACKER	14 Nov – 3 Dec 44	Attack on German bridgehead on Maas River
OBOE	1 May – 21 Jul 45	Amphibious operations in Borneo
OLIVE	25 Aug 44 – Mar 45	Attacks on the Gothic Line, Italy
ORATION	19 – 21 Apr 43	Assault on Enfidaville, Tunisia
OVERBOWL	44	SOE operation in Burma
OVERLORD	6 Jun 44 – 8 May 45	Liberation of northwest Europe
PADDLE	17 – 21 Aug 44	Closure of Falaise Pocket, France
PANTHER	17 Jan 44	Crossing of Garigliano river, Italy
PASSPORT	May 45	Cancelled advance to Minbya, Burma
PEDANTIC	44	SOE operation in Burma
PEGASUS	22 – 23 Oct 44	Evacuation of fugitive soldiers post MARKET-GARDEN
PENKNIFE	31 Jan – 28 Feb 45	Deception operation in northern Italy
PERCH	7 – 14 Jun 44	Attempt to encircle and capture Caen, France
PHEASANT	20 Oct – 4 Nov 44	Liberation of North Brabant, Netherlands
PIGSTICK	Spring 44	Proposed landing on Ayu peninsula, Burma
PIKE	39 – 41	Planned operations against the Soviet Union
PILGRIM	41 – 42	Planned invasion and occupation of Canary Islands
PISTOL	Sep 44	SAS anti-railway operations, France
PLUNDER	23 – 27 Mar 45	Crossing of Rhine river, Germany
POLLUX	Oct 44	11 Armd Div clearance of Venlo salient, Netherlands
POMEGRANATE	12 Jan 44	SAS raid in Italy in support of SHINGLE
POMEGRANATE	16 – 18 Jul 44	Preparation for GOODWOOD
POSTAGE ABLE	43 – 44	Topographic preparation for NEPTUNE/OVERLORD
POSTMASTER	14 Jan 42	Raid on Fernando Po island, west Africa
PUGILIST	Mar 43	Attack on Mareth Line, Tunisia
PRIMROSE	16 – 19 Apr 40	Small scale landings in southern Norway

Name	Date(s)	Location & Purpose
QUAIL	Mar 45	Reception party to meet/assist IBROX
QUICKSILVER	44	Deception, part of FORTITUDE SOUTH
R4	Apr 40	Proposed invasion of Norway and Sweden
RAINCOAT	2 – 10 Dec 43	Breakthrough of Bernhardt Line, Italy
RAMROSE	Jan 45	Abortive SOE operation in central Burma
RANKIN	45	Scenarios for APOSTLE
RAPIER	Aug 41	Part of COUNTENANCE
RAVENOUS	Nov 42	Plan for advance into Burma in concert with CANNIBAL
RENDEZVOUS	Dec 44 – Jan 45	SOE patrol ops forward of Fourteenth Army, Burma
RIMAU	10 – 16 Oct 44	Commando raid on shipping in Singapore harbour
ROAST	1 – 2 Apr 45	Commando operation in Comacchio lagoon, Italy
ROMULUS	13 – 31 Dec 44	Clearance of western Arakan, Burma
ROSE	42	Landing at Tulear, Madagascar
ROSE	7 Mar – 21 Apr 45	Clearance of Ruhr pocket, Germany
ROUNDUP	43	Planned early invasion of Europe during 1943
ROUNDHAMMER	43	Planned development of ROUNDUP
ROYAL FLUSH	44	Deception operations involving Spain, Sweden & Turkey
RUPERT	Apr – May 40	Operations in Norway except AVONMOUTH
RUTTER	Jul 42	Early name for JUBILEE
SABINE	Apr, May 41	Suppression of Iraqi insurgency
SAMWEST	6 Jun 44	4SAS parachute drop in Brittany in support of OVERLORD
SANKEY	Jan 45	Landing of Wellington Force RM, Arakan, Burma
SATIN	Jan 43	Proposed advance to Sfax/Gabes, Tunisia
SAUCY	Autumn 43	Planned smaller version of ANAKIM
SAVANNA(H)	Mar – Apr 41	SOE operation in NW France
SAXIFRAGE	27 Oct 43	SAS raid on eastern Italy
SCIPIO	6 – 7 Apr 43	Battle of Wadi Akarit, Tunisia
SICKLE	18 Apr – 2 May 40	Landings at Andalsnes, Norway
SIESTA	Nov 44	Planned offensive on the Nijmegen salient, Netherlands

Name	Date(s)	Location & Purpose
SIRIUS	Oct 44	15th Inf Div operation
SHINGLE	22 Jan 44	Landings at Anzio, Italy
SKYE	Mar – Nov 44	Deception radio traffic in support of FORTITUDE NORTH
SKYSCRAPER	43	Planned early invasion of Europe during 1943
SLAPSTICK	9 Sep 43	Amphibious invasion of Taranto, Italy
SLEDGEHAMMER	42	Planned early invasion of Europe during 1942
SLIPPERY	Jul 45	Deception operations in Thailand
SNOWDROP	Sep 42	Alternative name for BIGAMY
SPAN	44	Deception in support of DRAGOON
SPEEDWELL	7 Sep 43	SAS raid on Italian rail targets near Genoa, in support of SLAPSTICK
SPIERS	Dec 43 – Sep 44	SOE operations in Kokang, north east Burma
SPRING	25 – 27 Jul 44	II Canadian Corps offensive in Normandy, France
SQUATTER	16 – 17 Nov 42	SAS Parachute raid against German airfields, Libya
STARKEY	43	Deception operations in Boulogne area, France
STREAM	10 – 11 Sep 42	Landing at Majunga, Madagascar
STREAMLINE JANE	42	Operations STREAM, LINE and JANE (Madagascar)
STRIKE	6 – 12 May 43	Final attacks to secure Tunisia
SUNRISE	Feb – May 45	Negotiations for German surrender in Italy
SUNSTAR	22 – 23 Nov 42	Commando raid on Houlgate, France
SUPERCHARGE	2 – 5 Nov 42	Second phase of Battle of El Alamein
SUPER GYMNAST	42	Early version of TORCH
SWITCHBACK	6 Oct 44	Clearance of south bank of River Scheldt, Netherlands
TABARIN	43	Denial of bases in Antarctica
TALISMAN	45	Early version of ECLIPSE
TALON	3 Jan 45	Landing at Akyab, Burma
TAMPER	42	Landing at Morondava, Madagascar
TARBRUSH	15 – 18 May 44	Beach reconnaissance of French coast
TELESCOPE	May 44	Early version of COPPERHEAD
TENDON	Mar 43 – Aug 45	SOS operations in northern Burma
THISTLEDOWN	Jan 44	2 SAS operation in Italy, part of MAPLE

Name	Date(s)	Location & Purpose
THURSDAY	Mar – Apr 44	Second Chindit incursion into northern Burma
TIDERACE	2 – 12 Sep 45	Reoccupation of Singapore
TINDALL	30 Jun – 31 Oct 43	Deception operation in Stavanger, Norway
TITANIC 1 – 4	5 – 6 Jun 44	Dropping dummy parachutists in support of OVERLORD
TOMBOLA	Mar – Apr 45	SAS operation in Italy
TONGA	5 – 7 Jun 44	Airborne operations in support of OVERLORD
TORCH	8 – 16 Nov 42	Invasion of French Morocco and Algeria
TOTALIZE	8 – 9 Aug 44	Attack towards Falaise, Normandy
TRACTABLE	14 – 21 Aug 44	Capture of Falaise, Trun and Chambois, Normandy
TRANSCEND	Mar 45	'R' Force deception in support of PLUNDER
TRANSFIGURE	Aug 44	Planned airborne op to prevent German escape through Paris-Chartres gap
TREATMENT	Sep – Oct 42	Deception plan, part of BERTRAM
TURPITUDE	44	Follow-up to ZEPPELIN
TURRET	13 Mar 45	Landing at Letpan, Arakan, Burma
UNDERDONE	44	Part of NOAH's ARK, in Albania
UNDERGO	25 Sep – 1 Oct 44	Reduction of Calais pocket, France
UPSHOT	43	Early version of TINDALL
UNTHINKABLE	45 – 46	Concept for attack on USSR
VACUUM	40 – 45	Movement of troops from UK to overseas
VALEDICTION	Nov 44	Early version of VERITABLE
VALENTINE	Apr 40	Occupation of the Faroe Islands
VAMPIRE	27 – 28 Mar 45	Canadian crossing of Rhine River, Germany, part of PLUNDER
VANDAL	3 – 9 Aug 44	X Corps attack on Bibbiena, Italy
VANGUARD	Mid 44	Planned capture of Rangoon
VARSITY	24 Mar 45	Airborne operations in support of PLUNDER
VENDETTA	44	Follow-up to ZEPPELIN
VERITABLE	8 Feb – 11 Mar 45	Battle of the Reichswald
VITALITY	24 – 29 Oct 44	Attacks on South Beveland, Netherlands
VULCAN	22 Apr – 6 May 43	Advance to Tunis

Name	Date(s)	Location & Purpose
WADHAM	Jul – Sep 43	Proposed deception operation indicating a landing in Brittany
WALK	16 – 17 Mar 43	Diversionary operation in preparation for PUGILIST/GALLOP
WALLACE	19 Aug – 17 Sep 44	SAS operations in Cote d'Or, France
WATERFALL	Autumn 43	Deception operations in support of HUSKY
WELLHIT	17 – 22 Sep 44	Capture of Boulogne, France
WHIPCORD	41 – 42	Proposed invasion of Sicily
WINDSOR	4 – 5 Jul 44	Capture of Carpiquet airfield, Normandy, France
WINTERTON	Mid – 44	Proposed SOE/PWE operation in Arakan, Burma
ZEPPELIN	44	Deception operations in Balkans in support of OVERLORD
ZIPPER	45	Planned liberation of Malaysia and Singapore
ZOMBIE	Feb 45	2 SAS operation with partisans in northern Italy

ENDNOTES

Introduction

1. If in doubt, my mantra has been to include it anyway. For example, I am not at all certain that the abbreviations JNCO and SNCO were in common use during World War 2, but, just in case...

Part 1: A Glossary of Official Military Terms

1. Sydney Jary *18 Platoon* The Light Infantry (2003) p74
2. For many years, despite many tears and tantrums, the authr had been unable to discover what I.T. in this context stood for...but it can now be revealed to a waiting world: *Izod Test*, a method of determining the impact resistance of a material.
3. AB64 was the soldier's pay book.
4. When a soldier or officer made a permanent move from one unit to another, he would be SOS – struck off strength – from his original unit, and TOS – taken on strength, by his new unit. Where soldiers or officers were in between permanent postings, they could be placed in a sort of limbo, known as *held strength*, of another unit. If officers were in none of these categories, they were held on an "Unemployed List".
5. The numbers were roughly equivalent to, but not exactly the same as, the weight of the vehicle, as the dynamic load imposed by a moving vehicle had to be taken into account, rather than just the nominal weight. The capability of bridges could be increased beyond Class 70: Bailey Bridges were capable of being configured from Class 80 up to 240.
6. Within the RAC, some armoured brigades operated independently without any change of nomenclature.
7. Pre-war, Regiments of Royal Artillery had been referred to as artillery brigades.
8. The census organisation was based in Chilwell, Nottingham.
9. A 1941 RAOC publication lists the Commands as: Aldershot, Eastern (including London District), Northern, Scottish, Southern, Western, (Jersey and Guernsey!), N Ireland, and overseas as Bermuda, Ceylon, China, Egypt, Gibraltar, Jamaica, Malaya, Malta and Mauritius. This tells us that this is a pre-war list that had not been kept up to date. SE Command was abolished on 30 November 1944, at the same time Aldershot District (formerly Aldershot Command and subsequently Aldershot Area) was placed under Southern Command.
10. The names could be abbreviated, for example WESTCO for Western Command, SECO for South-Eastern Command etc.

11. The exception was London District, which did not form part of a larger Command, although it was located within the South-Eastern area.
12. The names of districts were frequently abbreviated, eg NOMDIST for the North Midlands District.
13. Denys Biden quoted in Glynn B Hobbs *From Sicily to the Alps* Mallard (1999) p68
14. It was necessary, again for reasons of clarity, to specify which unit of time was in use, for example, H minus 15 hrs, as opposed to H minus 15 mins. H minus 15 was not acceptable. Additionally, the words *plus* and *minus* were meant to be used rather than the mathematical equations, but once again this was not always followed and + and – were often seen.
15. The term *Locating* was in use during WW2 but would not be incorporated into unit designations until after the war.
16. The word Haversack is believed to come from two similar words used in German and Dutch, *Hafersack* and *Haversak* respectively, and referring to a sack of oats carried for the feeding of horses.
17. Within the RE, the term company was used for most sub-units, whereas squadron was used for those sub-units working within armoured formations. For example, 17 Field Company, 14 Field Squadron.

Part 2: Slang Expressions

1. A similar word used by some units was "boning". Why the authorities persisted with issuing boots (c 36 million during the conflict) that, when new, had a "pebblegrain" finish that required burning down using the red-hot end of a spoon in order to make them smooth enough so that they could be properly "bulled" using spit and polish is one of the greatest military mysteries of all time.
2. *The Story of the RASC 1939-1945* commented that "there must have been few items of equipment which were cursed so much as the flimsy." P45
3. Until July 1945 British troops were officially forbidden even to talk to Germans unless for official reasons, and it was not until September that they were allowed to enter a German shop.
4. Many years after the conflict, this author got into trouble in Cyprus by going into the Episkopi NAAFI and asking a local woman working there if they sold housewives; she thought that I was trying to acquire the services of a prostitute, and made her feelings very well known to me and to the rest of the shop.
5. Queer in this sense meant strange or weird and did not refer to the modern connotation.
6. MJ Trow *Swearing Like a Trooper* Constable (2013) p37

Part 3: Abbreviations

1. Bob Crisp *Brazen Chariots* Norton (2005) p 34 In fact, MET was a signal code used by reconnaissance aircraft simply meaning Mechanical Transport.
2. Because of this complexity, some arms and services felt the need to issue their own booklets containing the terminology specific to their trade, for example the RAOC issued a pamphlet covering only the various ammunition abbreviations.
3. Naturally, because this is the British Army after all, other abbreviations were used. For example, the Lancashire Fusiliers official abbreviations were LF and Lan Fus respectively, but both Lancs F and Lancs Fus were also used.
4. There is at least one official variation to this rule, and it concerns the Africa Star medal. Three clasps were authorised for wear with the medal, and for unknown reasons (presumably of space), two of these are inscribed as 8th Army and 1st Army. However, the knowledgeable reader will no doubt comment that clasps on other medals seem to have had no problem with space and can easily fit in wording such as *Bomber Command* or *France and Germany*.
5. However, in the main list of abbreviations in this work, for reasons of consistency, I have chosen to capitalise the main words within each definition.

Part 4: Regiments And Corps

1. Such things made for an unhelpfully complicated organization. For example, it was necessary to issue a pamphlet in 1939 detailing the range practices each soldier must complete annually, entitled: “Range Courses – Territorial Army (less Cavalry Armd Car Regts, Cav, Lt Tk Regts, and RTC Bns) and Supplementary Reserve (less Infantry)”.
2. Royal from November 1946.
3. The SR was largely in suspended animation between the two wars, although in theory they still existed in the overall order of battle.
4. eg The King’s Own Malta Regiment, The Bermuda Rifles.
5. Although not explicit in the original document, this refers to units of the Universities (Senior Division), and the grammar and other schools and colleges (Junior Division) that made up the Officers’ Training Corps, but not the CCF or the ACF who were listed separately within the Army List.
6. This does not make them, as members of the RHA often and erroneously claim, the most senior regiment in the army. Rather, it places them at the head of a line of marching or riding troops in a very specific circumstance only.
7. RAC Regiments were numbered 107-116, and 141-163.
8. In 1939 upon the formation of the RAC, the Royal Tank Corps had to change its name to become the Royal Tank Regiment in order to avoid the situation of having a “corps within a corps”. However, in 1941, the Army Catering Corps was formed and was in effect part of the Royal Army Service Corps, and in January 1944, the Reconnaissance Corps was absorbed by the RAC thus becoming…a corps with a corps!
9. The precedence of the GAD in relation to the other armoured divisions is a bone of contention. Many documents list the GAD before the numbered armoured divisions, but as the Foot Guard regiments were lower in precedence to the Calvary and units of the RAC, it should be the other way round, with the GAD following immediately after 79th Armoured Division.
10. Only regular units are listed in the AL.
11. Horsed initially; to the RAC on mechanization early 1941.
12. Horsed initially; to the RAC on mechanization July 1941.
13. Numbered 1-12 and 40-51.
14. The NIH were an oddity; an Irish regiment, it was formerly a Special Reserve unit and was was remustered as a Militia unit in October 1921, and thus did not form part of the grouping of Yeomanry cavalry regiments. Because the Militia took precedence over the TA, it thus “went to the “top of the list”.
15. Two units, 3CLY and 4CLY; these were amalgamated in the field in 1944, becoming 3/4CLY.
16. Use is often made of the term “Corps & Services”, referring to the majority of the army and largely meaning those parts that were not part of “The Arms” – the cavalry and infantry (including the guards). For the purpose of differentiation here , they are all in effect corps, but the word “corps” in this context usually indicates those which have a more forward role supporting the arms, whereas “services” normally implies a more rearward, administrative role. There is in fact little practical difference in a non-linear battlefield; there will have been times in all campaigns when the furthest soldier forward was a driver of the RASC, or a Padre, or a military policeman.
17. Normally, the precedence order used seems to have been: RHA, Field, Medium, Heavy, Super-Heavy, Anti-Tank, LAA, HAA, Searchlight, Coast, Parachute/ Airlanding, Survey, Regiments RA, although there were variations.
18. Z regiments used rockets.
19. “Infantry Regiments RA” were formed from surplus regiments at the beginning of 1945; officially called simply “Regiments RA”, the word *infantry* was often included for clarity. They were numbered in the 600 range, starting from 600.